Religion, Conflict, and Peacemaking

RELIGION, CONFLICT, & PEACEMAKING

An Interdisciplinary Conversation

EDITED BY **MURIEL SCHMID**

Foreword by Thomas N. Maloney

THE UNIVERSITY OF UTAH PRESS | *Salt Lake City*

The Defiance House Man colophon is a registered trademark
of The University of Utah Press. It is based on a four-foot-tall
Ancient Puebloan pictograph (late PIII) near Glen Canyon, Utah.

LIBRARY OF CONGRESS CATALOGING-IN-PUBLICATION DATA

Names: Schmid, Muriel, 1965- editor.
Title: Religion, conflict, and peacemaking : an interdisciplinary conversation /
edited by Muriel Schmid.
Description: Salt Lake City : The University of Utah Press, [2017] | Includes
bibliographical references and index. |
Identifiers: LCCN 2017023358 (print) | LCCN 2017025744 (ebook) |
ISBN 9781607815877 () | ISBN 9781607815860 (pbk.)
Subjects: LCSH: Social conflict--Religious aspects. | Peace—Religious aspects. |
Culture conflict—Religious aspects. | Religions—Relations.
Classification: LCC BL65.S62 (ebook) | LCC BL65.S62 R43 2017 (print) |
DDC 201/.7--dc23
LC record available at https://lccn.loc.gov/2017023358

Elaine Enns and Ched Meyers, "Confronting Historic Injustice" appeared in an earlier
version as "Confronting Historic Injustice: Truth and Reconciliation," chapter 7 from
Ambassadors of Reconciliation, Vol. 2. Orbis Books, Maryknoll, NY. © 2009 by Elaine
Enns and Ched Myers. Reprinted with permission.

James L. Heft, "John Paul II and the 'Just War' Doctrine: 'Make Peace through Justice
and Forgiveness, Not War,'" (pp. 203-19) was originally published in *Religion, Identity,
and Global Governance: Ideas, Evidence, and Practice,* edited by Patrick James. © 2011
by the University of Toronto Press. Reprinted with persmission.

John Paul Lederach, "In the Beginning Was Conflict: Creation," was originally
published as chapter 4 in *Reconcile: Conflict Transformation for Ordinary Christians*
by John Paul Lederach. © 2014 by Herald Press, Harrisonburg, VA. Used with
permission.

Printed and bound in the United States of America.

To all the peacemakers who are changing the world

CONTENTS

FOREWORD

The Tanner Human Rights Center Conference on Religion, Conflict, and Peacemaking

THOMAS N. MALONEY

In February 2013, the Barbara L. and Norman C. Tanner Center for Nonviolent Human Rights Advocacy (the Tanner Human Rights Center) convened a conference on "Religion, Conflict, and Peacemaking" at the University of Utah. This was the seventh annual conference organized by the center. Past conferences have examined a variety of dimensions of human rights and conflict resolution, including terrorism, the rights of migrants, evolutionary aspects of human aggression, gender identity and the social control of sexuality, water as a human right, and economic globalization and the common good.

Planning for Tanner Human Rights Center conferences typically begins about a year ahead of the conference date. This schedule means that there is always some tension between wanting to address very current and timely matters, on the one hand, and some concern that the issues of the moment when we begin planning might appear much less compelling by the time the conference actually takes place. This tension was not much of a concern in planning for the 2013 conference: the entanglement of religion with social conflict presents a perennial, sadly reliable challenge. In developing the program, though, the organizers placed considerable emphasis on not simply documenting, again, the apparent connections between religion and conflict. Rather, they hoped to also highlight methods of ameliorating such conflicts, as well as cases in which religious values and religious communities play an important role in conflict resolution.

The conference opened with a keynote address by Mohammed Abu-Nimer, associate professor in the International Peace and Conflict Resolution Program and director of the Peacebuilding and Development Institute at American University. Panels the following day included a dialogue on challenges to peace in Israel-Palestine (led by S.J. Quinney College of Law faculty Hiram Chodosh, Amos Guiora, and Chibli Mallat); an examination of peacebuilding and cultural values (featuring John Carlson of Arizona State University, Stacey Horn of the University of Illinois–Chicago, and Zeena Zakharia of the University of Massachusetts–Boston); an open dialogue on religion, conflict, and peace (led by Professor David Derezotes of the University of Utah College of Social Work); and a panel discussion on "Peacebuilding in Practice" (featuring Laura Bennett-Murphy of Westminster College, Tim Nafziger of *Christian Peacemaker Teams*, and Hiram Chodosh).

This volume pulls together several of these conference papers along with additional contributions from Abbas Aroua, Elaine Enns, Ched Myers, and James L. Heft. The themes running through these chapters reflect many of the values at the core of the work of the Tanner Center. Several authors emphasize the notion that violence and conflict are part of the human condition, extending beyond the specific influence of religious motivations (and of the secular state), and that the role of religion in creating conflict can therefore be hard to clarify. Frank and informed dialogue between diverse parties thus takes on an important role in helping us to understand the true sources of conflict as well as potential areas of common ground between groups in conflict. Because conflict is so basic to the human condition, "Peace is not the absence of conflict but rather its good management."[1] The Tanner Human Rights Center's approach to understanding conflict resolution is consistent with this vision. The center's programs place great emphasis on the importance of dialogue and debate across communities—between groups in conflict, and also across academic disciplines and between the academy and the wider community—as a means to promote understanding and the "good management" of social conflict.

Several pieces in this volume also note the role of religion as a force of peace and healing, through the evolution of religious teaching, through the inspiration religion provides to individuals and groups to redress injustice nonviolently and creatively, and through the role of religion as a source of community and healing for individuals traumatized by conflict. These chapters span the experiences and insights of refugee children, community organizers and activist groups, and religious leaders. They reflect the center's emphasis on moving beyond understanding the causes of conflict to identifying creative solutions, as well as an emphasis on connecting global, national, local, and individual dimensions of human rights, conflict, and peacebuilding.

*

The conferences, programming, and publications of the Tanner Human Rights Center are a direct result of the generosity of the Tanner family—Barbara and Norman Tanner and Deb Sawyer. We are grateful for their vision in establishing the center and for their extraordinarily generous ongoing support. Each Tanner Center conference is organized by a distinct team of University of Utah faculty and other members of the Salt Lake City community who develop the theme, invite the speakers, and organize the program. The organizers of the 2013 conference included Muriel Schmid, the director of the Religious Studies Program at the University of Utah, who served as the committee chair and whose vision shaped the program. Her colleagues on the committee were Cecilia Wainryb of the Department of Psychology, Nathan Paul Devir of the Department of Languages and Literature, and David Derezotes of the College of Social Work, all at the University of Utah.

Beyond the core faculty team, a number of departments and centers at the University of Utah, as well as local organizations, made the conference possible through a variety of kinds of support. These included the College of Social and Behavioral Science, the S.J. Quinney College of Law, the College of Humanities, the Tanner Humanities Center, the Office of the Vice President for Academic Affairs, the Office of the Vice

President for Institutional Advancement, and the Office of the Vice President for Student Affairs, all at the University of Utah; the Salt Lake City Public Library; and the College of Religious Education at Brigham Young University. Additional funding was provided by the Departments of Economics, Languages and Literature, and Psychology, the Honors College, the International Center, the International Studies Program, the Peace and Conflict Studies Program, and the Dee Endowment, all at the University of Utah, along with the Utah Humanities Council. Finally, the success of the conference and of related programming that provided the inspiration for this volume was to a great degree a result of the skillful work of the staff of the Tanner Center, including Aleta Tew and Victoria Medina, and the center's intern, Marianne Carpenter.

Notes
1. See chapter nine of this volume, Abbas Aroua, "Peace, Conflict, and Conflict Transformation in the Islamic Tradition."

ACKNOWLEDGMENTS

First, I want to thank the Barbara L. and Norman C. Tanner Center for Nonviolent Human Rights Advocacy at the University of Utah and its staff for their support in organizing the conference that led to this volume and its publication, and also Barbara and Norman Tanner for their generosity and vision in establishing the center. Thank you to John Alley, our acquiring editor at the University of Utah Press, who diligently worked with us on the manuscript; to Patrick Hadley, the press's managing editor; and to copyeditor Ginny Hoffman. Thank you to Dr. Catherine Morris and Dr. Michael Minch for their valuable comments. Thank you to Katie Sexton, student at the University of Utah, who was our final editor. Thank you to James Heft, Elaine Enns, Ched Myers, and John Paul Lederach who generously agreed to republish their work here.

I

Religion's Long Shadow

A Brief Overview of the Conversation

MURIEL SCHMID

When William Cavanaugh first introduced in 2007 the idea that religious violence was a myth contributing to justifying the war ideology of the West, he counterbalanced to some extent the plethora of sociopolitical analyses that had invaded the public sphere in the aftermath of 9/11 and quasi-univocally equated religion with violence and terrorism.[1] In the spring of 2004, *The Hedgehog Review* dedicated an issue to the discussion of the long and complex relationship between religion and violence analyzing some of the perspectives put forth after 9/11; at the end of the volume, Charles Bellinger offered an excellent bibliography on the topic, reminding his readers that "[t]he literature on religion and violence was already substantial before the Sept. 11 attacks, and it has swelled at an increased pace since then."[2] In the last ten years, many titles have been added to the list and prominent voices have addressed the issue in a variety of ways; among them, public intellectuals such as Sam Harris (*The End of Faith: Religion, Terror, and the Future of Reason*, 2005) or Reza Aslan (*Beyond Fundamentalism: Confronting Religious Extremism in the Age of Globalization*, 2010), Navy reservist and former politician Douglas Johnston (*Religion, Terror, and Error: U.S. Foreign Policy and the Challenge of Spiritual Engagement*, 2011), former president

Jimmy Carter (*A Call to Action: Women, Religion, Violence, and Power*, 2014), and popular theologian Karen Armstrong (*Fields of Blood: Religion and the History of Violence*, 2015). Following the 9/11 events, the link between religion and violence became particularly powerful and very few voices challenged this equation. However, as Cavanaugh laments, "*The Myth of Religious Violence* promotes a dichotomy between *us* in the secular West who are rational and peacemaking, and *them*, the hordes of violent religious fanatics in the Muslim world. *Their* violence is religious, and therefore irrational and divisive. *Our* violence, on the other hand, is rational, peacemaking, and necessary."[3] Cavanaugh suggests deconstructing the simplistic dichotomy between secular (politics, institutions, societies) and religious in order to challenge what he calls *The Myth of Religious Violence*.

The increase of literature on religion and conflict transformation theory or peacemaking practices has also been significant since 9/11 and has represented another powerful way to challenge the dominant discourse that has established a direct relationship between religion and violence. Exactly ten years before Cavanaugh, Marc Gopin was advocating for the necessary development of "a new course of study of religion that examines its relationship to conflict and conflict resolution methodologies."[4] Little did he know that one of the few constructive effects of 9/11 would emphasize the role of religion in peacebuilding as Gopin wished it in his 1997 essay. A second post-9/11 wave of scholarship has now emerged, delineating the positive role religion plays in conflict resolution. In this scholarship, scholars and practitioners alike seek to find ways to utilize religion as a positive force and to integrate religious communities and leaders into peacebuilding processes. Today, Gopin has become one of the most important voices in the field, writing extensively on religious peacemaking. Over the years, several scholars became landmark names in this conversation, in particular David Little and his work with the Tanenbaum Institute (*Peacemakers in Action: Profiles of Religion in Conflict Resolution*, 2007) and Scott Appleby and the research conducted under the umbrella of the Kroc Institute at the University of Notre Dame (*The Ambivalence of the Sacred: Religion, Violence, and Reconciliation*, 2000). Both Little and Appleby contributed to a seminal collection of essays edited by Harold Coward and Gordon Smith, *Religion and Peacebuilding* (2004) that has become a reference for this conversation. The present volume offers essays by other renowned scholars in the field: John Carlson (*From Jeremiad to Jihad: Religion, Violence, and America*, 2012), Mohammed Abu-Nimer (*Nonviolence and Peace Building in Islam: Theory and Practice*, 2003), John Paul Lederach (*The Moral Imagination: The Art and Soul of Building Peace*, 2005), and James Heft (*Beyond Violence: Religious Sources of Social Transformation in Judaism, Christianity, and Islam*, 2004). The four of them share elements of their expertise: Carlson centers the discussion on religion and violence in the American context; Abu-Nimer discusses models of interfaith dialogue as a peacebuilding tool which he used in the context of the Israeli-Palestinian conflict; Lederach offers a reading of the biblical narrative of the Creation that emphasizes the intrinsic need to address conflict; Heft gives an overview of the Just War theory in the Catholic tradition.

This recent field of inquiry has grown out of case study and empirical research. Much of the scholarship published on religious peacemaking stems from specific contexts and is grounded in practical experiments. Religion, in this conversation, is a living faith with a specific tradition and set of beliefs that function as the grounding or inspiration of peacemaking initiatives, strategies, and processes. This volume presents several examples of such an approach. Abbas Aroua (*The Quest for Peace in the Islamic Tradition*, 2013) is the founder and director of the Cordoba Foundation in Geneva, Switzerland, dedicated to fostering respectful dialogues and peace initiatives between groups of different cultural background and faith traditions; his essay revisits the Islamic textual tradition around the concepts of peace and conflict transformation. Kathleen Kern (*In Harm's Way: A History of Christian Peacemaker Teams*, 2009) and Tim Nafziger are long-standing members of *Christian Peacemaker Teams*, an organization launched in the late 1980s by the members of the peace churches in order to advocate for a nonviolent approach to conflict resolution in partnership with various groups in the United States and abroad; their essay provides both a general history of the organization and a few specific examples of their work. Elaine Enns and Ched Myers (*Ambassadors of Reconciliation*, 2009) are at the heart of the Bartimaeus Cooperative Ministries, a center that explores various ways in which the Christian tradition can be active in developing models of restorative justice; their essay talks about historic trauma and the role of truth and reconciliation committees in North America.

Between June 2011 and December 2012, the *Journal of the American Academy of Religion* published a back-and-forth between two scholars of religion, Atalia Omer and Russell McCutcheon, on the intricate role religion can play in peacebuilding; both ended up at opposite ends of the spectrum. In her essay, Omer argued that religious studies had a unique approach to conflict resolution and could serve as a platform to address issues of power, relationship between dominant and subaltern narratives, construction of identities, and so forth; whereas McCutcheon affirmed that the role of the scholar of religion does not include any normative insight or expertise into notions such as justice, peace, or reconciliation.[5] Beyond the personal aspect of this debate, a legitimate question arises: is religious peacebuilding dependent on a disciplinary approach to conflict transformation? Or, on the contrary, does religious peacebuilding emphasize the pluridisciplinary nature of conflict resolution theory itself? Around the growing interest in peace studies for practices that revolve around just peacebuilding and strategic peacebuilding,[6] an understanding of religion as a social and cultural force is needed—this is what Omer defends against McCutcheon.

This volume offers three essays that allow for the exploration of an interdisciplinary approach to the relationship between religion, conflict, and conflict resolution. Coming from a legal and political perspective, Chibli Mallat (Introduction to Middle Eastern Law, 2007) discusses the Arab Spring context and offers an in-depth analysis of the various factors at play in the changes we witnessed in the Middle East at that time. As a professional psychotherapist, Laura Bennett-Murphy's contribution exemplifies how the integration of religious identity can help understanding and healing personal traumas. Finally, David Derezotes (*Transforming Historical Trauma through Dialogue*, 2013) shares his experience as a social worker who facilitates dialogues between groups of different religious identities.

In an essay on religion and peacebuilding, Gerard Powers insists that successful religious peacemaking depends on "a strong public role for religion":

If the secularists are mistaken in their assumption that the antidote to religious conflict is to marginalize and privatize religion, then strategic religious peacebuilding cannot be limited to motivating individuals to be peacebuilders and transforming interpersonal relationships; it must be tied up to a strong public role for religion.[7]

The growing field of inquiry in religious peacemaking has definitively drawn attention to religious leaders, communities, and traditions and their role in both igniting and resolving conflicts. In recent years, religion has been part of a public and political discourse addressing various types of conflict, generating healthy debates about the sociocultural construction of religious violence (Cavanaugh) and the sociocultural construction of religious peacemaking (McCutcheon). This volume seeks to contribute to this debate and invite the reader to explore a wide array of approaches to the relationship between religion, violence, and peace. This opportunity would not have been possible without the support of Tom Maloney, the director of the Barbara L. and Norman C. Tanner Center for Nonviolent Human Rights Advocacy, and all the people who organized its 2013 conference.

Contributions have been arranged into thematic sections, and each section starts with a brief introduction. Keeping with the terminology often used in the field of peace studies, the title of this volume chooses the term "peacemaking" (over peacebuilding) to indicate that on the continuum that stretches from negative peace (peacekeeping) to positive peace (peacebuilding), many of our practices stand in the transition that leads to the establishment of a just peace.

Notes

1. William Cavanaugh, "Does Religion Cause Violence?" *Harvard Divinity Bulletin* 35, nos. 2–3 (spring/summer 2007). The extended book version was published by Oxford University Press in 2009 under the title *The Myth of Religious Violence*.
2. Charles K. Bellinger, "Religion and Violence: A Bibliography," *The Hedgehog Review* 6, no. 1 (spring 2004): 111.
3. Cavanaugh, "Does Religion Cause Violence?," 1.

4. Marc Gopin, "Religion, Violence, and Conflict Resolution," *Peace & Change* 22, no. 1 (January 1997): 1.
5. Atalia Omer, "Can a Critic Be a Caretaker Too? Religion, Conflict, and Conflict Transformation," *Journal of the American Academy of Religion* 79, no. 2 (June 2011): 459–96; and her subsequent response to McCutcheon, "Rejoinder: On Professor McCutcheon's (Un)critical Caretaking," in *Journal of the American Academy of Religion* 80, no. 4 (December 2012): 1083–97. Russell T. McCutcheon, "A Direct Question Deserves a Direct Answer: A Response to Atalia Omer's 'Can a Critic Be a Caretaker Too?,'" *Journal of the American Academy of Religion* 80, no. 4 (December 2012): 1077–82.
6. See, for instance, Daniel Philpott and Gerard Powers, eds., *Strategies of Peace: Transforming Conflict in a Violent World* (Oxford: University of Oxford Press, 2010), and Pierre Allan and Alexis Keller, eds., *What Is a Just Peace?* (Oxford: Oxford University Press, 2006).
7. Gerard Powers, "Religion and Peacebuilding," in Philpott and Powers, Strategies of Peace, 333.

PART I

RELIGIONS IN DIALOGUE

Interfaith work has a very long history (the first formal gathering of representatives of Eastern and Western religions was held in Chicago in 1893) and the interfaith movement has become significantly bigger in the post-9/11 era and indicates today a desire to portray religion, religious communities, and religious leaders as potential partners in building a more peaceful and more tolerant global world.[1] More specifically, interfaith dialogue has been regarded as a unique tool that religious peacemaking can develop in order to support peace processes, and international organizations (see for instance the October 2007 United Nations initiative on interfaith dialogue)[2] have fostered interfaith dialogue as a tool for change.

However, as Reina Neufeldt aptly notices, the status of interfaith dialogue in diplomacy and peace processes is not always recognized; she goes on to mention that "[w]hen interfaith dialogue fails, it reinforces arguments that religious-based actors have no bearing on peace processes and religion is more effective at mobilizing people for violence than for peace. When it succeeds, it is seen as a minor footnote to a major political peace process."[3] Worse yet, because of how interfaith dialogue is sometimes portrayed, suffering from what Atalia Omer calls the "kumbaya syndrome,"[4] it is altogether dismissed as a potential actor in peacebuilding efforts.

The two essays in this section address some of the issues linked to the very principle of interfaith dialogue and the broader use of dialogue to resolve conflicts. Both contributions come from practitioners who have extensive experience in developing models of dialogue to work through conflicts. Mohammed Abu-Nimer draws his observations from the Israeli-Palestinian context, David Derezotes from community-based religious dialogues in the United States.

Notes

1. See, for instance, the work done by the World Conference of Religions for Peace which started in 1970 (http://www.religionsforpeace.org/) or the work of the Council for a Parliament of the World's Religions which stems from an initial gathering held in Chicago in 1893 during the Columbian Exposition (http://www.parliamentofreligions.org/); the Parliament was founded officially in 1988.

2. Following an unprecedented resolution, the United Nations organized an interfaith consultation in October 2007 in order to promote a strong culture of cooperation for peace: "The General Assembly, in its resolution 61/221 of 20 December 2006 (OP. 14) decided 'to convene in 2007 a high-level dialogue on interreligious and intercultural cooperation for the promotion of tolerance, understanding and universal respect on matters of freedom of religion or belief and cultural diversity, in coordination with other similar initiatives in this area.'" See http://www.un.org/ga/president/62/issues/hld-interreligious.shtml. A report (63/262) was then published.

3. Reina C. Neufeldt, "Interfaith Dialogue: Assessing Theories of Change," *Peace & Change* 36, no. 3 (July 2011): 345.

4. Omer, "Can a Critic Be a Caretaker Too?," 472.

Interfaith Dialogue and Religious Leaders in the Israeli-Palestinian Context
Needs and Limitations

MOHAMMED ABU-NIMER

Introduction

Following the collapse of the Soviet Union and the end of the Cold War, the world has witnessed a rise in identity-based conflicts. Most of these conflicts have economic and territorial root causes. Unfortunately, however, a large number of these conflicts have been framed by both international and national agencies as religious. Some of these include conflicts in Myanmar with the Rohingy, a Muslim minority; in southern Thailand with the Muslim Patani minority, who are seeking autonomy from the Buddhist majority government; in Mindanao Philippines with the Moro, a Muslim minority group who are also seeking autonomy from the Philippine government; in Sri Lanka with the Tamil Hindu and Muslim minorities, who are seeking autonomy from the Sinhalese, Buddhist majority; as well as civil wars in Iraq and Syria and the Central African Republic.

Debate about the nature of these conflicts notwithstanding, it is clear today that without addressing the grievances related to the religious identity of certain groups in these conflicts, there is little hope that such countries can experience stability and peace in the near future. Thus, religious identity becomes an important factor and force in resolving such identity-based conflicts. Obviously, most research on religious identity and conflict has focused on how religious identity can be manipulated to trigger and sustain violence in conflicting societies. The danger of such overexplanation or exaggeration of the effect and role of religious forces and identity in a political setting can be clearly seen in Iraq, Somalia, Iran-United States, Israel-Palestine, and Northern Ireland, where policymakers frame political and economic conflicts as exclusively religious or sectarian conflicts. For example, in the context of Iraq, social scientists appear aligned with particular political agendas and policymaking debates when they present Islamic theology as a root cause of the ongoing "war on terror," pointing to religious identity as the primary cause for war and consequently the only path to resolve the conflict. But, as a social scientist, when framing the "war on terror" as a religious war, to what extent are we serving specific and partisan political agendas? There are other root causes for these conflicts (e.g., distribution of resources, globalization forces, hegemonic power policies, discrimination, lack of citizenship rights, persecution, etc.).

Countering this tendency, and refocusing the research and practice on the distinct set of functions and roles that religious actors can adopt in their efforts to contribute to peacebuilding, is a crucial step in repositioning religious identity in its proportional location and function within the local, social, and political structures. This task is urgently needed in the Israeli-Palestinian conflict in order for local leaders on all sides to claim their constructive role in advancing the peace and justice agenda.

Religion in the Arab-Israeli Peace Process: Background

The formal Arab-Israeli peace process began in the early 1990s with the Madrid talks. Since then Jordan and Egypt have maintained their peaceful or non-state-of-war relations with Israel, while the Israeli-Palestinian track has its own fluctuations. Twenty-one years after the Oslo breakthrough and many rounds of negotiations and multiple international and local initiatives, Israeli and Palestinian communities and representatives find themselves in another deadlock with a high level of threat for reverting to full-fledged violent confrontation. Similarly, little progress has been made on the larger Arab-Israeli track. The remaining Arab countries can be divided between total and partial diplomatic disengagement with Israel. There is no unified Arab-Israeli peace process. It is necessary to discuss or analyze the role of religious leaders in these two tracks rather than treat them as one unified process. The level and nature of involvement are different in the two processes.

Nevertheless, religious ideologies have had significant impact on the dynamics and course of the Arab-Israeli conflict, mainly provoking and inciting violence and exclusion of the other. Historically both Arabs (Muslims and Christians) and Jews have deployed their religious identity in the political and military battlefields of these conflicts. In fact, both religious and political leaders continue to utilize their constituencies to mobilize and cultivate political support.[1]

Zionist movement leaders have linked their political agenda and ideology with Judaism and the debates between secular Jews and religious Jews. For example, Theodore Herzl and other founders of Zionism used Judaism to legitimize their demands for a homeland for European Jews in historic Palestine and sealed the link in the late 1890s. Also, since 1948 Israeli governments have used the Jewishness of the state to oppose the return of Palestinian refugees from the 1948 war to their homes inside Israel. In fact, the Jewish religious identity and biblical discourse are often used by many Israeli right-wing politicians to justify the government policy of territorial expansion and increasing settlements in the Occupied Palestinian Territories.

The main leadership of the Palestinian national movements has included a number of religious figures since the early 1920s—such as al-Qassam and al-Husseini—who have claimed the front seat in defending and speaking on behalf of Palestinian nationalism. The mobilization of the Muslim world to sympathize and support the Palestinian national cause often relied on the religious importance of Jerusalem. However, a clearer example is the discourse of a number of Hamas leaders in emphasizing the religious roots of the conflict in their speeches and mobilization to resist Israeli occupation of Palestine.

The nature of the conflict and its evolving issues determine to a large extent the role of various actors in its resolution. Thus there is a debate whether the Israeli-Palestinian conflict is mainly over religious identity and ideology or over national self-determination shaped by external and internal colonial policies and dynamics.

The role of religious leaders in these two analytical approaches to the conflict can be different. Historically, religious leaders in the Arab-Israeli conflict have mainly claimed the spoiler role. There are hundreds of examples and illustrations in which religious verdicts and decrees were issued by Jewish, Muslim, and Christian religious leaders evoking their followers' religious sentiments to resist and oppose a political compromise, and to declare an exclusive ownership and right over the disputed land. For example, on the Jewish side, such decrees were utilized to resist the withdrawal of Israeli forces form Sinai in 1979 and Gaza in 2005, and to provide religious justification for the occupation and settlement of the West Bank and Gaza since 1967.[2]

On the Arab side, Muslim claims of exclusive rights to establish an Islamic state in the land of Palestine are often repeated by Islamic groups in the Arab world, as well as Hamas in Palestine. For example, the Muslim-Jewish conflict during the Prophet Muhammad's life (for example, the Battle of Khaybar 1,400 years ago) is linked to the current conflict with the Jewish Zionist movement (e.g., use of the term of Yahud Khaibar in reference to Jews who fought the Prophet in Medina). In addition, there is the use of the Friday *khutba* (preaching) and the rhetoric of revenge for the occupation of Palestine, especially when Israeli security forces violate Islamic holy sites in Hebron or Jerusalem.

Hamas leaders have become powerful figures in Palestinian politics, prominent in the national discourse about winning popular elections in Gaza. The Palestinian Christian minority's leaders often appeal to the western Christian public and their leaders to save them from the conflict and Israeli occupation and the migration of Christians from Palestine.

Despite the intense destructive manipulation of religious identity by politicians in the Israeli-Palestinian conflict, the involvement of religious leaders in the formal peace processes remains absent or extremely minimal. For example, after a few years of shuttle diplomacy by the various American envoys to broker a peace deal between the Israeli government and Palestinian president Abbas, there has been no formal meeting between any of these envoys and Jewish, Christian, or Muslim religious leaders to explore possible ways to engage them in the process.[3] Such a reality is not new. Historically this marginalization of religious leaders from the formal peace processes has also been supported by local politicians.

Secular national Palestinian analysts have refused to acknowledge the potential positive role of religious leaders and urged the separation of religion from the political conflict over national self-determination (Fatah, PFLP, DFLP, and the People's Party). The emergence of Hamas in the late 1980s only intensified their arguments against engaging the religious dimension of the conflict and opposition to involvement of religion in the conflict. These analysts argue that it is against the Palestinian national interest to incorporate religion in the conflict, and that the link mainly serves the Zionist national movement by diverting the conflict from issues of colonialism, and more recently that it contributes to the Islamization of the Palestinian conflict and might drag it into an al-Qaeda–United States war.

Israeli secular negotiators, whether they belong to Labor or Likud, have repeatedly excluded religious figures from their efforts to reach a settlement with the Palestinians or Arabs (Oslo 1, Camps David I and II, Road Map, etc.), and they have alienated the religious right as well as small religious peace groups.

Despite being sidelined in the formal peace processes, religious leaders in Israel-Palestine can play an important role in various ways. For example, they can provide input in the actual negotiation process, monitor agreements, advocate for rights and justice of all marginalized groups, raise awareness among Arab and Jewish youth through formal and informal peace education programs, engage in programs to contribute to social and economic development, and appeal to moral common ground and the moral discourse within their own communities.[4]

In a 2004 interview, Abdul Salam Manasra said, "There will be no peace between Muslims and Jews here without religious people intervention."[5]

A Palestinian interviewee said:

> Religion is not only concerned with the theological. Religion is a connecting and disconnecting point. Jews and Arabs have cultural and religious stereotypes. With the time passing, I

understood that religion can contribute in positive ways, it has the potential to remove the intolerance and misunderstanding.[6]

Religious actors can also play specific and unique roles in various areas or application of peacebuilding, including: education, advocacy, pastoral diplomacy, observation, presence, accompaniment, fact finding, assessment, good offices, conciliation, providing auspices, facilitation, mediation, and witnessing to truth.[7]

Obviously, there have been many examples of community-based interreligious peacebuilding carried out in Israel-Palestine. Examples of these include the various Quaker initiatives, especially in Al-Haq Center in Palestine, which since the 1950s have focused their contribution on relief and development, and legal advocacy. Mennonite groups have worked on capacity building, monitoring, and advocacy of human rights. United Religious Initiative (URI) managed to formulate a regional and local Israeli Jewish and Arab initiative to foster greater interreligious understanding among its participants. The Interfaith Encounter Association (IEA) organized ongoing interfaith dialogue meetings in Israel between Arabs and Jews. Sulha is an organization that focuses on large gatherings of Arabs and Jews in various regions to publically celebrate peace work through art and music, traditional and cultural ceremonies, and training. The Truman Institute is an academic center that focuses on interfaith dialogue, especially between Jewish and Christian theologians through lectures, panelists, conferences, and publications.

Religious Leaders' Constructive Roles in Advancing Peace

In general, there are three categories or types of religious peacebuilding activities:

1. Monitoring and advocating for human rights. These types of activities include mainly campaigns to reveal the level of human rights abuse by certain policies and structures, and lobbying (domestically and internationally) to change such conditions. In addition to serving as witnesses and accompanying and supporting victims through legal processes and investigations, the

primary tactics are often to appeal to media and to local and international legal and religious institutions.[8]

2. Dialogue and conflict transformation. These activities are carried out mostly though civil society groups and NGOs to promote deeper understanding of the other (through skills training or dialogue encounters), and in some cases focus on specific issues of the conflict (interfaith dialogue groups in Northern Ireland, and in the United States, Christian-Muslim groups post-9/11).

3. Liberation and nonviolent resistance. These activities often focus on nonviolent resistance and active confrontation of injustice with an objective to remove or change the oppressive structure (the anti-Apartheid movement in South Africa and Oscar Romero's campaign in El Salvador are classic examples).

In Israel-Palestine, a majority of the groups have focused their work on interfaith dialogue and advocacy for human rights. There are no joint Arab-Jewish religious groups who have adopted liberation theology as a method of peacebuilding. However a few organizations that operate out of their particular faith tradition have framed their activities with a liberation theology approach.[9] The majority of interreligious activities have focused on interfaith dialogue, especially inside Israel between Arabs and Jews.[10]

Interfaith Dialogue Efforts on Grassroots and Midlevel Leaders

Relative to other forms of peace intervention (secular human rights and other peace movement groups in Israel) there is a limited number of religious initiatives promoting Arab-Jewish peace, most of them launched in the last two decades (since Oslo).[11] In addition, their activities have fluctuated and often come to a full stop due to the deterioration of the security on the ground, especially after the eruption of the Second Intifada in 2000, and the repeated Israeli invasions of Gaza, Lebanon, and the West Bank.

A majority of the existing organizations are mainly based on efforts by certain local figures or individuals, who have carved out for themselves a distinct role in the interreligious field. As a result, many of these one-person organizations or initiatives have limited capacity to reach out to the general Israeli or Palestinian public. For example, among Palestinians there are few figures who are defined as experts and are experienced in interfaith dialogue and who are willing to meet with Israeli Jews in such forums.

Due to the nature of the activities carried out by the Jewish-led interfaith organizations in Israel (panel discussion, symbolic and ritualistic events), there is the lack of a large constituency supporting them or their role. In most cases, a U.S.-led NGO provides the umbrella for Arabs and Jews to be involved in such efforts. However, in general, Jewish organizations and NGO leaders remain more involved in launching such initiatives.

The motivations for participating in these interfaith activities are slightly different for Jews, Muslims, and Christians. Palestinian Muslims and Christians are motivated by their desire to bring political change, thus in their discourse of explaining and justifying their participation, they emphasize the need to explain their reality and the conflict's structural causes (such as occupation, system of discrimination). Also, for some, interfaith dialogue is a substitute for protest, which they either have tried or were unable to participate in public protest. Thus, Arab, Muslim, and Christian leaders tend to look for concrete, political outcomes, while Jewish participants seek mutual understanding and an opportunity to learn more about Islam and Christianity.

For many Jewish participants, rehumanizing the other in order to reduce prejudice is the primary motivation: "We do not only meet but also call each other on the phone and visit each other's homes. This deepens the understanding, breaks preconceived notions, and gives a feeling of humanizing the other. For many Jews, Arabs have no figure; but if we meet them they become a 'person.'"[12]

These different sets of motivations are not unique to either interfaith dialogue participants or to the Israel-Palestine context. Research on dialogue and encounter has documented these tendencies based on power differences between minority and majority groups.[13]

Interfaith Dialogue Processes and Content

Like other dialogue programs in conflict areas, interfaith dialogue organizers in Israel-Palestine have generally adopted a harmony process of dialogue, one that focuses on identifying theological and ritualistic similarities and differences. As shown in table 2.1, however, they often avoid political discussions and emphasize ways to reduce stereotypes and establish personal and group human relationships beyond the religious differences. Such interfaith dialogue group processes, especially in Israel, avoid political actions, advocacy, or critical examination of the structural violence in their society. As mentioned above, in Israel there is no Arab-Jewish organization that focuses on or has adopted a liberation theology approach.

TABLE 2.1. INTERFAITH DIALOGUE PROCESSES/DESIGN.

Harmony	Conflict/Political	Liberation Theology
Nonpolitical	Political	Critical examination of text
Educational	Conflict issues	Nonviolent action
Ritualistic	Critical/confront	Justice- and rights-oriented
Individual spirituality	Collective institutional	Individual and collective transformation
Mainly similarities (cultural and religious)	Confront and appreciate differences	Universal message

In terms of content, the majority of these interfaith dialogue meetings focus on basic theological explorations of beliefs, rituals, and cultural practices of Islam, Christianity, and Judaism. The participants either talk about their own individual practices or a group of expert panelists lecture to the audience about the specific themes. This cognitive learning of theological differences and similarities is most popular among Arab and Jewish academics and clergy (see activities of Women Dialogue Group, Interfaith Encounter Association [IIE], ICCI, Yisodot, Hartman Institute, Bar Ilan University, and Liqa'a).

During many interfaith meetings, issues that relate to daily life and collective problems of the Palestinians and Israelis are avoided. Thus, in the context of Israeli-Palestinian interfaith dialogue, there is too little focus on the "dialogue of life" approach, where the conversation or content is framed around the issues related to how each participant is able to express his or her religious identity on a daily basis and in daily matters. On the other hand, theological dialogue occupies the center of the interaction, where the conversation or the issues raised are centered on the way in which each participant views his or her religious beliefs and rituals (often led by a religious authority). (Table 2.2 illustrates some of these categories.)

TABLE 2.2. MODELS OF INTERFAITH DIALOGUE: THEOLOGICAL DIALOGUE VERSUS DIALOGUE OF LIFE.

Theological Dialogue	Dialogue of Life
Theological differences/similarities	Family planning and faith
God, Holy Spirit, Mary, Abraham, land of Israel, martyrdom, etc.	Economic development
State of women, Jihad, etc.	Policies of discrimination and prejudice
Clergy, religious scholars	Grassroots celebrations of rituals and learning more about the other religion

When combining tables 2.1 and 2.2, there are four possible cells in which we can classify many of the interfaith dialogue processes and content as they are carried out by religious leaders in this context (see table 2.3).[14] In fact, a number of participants in interfaith encounters in Israel-Palestine expressed their frustration with the dominant public perception that the theological harmony model overemphasizes similarities between the Jewish and Islamic faiths in terms of rituals and certain beliefs or values. A number of Palestinian interviewees warned that such an emphasis can be easily used by politicians to mask the real issues of the conflict (territory and self-determination).

Effects of Interfaith Dialogue: Reflections

There is no doubt that interfaith dialogue efforts in the context of the Israeli-Palestinian conflict have contributed to peacebuilding efforts

TABLE 2.3. INTERFAITH DIALOGUE THEMES AND PROCESSES.

Content and Processes of Dialogue	Theological Dialogue	Dialogue of Life
Harmony	A All children of God/ Abraham	B Civic education and shared citizenship issues
Conflict/political Differences	C Holy Trinity Muhammad's prophecy	D Profiling of Muslims Christian minority status and issues in Muslim countries

on various levels. These contributions can be summarized into several categories:

First, learning and understanding other faiths. Participants explained that as a result of their participation in these workshops they have learned more about the other faith groups. This increased knowledge about Islamic, Christian, and Judaic belief systems enhances the capacity of individuals to understand certain rituals, symbols, and values expressed by different groups. However, such cognitive learning often remains confined to individuals and a small group of experts.

Second, rehumanizing the other. This is probably the most influential outcome of the interfaith dialogue. Most participants expressed their surprise in discovering the similarities that they discovered in the other community. People from each faith gave examples illustrating that they did not expect to find feelings of pain and insecurity, as well as deep spiritual connections to certain values and devotion among other faith groups.

The psychological divides between Arabs and Jews in Israel-Palestine have produced a high level of alienation and dehumanization of the enemy, to the extent that through interfaith group dynamics, participants rediscover the humanity in the other. Thus, a simple visit to a home, or listening to people of another faith explaining their deep connections to land, children, etc., produce this sense of close human connectedness among participants. One dialogue participant put it this way:

> As a Christian believer I try to implement this [forgiveness] in all my life. When Jenin events took place, a nephew of one Jewish participant was killed, I forgot I am Palestinian and that Jews entered Jenin and I went to visit her. I wanted to share her pain, and I rejected my Palestinian and her Israeli identity. She was very touched and affected by my visit. I encouraged her to return to the meetings.... [F]ollowing this we decided to visit each other in our houses.[15]

Third, spreading the message of interfaith peace. Interfaith dialogue groups will not resolve the Arab-Israeli conflict; however, they contribute to a peaceful public message that religious actors and clergy should have a constructive role in society. This peaceful activity becomes especially important when a majority of the religious actors in both Arab and Jewish societies are engaged in spreading hatred, disconnections, or justifying violence and injustice.

Despite this qualitative data evidence of effect and impact of the interfaith efforts on the leaders and participants of these encounters, the reality is that there is very little systematic research to comprehensively document the macro- and micro-impacts of these interreligious efforts in the various communities or target audiences. Thus, it is hard for the proponents of these programs to establish a case for major impact and even relevance to the conflict dynamics in this context. However, one must be cautious in expecting such initiatives to produce the type of desired impact that many donors, public-opinion makers, and even followers of each faith expect or use to measure the success of any peace intervention initiative.

The success of the interfaith organizations in Israel-Palestine can be measured through their symbolic contribution to the overall message that peace is possible between Israelis and Palestinians, despite their painful and complex historical and religious differences. The fact that religious leaders take a stand against the voices of war and exclusion in their community is an important step to maintaining hope that the discourse of religious violence can be countered from within.

An example of this symbolic effect of interfaith dialogue can be illustrated through the Alexandria Declaration, which was launched by top religious leaders in the region. This initiative in which Jewish, Muslim, and Christian leaders met for the first time in Alexandria, Egypt, in 2002, resulted in a declaration of peace that was certainly a breakthrough in the role Middle Eastern religious leadership can play in conflict. The initiative started as a three-day summit between senior Christian, Jewish, and Muslim leaders and resulted in the First Declaration of Alexandria of the Religious Leaders of the Holy Land, which condemned violence and pledged to work for peace. A Permanent Committee for the Implementation of the Alexandria Declaration (PCIAD) was established from the signatories and other spiritual leaders and has since met regularly.[16]

> First Declaration of Alexandria of the Religious Leaders of the Holy Land
>
> *In the name of God who is Almighty, Merciful and Compassionate*, we, who have gathered as religious leaders from the Muslim, Christian and Jewish communities, pray for true peace in Jerusalem and the Holy Land, and declare our commitment to ending the violence and bloodshed that denies the right to life and dignity.
>
> *According to our faith traditions*, killing innocents in the name of God is a desecration of his Holy Name, and defames religion in the world. The violence in the Holy Land is an evil which must be opposed by all people of good faith. We seek to live together as neighbors, respecting the integrity of each other's historical and religious inheritance. We call upon all to oppose incitement, hatred, and the misrepresentation of the other.
>
> The Holy Land is holy to all three of our faiths. Therefore, followers of the divine religions must respect its sanctity, and bloodshed must not be allowed to pollute it. The sanctity and integrity of the Holy Places must be preserved, and the freedom of religious worship must be ensured for all.
>
> Palestinians and Israelis must respect the divinely ordained purposes of the Creator by whose grace they live in the same land that is called Holy.

We call on the political leaders of both parties to work for a just, secure, and durable solution in the spirit of the words of the Almighty and the Prophets.

As a first step now, we call for a religiously sanctioned cease-fire, respected and observed from all sides, and for the implementation of the Mitchell and Tenet recommendations, including the lifting of restrictions and return to negotiations.

We seek to help create an atmosphere where present and future generations will co-exist with mutual respect and trust in the other. We call on all to refrain from incitement and demonization, and to educate our future generations accordingly.

As religious leaders, we pledge ourselves to continue a joint quest for a just peace that leads to reconciliation in Jerusalem and the Holy Land, for the common good of all our peoples.

We announce the establishment of a permanent joint committee to carry out the recommendations of this declaration, and to engage with our respective political leadership accordingly.

Signatories:
>   His Grace the Archbishop of Canterbury, Dr. George Carey
>   The Sephardic Chief Rabbi Bakshi-Doron
>   The Deputy Foreign Minister, Rabbi Michael Melchior
>   Rabbi David Rosen, President of the WCRP
>   The Rabbi of Savyon, Rabbi David Brodman
>   Minister of State for the Palestinian Authority, Sheikh Tal El Sider
>   Representative of the Greek Patriarch, Archbishop Aristichos
>   The Melkite Archbishop, Archbishop Boutrous Mu'alem
>   Representative of the Armenian Patriarch, Archbishop Chinchinian
>   The Bishop of Jerusalem, the Rt. Revd. Riah Abu El Assal

However, a critique of such a high-level initiative is that it does not go beyond the declaration mode or the "halls of luxurious hotels." There were no significant follow-up activities to link accomplishments and breakthroughs to the local religious institutions or actions on the ground to confront structural violence sustained by religious groups and institutions. The initiative fell short of addressing real conflict issues and remained generic in calling for unity, harmony, and peace. The religious leaders did not take a meaningful and calculated risk to signal to their followers the need for political compromise on core issues. In addition, religious leaders who participated were associated with the political establishments on both sides (e.g., the state mufti, chief rabbis, etc.) and were often sponsored or hosted by foreign and not local organizations.

Despite this critique, it is important to recognize the historic breakthrough of a regional declaration such as the one coming out of Alexandria. When Israel's chief rabbi attended and endorsed the Alexandria Declaration of Interfaith Coexistence and called for peaceful resolution, this resulted in greater media coverage—and recognition of the important role that religious leaders can play in the informal peace process.

But regardless of its visibility, this initiative was unable to shift the reality on the ground within a short period of time (even within a two-year period!). In interviews with Muslim and Christian Palestinian clergy in 2003, they cited the failure of the Alexandria Declaration in achieving peace between the Israelis and Palestinians. Developing a realistic set of expectations and agreeing upon the short-term and long-term intervention objectives, without relying solely on "divine miracles," is certainly a necessary preparatory step for interreligious peacebuilding.

Overcoming Obstacles in Interfaith Dialogue

The dynamics of the Israeli-Palestinian conflict are constantly shifting and being affected by the larger geopolitical forces in the region. For example, the recent political upheaval in the Arab world, especially in Egypt, Syria, and Iraq, have introduced new factors in the Israeli-Palestinian conflict and the discourse of religious identity. The fact that a Shia-Sunni divide has emerged as a regional discourse and the increasing presence of al-Qaeda affiliate groups in Syria and Sinai forces interreligious leaders in Israel-Palestine to adjust their strategies in responding to a new set of fears and priorities in exploring ways to constructively speak against religious exclusion and radicalization. This is especially the case when Israeli religious settlers and their radical discourse are taking a more central stage in Israeli politics.

In addition to these challenges, there are many external obstacles and internal limitations facing interfaith dialogue organizations in Israel-Palestine.

There is a disconnect from Arab-Jewish public concerns. Most interfaith groups are limited to a small number of participants who focus their conversation on ritualistic and cultural explorations of people from different faith groups. For example, when the Grand Imam of Al-Azhar and the Chief Rabbi met, it was only symbolic, avoiding talk about real problems. Rabbi Jeremey Miligram stated:

> Even when youth from Ramallah meet with Israeli youth, it is highly frustrating and demoralizing for Palestinians, when they do not talk about the killing of children and only focus or highlight the similarities in their faith by explaining a few verses from the Qur'ān or Bible to each other, and avoid demanding rights and talking about religious political issues.[17]

An active Jewish participant explained her frustration with this interfaith dialogue process: "[W]hen we are dealing with Palestinians who truly are suffering enormously every day in their situation, they feel that to not talk about this is almost a betrayal. Whereas the Jews who are suffering in their own way from the bombings and from the terrorism that is coming from these same towns, feel like talking with these people is almost traitorous."[18]

When examining Arab-Jewish power relations in this context, attending an interfaith dialogue activity becomes an excuse for no further action to address structural violence in Israeli-Palestinian relations. Thus, avoiding the "dialogue of life" (conflicting issues) and focusing on theological similarities contributes to the gap between interfaith dialogue groups and real concerns of most Arabs and Jews. Obviously, such approaches serve the needs of the dominant majority members who are motivated by the desire to "talk and understand." While the existing status quo of majority privileges generates the desire to reduce the conflict to individual psychological issues, members of the dominated group (Palestinians) continuously point out that occupation and structural violence issues need to be addressed.[19]

This reality of ignoring the severe violations of human rights in the Occupied Territories continues to be a challenge for interfaith dialogue groups in Israel-Palestine. There has been no movement on the part of such organizations to engage in activities or raise their voices against the conditions of holy sites in Hebron or Bethlehem, or even against the Separation Wall. Interfaith groups in Israel-Palestine have a limited circle of participants, often working with the same individuals and rarely reaching out to new audiences (especially those who oppose dialogue or have antagonistic and strong prejudices against the other faith groups). "Preaching to the converted" is a symptom that characterizes most interfaith dialogue groups. The inability to reach out to mainstream Arab and Jewish segments of society is in part caused by the type of organizers, facilitators, and invited experts, and the lack of "collective representation" of those who participate. As indicated by one active interfaith dialogue participant: "[P]eople who come to these meetings do not necessarily have a large public constituency. They are often marginalized in their own communities."[20]

A major challenge for interfaith dialogue groups in Israel-Palestine is related to sustainability and long-term impact. Due to reliance on external foreign funds (an overwhelming majority of funds are from U.S. and European Jewish and Christian groups), interfaith activities are sporadic and seasonal. Interfaith work is linked to a donor's cycle and agenda. Sustainability is also reduced by the violent nature of the conflict. Violent escalation and constant episodes of violence that characterize the Israeli-Palestinian conflict have caused many of the interfaith dialogue groups to stop their activities during a surge in military or communal violence. For example, no interfaith dialogue group activities took place during the height of the Second Intifada in 2002.

The interfaith dialogue field in Israel-Palestine faces some internal limitations that also curtail its effectiveness in attracting a wider audience or becoming more effective with its existing target groups. For example, many facilitators and organizers have limited understanding of interfaith peace programming in general and are unable to contextualize their programs within larger peace efforts.

Due to a lack of resources, there are limited professional trainings offered to the interfaith facilitators or their organizations. There is a limited degree of professional capacity in facilitating and designing these programs. Their experience in the field is mainly based on trial and error. Some of the facilitators and organizers recognized these limitations and admitted that "faith alone is not enough" to become an effective interfaith dialogue organization. However, they also were quick to articulate their needs for further professional training and resources.

Another internal limitation is reflected in the asymmetric management and funding of interfaith programs in which a majority of the directors, managers, and donors are Israeli and American Jews, while the facilitators and field coordinators are a mix of Palestinians and Israelis. In addition, issues of a lack of financial transparency were raised by various participants when they explained lack of credibility and internal challenges.

Although between 2003 and 2007 there were over fifteen different interfaith organizations and initiatives in Israel-Palestine, there has been a lack of intentional linkages or networking among these groups or between them and other peace programs in the region or in Israel-Palestine. This disconnect is clear in conferences, communication networks meetings, and certain replications of activities and participants.

For Palestinian Christians and Muslims, and Israeli Jews who operate in this field of interreligious peace, addressing the above challenges requires resources and support both from their own communities and from the outside. Nevertheless, their limited efforts despite the difficult context are symbolically significant in conveying a clear message that religious identity can be a source of peace rather than a justification for war and conflict, and that the roots of the Israeli-Palestinian conflicts are political rather than theological.

Conclusion

Religious peace actors are active in the Israeli-Palestinian context. Their activities focus mainly on interfaith dialogue and on a grassroots level of participation. Their contribution to the peace processes and Israeli-Palestinian conflict is symbolic, but it is important to have religious peace actors as a part of the overall networks for peace in the region.

The interreligious peacebuilding field is gradually developing into an integral part of the wider peace efforts carried out by Arabs and Jews in general. Nevertheless, there are certain shortcomings that have impeded its effectiveness in reaching out to mass groups or in deepening its impact. For example, internal and external factors such as: its organizers, donors, staff, and volunteers' professional capacity; type of participants' representation; processes and models employed by organizers; and increased militarization and violence.

Different from other conflict areas such as South Africa, El Salvador, India, or Sri Lanka, where there have been religious leaders who declare their complete commitment to a theology of nonviolence action, in Israel-Palestine such figures and groups have not yet organized or captured the stage of peace work. Thus, there is a dire need for coordination and linkages among those authentic religious leaders who are genuinely committed to peace and willing to walk in the forefront of peacemaking rather than be "regime advisors."

Finally, in the context of Israeli-Palestinian conflict and peace work, there is no way around religious peacebuilding anymore. Religious actors from both sides are increasingly assuming a leadership role and voicing their desire for an active role in formal and informal peacemaking efforts. The spread of militant religious groups and the prevalence of exclusive religious discourse in Israeli and Arab societies imposed this need to address religion in every peace initiative possible. In this context, for any social or political change initiative to be effective and reach out to the masses, it has to go through the gates of "religious identity." Otherwise it will lack public credibility. This does not mean that effective peace processes have to be religious and led by religious figures or leaders, but they must look for creative ways to incorporate the voices of religious constituencies into peace processes.

Notes

1. The author is deeply thankful to Timothy Seidel, who assisted in editing and revising this chapter.

    See various examples of the religious dimensions in the Israeli-Palestinian conflict: http://www.ifamericansknew.org/cur_sit/religion.html (accessed April 2, 2014).

2. Such a political strategy is clearly manifested in the ideology of "Gush Emunim" ("Block of the Faithful"—a settler movement in Israel since 1967)

and the political parties Shas (the largest Sephardic Jewish political party and its link to Land of Israel) and the National Religious Party (NRP).

3. Based on an informal interview with a senior advisor to the Israeli Jewish chief rabbi and leaders of the Islamic Movement in Israel, Jerusalem, March 2014.

4. Some of the data for this article is based on a set of interviews and observations completed by the author in Israel-Palestine between 2003 and 2007. Over forty-five interviews with Muslims, Christians, and Jews were completed and analyzed.

5. Interview with Abdul Salam Manasra, Nazareth, July 2004.

6. Interview with a Palestinian participant, Jerusalem, 2003.

7. Based on training materials for a course on "Religious Sources of Conflict and Peace" led by Cynthia Sampson and Mohammed Abu-Nimer at Eastern Mennonite University's Summer Peacebuilding Institute (1997).

8. The role of the church in opposing Apartheid in South Africa is a classic example of such a function. The Organization of Islamic Cooperation has also adopted this role, especially when the victims are Muslim minorities, for example the OIC visit to Central African Republic in 2014.

9. Rabbis for Human Rights (an Israeli Jewish organization) and Sabeel (a Palestinian Christian center in Jerusalem) are two exceptional organizations that support advocacy of peace and human rights. They are uninational or unireligious organizations and operate from their own liberation theology framework.

10. Most of the interfaith groups are active within the 1948 Israeli borders with only two to three initiatives operating in the West Bank and no Arab-Jewish interfaith dialogue initiatives in Gaza.

11. Mohammed Abu-Nimer et al., *Unity in Diversity: Interfaith Dialogue in the Middle East* (Washington, D.C.: United States Institute of Peace, 2007).

12. Interview, Haifa, April 2004.

13. Abu-Nimer, *Dialogue, Conflict Resolution, and Change: Arab-Jewish Encounters in Israel* (Albany: State University of New York Press, 1999).

14. A full description of the various organizations and their activities can be found in Mohammed Abu-Nimer, Emily Welty, and Amal I. Khoury, *United in Diversity: Interfaith Dialogue in the Middle East* (Washington, D.C.: United States Institute of Peace, 2007).

15. Interview with Women Dialogue Group, Jerusalem, 2003.

16. For more information see David R. Smock, *Interfaith Dialogue and Peacebuilding* (Washington, D.C.: United States Institute of Peace, 2002), and the Network for Interfaith Concern (http://nifcon.anglicancommunion.org/work/declarations/alexandria2.cfm) (accessed May 18, 2014).

17. Interview with Rabbi Jeremey Miligram, Jerusalem, July 2005.

18. Interview with participant of Jerusalem Women Dialogue Group, Jerusalem, July 2004.

19. Amy S. Hubbard, "Understanding Majority and Minority Participation in Interracial and Interethnic Dialogue," in *Reconciliation, Justice, and Coexistence: Theory and Practice*, ed. Mohammed Abu-Nimer (Lanham, MD: Lexington Books, 2001).

20. Interview with David Neuhaus, Jerusalem, August 2006.

3

The Use of Dialogue in Transforming Religious Conflict

DAVID DEREZOTES

Religious conflict can be thought of as a disagreement about the rituals, beliefs, and doctrines that religions may teach. Such conflict is inevitable. We share a world of religious diversity, which includes people with many religions and a growing minority who have no declared religion at all. Frequently, there is also a local diversity of religion within our own families, institutions, and communities. Each individual may also have her own internal conflicts regarding the rituals, beliefs, and doctrines that she was taught to follow.

Although religious conflict may be a part of everyday human existence, we always have choices about how we respond to conflict. The suffering that comes from conflict may be unavoidable, but the suffering we experience from taking unhealthy actions in response to such conflict is avoidable. We may, for example, habitually try to avoid conflict, through distractions such as alcohol, drugs, or other compulsive activities. Or, we may respond to conflict with defensiveness or violence. Such activities inevitably lead to greater suffering.

In this chapter, I suggest that religious conflict, although often challenging and painful, can also be an opportunity for positive transformation. Such transformation is an intentional process in which the person uses conflict as an opportunity to develop self-awareness, self-acceptance, self-empowerment, and service to others. Dialogue is presented as a transformational process that can help bridge religious divides, and a variety of dialogue models are introduced that can be used to help develop the kinds of relationships necessary to peacefully resolve religious conflict.

What Is Religious Conflict?

Religious conflict is an ongoing disagreement about different rituals, beliefs, doctrines, and behaviors. A religious conflict is resolved, or transformed, when the disagreeing parties are "in relationship" with each other, despite their disagreements and differences. As Krishnamurti taught, when human beings are in relationship with each other, they recognize their interconnection and are in a communion based primarily upon what he calls a selfless love, instead of merely upon gratification, obligation, or power. Their nonviolent responses to conflict harm no one, and instead tend to promote peace both within and between themselves.[1]

In contrast, religious conflict remains unresolved when the parties still live "out of relationship" with each other. When people live out of relationship, they are in denial of their interconnection, and their interactions are based upon such motivations as gratification, obligation, or power. When people live out of relationship, they tend to respond with such behaviors as defensiveness, retaliation, and avoidance.

Religious conflict can be found at all three interrelated levels of human experience. First, religious conflict can be intrapersonal. Each of us has inner conflicts that need to be resolved as we make decisions about how we think and act from moment to moment. We may often have conflicting feelings, for example, about what to wear or what to eat, or what route to take to work. A person can have conflicting feelings or thoughts about religion as well. Many people may have doubts about the religion that they were brought up in, for example. Others may feel both desire and religious guilt about a pleasurable activity that they are interested in, or even about a passing thought or feeling they are having.

As suggested above, violent responses to conflict are those that cause harm to myself and/or others. A common example of a violent intrapersonal response to religious conflict would be denial or avoidance of the conflict through drugs, alcohol, or other potentially addictive activities. Another example of intrapersonal violence would be the imposition of guilt and shame on myself for having conflicting feelings or thoughts. Dialogue techniques that can help people develop nonviolent responses are offered later in this paper.

Second, religious conflict can also be interpersonal, when we have such conflicts with other people in our families, institutions, and local communities. We might encounter conflicts with our colleagues at work, for example, as ideas and behaviors related to religion are discussed. We may have religious conflicts at home, over family rules about sexual behavior that have religious roots. Common violent responses to such a conflict would include a judgmental verbalization (e.g., "that is a silly belief"), a defensive verbalization ("I am too intelligent to believe that"), or avoidance ("can we talk about something else?"). Dialogue techniques that can help people develop nonviolent interpersonal responses are offered later in this paper.

Finally, religious conflict can occur on a global level. Over 6 billion of the approximately 7.4 billion people currently living in our world profess belief in one of the twenty major religions, defined here as a religion with at least six hundred thousand followers.[2] Most of us are aware of the religious conflicts that exist in our global community. Today, it seems we are constantly hearing about violence that is perpetrated because of disagreements about religion. These might include a bombing in some city, acts of civil war in a divided nation, or the imprisonment and sometimes murder of religious minorities. Religious conflict can thus lead to religious divides within our families and communities, both local and global. A religious divide is an ongoing conflict that has resulted in a state of mutual separation, suspicion, and attack.

Although all religions have been involved in violent conflict, religions have also played significant peacemaking roles. In addition, other factors, such as cultural and ethnic identities, also play significant roles in violence that can be difficult to separate from religious identities.[3] Indeed, religion is just one of the many elements of human diversity that exist in ourselves, and in our families, communities, and world. As in all the etiologies of human behavior, religion interacts with other variables, such as race, culture, poverty, and power, often in complex and subtle ways.

Sociohistorical Trauma

Sociohistorical trauma is an ongoing negative reaction to the experience of interpersonal violence. Religious conflict can result in sociohistorical trauma. All violence is a monologue, a one-way conversation that silences the other (another person who seems different from me) and makes any true dialogue unsafe. The silencing can be ongoing and can result in disempowerment (disconnection from self), inhibition of cognitive, emotional, and social development, and disconnection from the world.

Each victim's trauma response reflects her own unique internal and external world. Thus, historical trauma is an *ecobiopsychosocialspiritual* process, in that ecological, biological, psychological, social, and spiritual elements are all involved. For example, a man who was sexually abused as a child may be ashamed because of cultural homophobia (ecological), he may develop an eating disorder (biological), he may become depressed (psychological) and isolated from others (social), and/or lose his faith that life is worth living (spiritual). The neurobiology of historical trauma is complex and still not well understood, and most researchers avoid simplistic explanations, such as the "chemical imbalance" theory, to explain observed symptoms.[4]

Non-Western scholars have expressed concerns that the Western mental health industry utilizes a technical rather than moral approach that focuses too much on such concepts as "emotional catharsis" and "chemical imbalance" and not enough on cultural and social contexts. Most refugees, for example, do well without mental health treatment,[5] and Western approaches to helping American Indian and Alaskan native populations are largely ineffective without the addition of approaches that draw from cultural traditions and build upon tribal strengths.[6]

Interpersonal violence can often lead to further violence. Victims of such violence may seek revenge and thus become perpetrators, creating cycles of perpetration and victimization. Both victims and perpetrators in these cycles may live in a state of disconnection, uncertainty, and hypervigilance.[7]

Sociohistorical trauma can be experienced by both individuals and by groups of people.

Interpersonal and global religious conflict can result in collective trauma that is passed down across many generations. For example, many children raised in Israel and Palestine may grow up with symptoms of sociohistorical trauma, even if they have not directly experienced violence in their own short lives. Religious sociohistorical trauma can thus be associated with religious divides in families and local institutions and communities.

Dialogue Is the Opposite of Violence

As described above, violence is always a monologue, because it silences the "other." In intrapersonal violence, the other is a "part" or voice inside myself, which I refuse to be aware of and accept. In interpersonal and global violence, the other is another person, or group of people.

The opposite of violence is dialogue. Dialogue can be defined as "a nonviolent relationship-building practice with shared commitment to parallel intrapersonal and interpersonal (or ecological) work directed towards increasing the mutual understanding, acceptance, and empowerment necessary for our collective transformation from 'trauma-repetition' towards sustainable, equitable, and peaceful communities."[8]

Some might argue that two people can be in violent conflict and in dialogue at the same time. Although it is true that an individual can, for example, listen for understanding, or speak respectfully and honestly in any situation, the other may still be unwilling or unable to reciprocate. When the other is violent or makes violent threats, personal boundaries are violated and need to be protected, and the values of dialogue (listening for understanding, speaking respectfully) may be practiced by only one side. Such "one-sided" dialogue may or may not lead to more reciprocal dialogue (where both people eventually practice in concert with the values of dialogue). Friedman described Martin Buber's dialogue practice as a "confirmation of otherness" in which the unique positions of each person are recognized and affirmed, regardless of whether they continue to strongly disagree about those positions.[9] Such confirmation was arguably part of the nonviolent resistance practiced by such leaders as Nelson Mandela, Martin Luther King, and Mahatma Gandhi, who taught the ideal of love for the other, regardless of their behavior.

The most important task of participants in any dialogue is first and foremost to listen. Deep listening, which is listening with presence and compassion for the purpose of understanding, is a valuable gift any person can give to another. Having "presence" means that the listener is able to put himself in the here-and-now moment, with his intent on understanding the other person. To have "compassion" means to think and act with loving kindness towards the other, particularly with the intent to help the other experience more joy and less suffering. Many people have difficulty bringing deep listening to the other, because they are not ready yet to forgive them and give up their own hurt and anger. These issues will be discussed further in the section on dialogue models below.

The phrase "parallel intrapersonal and interpersonal or ecological work" in the definition of dialogue, refers to the interrelationship between my own "inner" work, and my relationships with others and with what we call nature. Basically, as I learn to understand and accept myself, I learn to better understand and accept others. I especially seek to be mindful of my difficult emotional and mental reactions (such as fear, anger, or disgust) which means I notice these reactions without trying to judge or change them. Instead I focus on an attitude of compassion for myself and for the other. This kind of compassionate and nonjudgmental awareness is popularly called "mindfulness" today.

Chodron describes mindfulness work as striving to have a "soft" (or open) heart. This soft heart allows a person to notice and resist any initial tendency to react violently, towards violence. Instead, the person strives to cultivate a fearlessness, which allows her to be nonreactive to others, willing to stay open to whatever happens in the moment, and more patient with the process. For Chodron, a closed heart seeks a quick fix to the discomfort of conflict, and seeks a solid and fixed pattern of thinking and acting, which can lead to violence.[10]

Mutual understanding means that dialogue involves both speaking and, especially, listening. Dialogue can be thus thought of as similar to the "compassionate conversation" Hanh has written about. In such a conversation, I strive to understand and be understood, and especially to help others suffer less. Hanh suggests that people practice what he calls mindful breath work and mindful walking, as a preparation for mindfulness in relationship.[11]

Dialogue can help people break the learned pattern of trauma repetition and learn new patterns of relating with other people. Trauma repetition refers to the tendency of people with trauma to sometimes try to avoid suffering by either withdrawing into a pattern of avoidance or compulsively recalling and sometimes reenacting the original traumatic experience.[12]

The purpose of dialogue, then, is to create the kind of relationships necessary for cooperation across the differences that divide our families, communities, and world. Humans appear to desire and even require such relationships for our own wellbeing. Neuroscientists have found that humans are naturally "wired" to seek healthy relationships with others. In fact, we now know that social relationships foster physical and mental health in ourselves and in our communities.[13]

The Dialogue Facilitator

The dialogue facilitator strives to

> help co-create a *community of diversity* in which each participant is free to experience and express both individuality and interconnection. The effective dialogue facilitator is able to consciously shift her own awareness back and forth between her individual self (the "me") and the entire dialogue group she is interconnected with (the "we").[14]

The facilitator thus strives to help dialogue participants codevelop the kinds of relationships that may help them bridge the religious, and other, differences that divide them, and in doing so hopefully also transform the religious trauma that has fueled those divides.

The most important knowledge that the dialogue facilitator has is her own self-knowledge. She employs what social workers call "conscious use of self," in which the facilitator models mindful use of all the ecobiopsychosocialspiritual levels of human consciousness. The facilitator thus is aware of his own cognitions and emotions as he works, as well as the group environment, social interactions, and spiritual and religious issues in the group.

The facilitator is also a seeker of "little t" truth, rather than "big T" Truth. Although humans may never agree on the big T Truths (ultimate truths recognized by all) regarding religious rituals, beliefs, and doctrines, we certainly can recognize and confirm the little t truths, held by individuals or groups of people.

The facilitator usually introduces a set of ground rules for the dialogue. Many people are more familiar with debate, and often confuse the rules of debate with the rules of dialogue. A list of dialogue ground rules are offered below.[15]

TABLE 3.1. WAYS TO INTERACT WITH OTHERS IN A GROUP DIALOG.

Participants do:	Participants do not:
(1) Listen to others	(1) Debate
(2) Pay attention to my own reactions (e.g., sensations, emotions, and thoughts)	(2) Express judgements
	(3) Act violently
	(4) Analyze or diagnose other people
(3) Speak as honestly and directly as I can	(5) Interrupt others
(4) Speak for myself rather than speaking for others	(6) Speak longer than a few minutes during my turn
(5) Be respectful towards others	(7) Demand agreement or responses from others
(6) Give other people the opportunity to speak before taking another turn	
(7) Allow forgiveness to myself and others when we make mistakes	

The dialogue facilitator also seeks to develop her own spiritual maturity. One of the chief characteristics of spiritual maturity identified by both men and women is an acceptance of other faith systems.[16] The facilitator therefore models respect for different religions and spiritual perspectives in the dialogues, and strives to help participants do the same. Thus participants learn that it is possible to confirm the religious differences in the room, even though they may at the same time have strong personal reactions to the beliefs of other people in the dialogue. Such "confirmation of otherness" is, as described above, a practice of respectful listening and sharing, where differences are recognized and accepted. The facilitator sees that dialogue is not necessarily about finding a way to agree, but is more about how we treat each other when we disagree.

Five Dialogue Models

About forty years ago, Abraham Maslow identified four "forces" of modern psychology: the psychodynamic, the behavioral, the experiential, and the then-emerging transpersonal approaches.[17] Since then, an additional new "force" has arguably emerged in the literature that could be called the ecobio approach. Five dialogue models, for work with religious conflict, can be informed by these five forces. They are introduced below.

The common goal in all the dialogue models is to help people develop relationships with other people, particularly with people who belong to the other "side" of a religious divide. Each model emphasizes one of the ecobiopsychosocialspiritual dimensions described in this chapter. All the models share the assumption that personal- psychological transformation accompanies social-relational transformation. This means that as each person works on her own self-awareness and self-acceptance, she becomes more skilled at listening to and accepting others. When there is historical trauma that involves religion, these dialogue models may help participants establish the kind of relationships necessary to work towards transformation of the trauma.

Although these five models are described separately below, they can all be used in the same dialogue event. They are not mutually exclusive, and the most effective facilitator is flexible enough to draw from any combination of models, as needed.

Psychodynamic Dialogue: Telling Our Stories for Understanding

In the psychodynamic model, the facilitator invites people to take turns sharing stories about themselves, while the rest of the group listens for understanding. I have often discovered that storytelling activities can help dialogue participants transform the differences that divide them. For example, in a dialogue on gun control, the facilitator could ask participants to share a story about their first memories or experiences that have to do with guns. The stories that are generated might include stories about going hunting with a parent, playing with squirt guns on a summer day, or hearing that a neighbor had been shot in a street violence incident. Such stories can help participants better understand why the other might have a different view on guns than they do. As the ancient proverb says, "The shortest distance between two people is a story."

When a dialogue group first starts to meet, storytelling can also help "break the ice" in the relationship-building process. For example, there was considerable tension in a community over the "religious divide" between people in the local majority religion and people belonging to other religious minorities. The facilitator asked participants from both groups to share the stories of how they became affiliated with their current religions. Most participants were able to both share and listen, and the dialogue moved forward. Researchers have found that people can benefit psychologically and socially from telling their stories and being listened to.[18]

Cognitive Behavioral Dialogue: Exploring Attitudes and Behaviors

Cognitive behavioral dialogue is focused on the exploration of attitudes and behaviors. This dialogue model is based upon Cognitive Behavioral Therapy (CBT), which has been the most popular approach to counseling in the United States for decades, and which has also been attractive to researchers who study practice outcomes.[19] Many self-help books and other popular literature utilize CBT techniques, and neuroscientists have even developed, for example, a "brain science of happiness" that links cognitions and brain activity to mood states.[20]

Cognitive behavioral dialogue is relatively "safe" for dialogue participants, because most people like to talk about ideas, or as we say today, because most of us like to "stay in our heads." The dialogue facilitator can use this advantage of safety to help the dialogue get started, by framing the first dialogues as intellectual conversations. For example, one dialogue is being developed for people who want to talk about religion and same-sex marriage. The facilitator knows that people can get angry and defensive about their positions on this subject, so she sets up the first dialogue meeting to begin with a cognitive behavioral dialogue in which people are asked to talk about their beliefs. They may, for example, be asked to take turns responding to the question, "What is one thing you know for certain about the world?" The facilitator reminds participants that they are to listen to these ideas, rather than to react in judgment.

Experiential: Talking and Understanding from the Heart

Experiential dialogue is about the communication of feelings. I was once in a dialogue with American Indian people, and one of them said that he wanted us all to speak "from our hearts." I have also heard a refugee from a "Third World" country say that people can only understand someone else by listening "through the heart." What do these statements mean?

People can learn to speak and listen from the heart. There are arguably six basic emotions: sad, mad, glad, scared, excited, disgusted.[21] The dialogue facilitator can ask participants to be curious about which of the six emotions are coming up for them in the moment, as the dialogue conversation goes on, and to try sharing that information with others. As people do this, they begin to speak and listen from the heart.

Why would you want participants to speak and listen from the heart? There is considerable evidence that emotional intimacy, the sharing of emotions in genuine, mutually supporting, and nonviolent ways, is associated with positive physical and psychological wellbeing.[22]

Transpersonal: Talking from Spirit

Transpersonal dialogue includes the spiritual dimension in conversation. Spirituality can be thought of as associated with such individual experiences as a sense of connection with the world, a feeling of awe, an appreciation of what is sacred, an ability to love, and the temperance of ego. In contrast, religiosity can be understand as socially shared rituals, beliefs, and doctrines.

Although most people have spiritual experiences, just as they have emotional experiences, there may be few, if any, times in their life when they can share such experiences in an environment that feels safe. People can be religious or atheist and have spiritual experiences. Although spirituality may not be commonly discussed, the spiritual dimension is a part of human experience.[23]

In spiritual dialogue, the facilitator asks participants to share aspects of their spirituality with each other. When there is a religious divide in a community, for example, people may benefit from a dialogue in which participants respond to such questions as, when did you feel the most spiritual in the past month, or what was your earliest spiritual experience that you remember?

Ecobio: Communicating with Our Bodies and with Nature

In ecobio dialogue, participants communicate with and about their bodies, other living things, and the ecosystems that support all life. We are connected to our bodies and with nature. Scientists have discovered that most people can often experience healing and connection when they are out in nature, or when interacting with other living things.[24] We also know that we communicate constantly with other people through our body language, which includes all our nonverbal expressions.[25]

In ecobio dialogue, the facilitator engages participants in activities that encourage their reconnection with their bodies and with nature. Such activities can help people who are divided by religious conflict to build sustainable relationships. For example, in a dialogue between "conservative" and "liberal" Christians, the facilitator begins by asking participants to pair up in dyads with someone from the other group and take turns making a nonverbal movement with their bodies that shows how their week has been. One person jumps up and down, another drops to the floor, and soon many people are laughing.

Another example of an ecobio activity involves nature imagery. The facilitator asks participants to take turns describing their most "sacred landscape." One person shares about a beach she loves in Southern California. A second person talks about his favorite canyon, and another describes a waterfall in the mountains. Such sharing can often help people rediscover their common humanity and connectedness with each other and with nature, and can thus help them begin relationships.

Integration of Models in Addressing Religious Conflict in a Community Dialogue

Elements of all five models can potentially be used in any dialogue. To illustrate this, I will use an example of an intergroup dialogue, being held in a community where about half the population belongs to a religious majority, and the other half belongs to one of a variety of religious (or nonreligious) minorities. Participants in the dialogue reflect roughly the same percentages, so that about half the participants belong to the local religious majority, which we will call the "XYZ" church.

In the first meeting, the facilitator begins by welcoming the participants, who are all adults. Participants are asked to introduce themselves by giving their name, religious affiliation (if any), and their favorite food for dinner (the dialogue began following a light dinner). Guidelines for dialogue might be put up on a white board for discussion. Then a series of activities might be facilitated.

The facilitator might have each person who identified as belonging to the XYZ church pair up with someone who did not. The instructions are for them to take turns telling the story of their religious history. This history would include the faith(s) they may have been exposed to as children, the degree to which they participated in any religious or spiritual experiences as a child and adolescent, and the stability of the development of their faith in their adult years. The person who is listening is instructed to listen silently, with the intent to understand, for fifteen minutes. At the end of that time, the people in each pair switch roles, and the listener has a chance to tell her or his story. This is a psychodynamic exercise.

Another exercise could involve a CBT approach. In this case, the group comes back together, and people are asked to each share "one thing you know for sure about the universe." This involves the sharing of cognitions, or beliefs about the world. After everyone has an opportunity to share (people who want to "pass" are always allowed to) then the group engages in a discussion about what was shared.

Another exercise might involve experiential sharing. People are asked to talk about what has given them the most joy in the past two months. This kind of exercise challenges participants to reflect on their emotions, and to try to understand (empathize) with the emotions of the other. The topic of joy often is one that most people are willing to discuss, and can help reveal similarities across religions, cultures, and races.

A transpersonal exercise might involve the sharing of individual experiences of religion and spirituality. The facilitator could, for example, ask people to draw a picture of the relationship (without using words) between their spirituality and their religiosity, using crayons and a blank sheet of paper. Participants are allowed to define these terms however they wish. Then the facilitator sets up a "fish bowl" of seven chairs in the center of the room, with everyone else's chairs arranged in a larger circle facing inward, around the inner circle. The facilitator asks people who would like to share their pictures to sit in the inner circle. They do so, as the outer circle watches silently. Later, others can join the inner circle if they wish. At some point in the process, people can ask questions and make comments about the pictures, and about what they represent.

Finally, the facilitator can introduce some ecobio exercises. Here, for example, the participants can be asked to reflect on and share about the spaces in nature in which they feel the most spiritual or religious. Or, participants can be asked to share about the relationship they experience between their minds, their bodies, and their spirits. Such dialogue topics can help facilitate increased mutual understanding and, ultimately, may enhance relationships across a religious divide.

The effective facilitator utilizes "practice-based evidence (PBE)" to assess and evaluate her facilitation.[26] The PBE process utilizes monitoring and participant feedback to measure success. Thus, the facilitator asks participants how they feel and think about her facilitation, the group's progress, and their own individual participation. She also directly observes group dynamics, to help her determine if the methods she is using are assisting participants in achieving group goals.

In conclusion, dialogue is a transformational process that can help bridge religious divides. The facilitator can draw from a variety of dialogue models, as she strives to help people develop the kinds of relationships necessary to peacefully resolve religious conflict. The effective dialogue may utilize all five of the models presented in this chapter, as she selects and implements dialogue exercises.

Notes
1. J. Krishnamurti, *The First & Last Freedom* (New York: Harper & Row, 1975).
2. Robert E. Van Voorst, *RELG: World* (New York: Cengage Learning, 2013), and "Featured Religions and Beliefs," *Religions*, BBC (2013). http://www.bbc.co.uk/religion/religions/.
3. David R. Smock, *Religion in World Affairs: Its Role in Conflict and Peace* (Washington, D.C.: Unites States Institute of Peace, 2008).
4. Peter R. Breggin and David Cohen, *Your Drug May Be Your Problem: How and Why to Stop Taking Psychiatric Medications* (New York: Da Capo Press, 2000).
5. Derek Summerfield, "Childhood, War, Refugeedom and 'Trauma': Three Core Questions for Mental Health Professionals," *Transcultural Psychiatry* 37, no. 3 (September 2000): 417–33.

6. Maria Yellow Horse Brave Heart and Lemyra M. DeBruyn, "The American Indian Holocaust: Healing Historical Unresolved Grief," *American Indian and Alaska Native Mental Health Research* 8, no. 2 (1998): 60–76.

7. David Derezotes, "Ideology Identification as Psychosocial-Spiritual Disorder: A Framework for Assessment and Intervention," *Journal of Religion and Spirituality in Social Work* 32, no. 2 (April/June 2014): 145–59.

8. Ibid., 44.

9. Maurice Friedman, *The Confirmation of Otherness in Family, Community, and Society* (New York: Pilgrim Press, 1983).

10. Pema Chodron, *Practicing Peace in Times of War* (Boston: Shambhala, 2003).

11. Thich Nhat Hanh, *The Art of Communicating* (New York: HarperCollins, 2013).

12. Judith Herman, *Trauma and Recovery: The Aftermath of Violence—from Domestic Violence to Political Terror* (New York: Basic Books, 1992).

13. Matthew D. Lieberman, *Social: Why Our Brains Are Wired to Connect* (New York: Crown, 2013).

14. Derezotes, "Ideology Identification as Psychosocial-Spiritual Disorder," 68.

15. Adapted from David Derezotes, *Transforming Historical Trauma through Dialogue* (Thousand Oaks, CA: Sage Publications, 2013).

16. David Derezotes et al., "Spiritual Maturity: An Exploratory Study and Model for Social Work Practice," *Currents: New Scholarship in the Human Services* 7, no. 1 (2008): 1–18.

17. Abraham H. Maslow, *The Farther Reaches of Human Nature* (New York: Viking Press, 1971).

18. Jon Frederickson, *Psychodynamic Psychotherapy: Learning to Listen from Multiple Perspectives* (Hove, UK: Psychology Press, 1999).

19. Daniel J. Moran, "The Three Waves of Behavioral Therapy: Course Corrections or Navigation Errors?," *The Behavioral Therapist* (Winter 2008): 147–57.

20. Rick Hanson, *Hardwiring Happiness: The New Brain Science of Contentment, Calm, and Confidence* (New York: Harmony, 2013).

21. George Norwood, "Emotions," *Deepermind.* http://www.deepermind.com/02clarty.htm.

22. Richard C. Page, James F. Weiss, and Germain Lietaer, "Humanistic Group Therapy," in *Humanistic Psychotherapies: Handbook of Research and Practice*, ed. David J. Cain and Julius Seeman (Washington, D.C.: American Psychological Association, 2002), 339–68.

23. Ken Wilber, *The Spectrum of Consciousness* (Wheaton, IL: Theosophical Publishing House, 1977).

24. Howard Clinebell, *Ecotherapy: Healing Ourselves, Healing the Planet* (New York: Haworth Press, 1996).

25. Alexander Lowen, *The Voice of the Body* (Alachua, FL: Bioenergetics Press, 2005).

26. Timothy Anderson, Kirk M. Lunnen, and Benjamin M. Ogles, "Putting Models and Techniques in Context," in *The Heart and Soul of Change: Delivering What Works in Therapy*, ed. Barry L. Duncan et al., 2nd ed. (Washington, D.C.: American Psychological Association, 2010).

PART 2

RELIGIOUS IDENTITY
AND AMERICAN PERSPECTIVES

This section offers two contributions that explore the relationship between religious identity and narratives in the American context. Building on his volume, *From Jeremiad to Jihad: Religion, Violence, and America*, coedited with his colleague Jonathan Ebel, John Carlson revisits the myths that have informed American history and national identity, and deconstructs their religious tone and propensity to violence. In the spirit of Robert Bellah's seminal essay on "Civil Religion in America,"[1] Carlson offers a critical analysis of the myths that define the "American way." Throughout his analysis, he addresses the question of violence and whether or not such myths have contributed to the justification of the use of violence. After reviewing important figures of the American political landscape, Carlson concludes that American exceptionalism has entailed violence and conflict all along, albeit with different effects. Many scholars[2] have discussed the use of biblical imagery and references in American public discourse; Carlson reviews those positions with clarity and suggests that a strong link exists among American religious identity, American exceptionalism, and forms of both inclusion and exclusion within American society.

Ched Meyers and Elaine Enns analyze another element of American history and its narratives, namely the relationships between the population who settled on this continent and the indigenous population. The historical narrative about the colonial period generally erases most of its violent elements and thus often prevents the possibility to enter into a restorative process. Meyers and Enns give voice to those who have been silent and present the work of "Truth and Reconciliation" committees that are attempting to reframe historical narratives. In many contexts, the role of narratives is regarded as being central to peacemaking initiatives;[3] inspired by the prophetic visions of the Christian tradition, Meyers and Enns remind us that such work needs to happen in the American context as well.

Notes

1. Robert N. Bellah, "Civil Religion in America," *Daedalus: Journal of the American Academy of Arts and Sciences* 96, no. 1 (winter 1967): 1–21.

2. See, for instance, Michael Long and Tracy Wenger Sadd, eds., *God and Country?: Diverse Perspectives on Christianity and Patriotism* (New York: Palgrave Macmillan, 2007); Jacques Berlinerblau, *Thumpin' It: The Use and Abuse of the Bible in Today's Presidential Politics* (Louisville, KY: Westminster John Knox Press, 2008); and Andrew Hogue, *Stumping God: Reagan, Carter, and the Invention of a Political Faith* (Waco, TX: Baylor University Press, 2012).

3. See, for instance, Vamık D. Volkan, "Transgenerational Transmissions and Chosen Trauma" (opening address, XIII International Congress, International Association of Group Psychotherapy, London, August 1998); Yehudith Auerbach, "National Narratives in a Conflict of Identity," in *Barriers to Peace in the Israeli-Palestinian Conflict*, ed. Yaacov Bar-Sima-Tov (Jerusalem: Jerusalem Institute for Israel Studies, 2010), 99–134.

4

The American Way of Religion and Violence?

JOHN D. CARLSON

The American experience of religion and violence is charged with contradiction and moral ambivalence. This has been so from the beginning. For example, on one hand, the nation that Thomas Jefferson helped found on the principle of separation of church and state, having ably learned from Europe's wars of religion, successfully eluded temptations to wage religious wars of its own. On the other hand, individual colonies—and later states—maintained their own established religions, which were often imposed upon religious minorities—through the coercive force of government. Some might point to these latter historical moments as evidence that the separation of church and state is a myth—a fiction or falsehood. But paradoxically, the very same myth can also comprise its opposite: a profound and enduring truth. The truth embedded in myth is taken for granted not because it consistently represents the historical record but, rather, because it is so deeply entrenched in the minds of citizens—a resilient premise that pervades their thought and culture. The belief that something ought to be true becomes an aspiration, a guiding principle—a myth or truth that people live by. The contradictory (at times, ironic) relationship between truth and falsehood in political life is well established, going back as far as Plato's *Republic*, whereby a noble lie or myth becomes the carrier of the highest truths. More often, though, there is simply a gap between the ideals citizens hold true and certain events and interpretations that belie them. In any case, truth is not diminished simply because it accompanies or is purveyed by fiction. As with novels, so too with political myths.

Every culture has myths it lives by, and the United States is no exception.[1] When Americans claim certain "truths to be self-evident, that all men are endowed by their Creator with certain inalienable rights," they evoke the language of myth. In the United States, religion has played a central role in such myths, as invocations of "Creator" and "Nature's God" reveal.[2] Such myths are particularly ripe for scholarly investigation, and scholars have a tendency—indeed a responsibility—to scrutinize them. The Declaration of Independence, for example, did not mean originally (and was not interpreted to mean) that all men or all people were to be treated equally. Yet the tendency to critique can devolve into a tendency to deconstruct in ways that reduce multiple meanings, flatten out moral ambivalence, and overlook how myths also provide enduring frameworks for affirmation. The Declaration, for example, has provided a framework, however imperfectly realized, for the gradual expansion of equality and inclusivity for marginalized peoples.

The place of myth becomes particularly germane when it comes to the American experience of religion and violence. This chapter, framed in the form of a question, asks whether there is something we might recognize as an American way of religion and violence, including what parts of it are worthy of affirmation or critique. Its purpose is to consider some different ways that question might be interpreted and answered by examining several myths about religion and violence. In what follows, I largely build on ideas and insights first set out in the collection *From Jeremiad to Jihad: Religion, Violence, and America*, which my colleague Jonathan Ebel (a historian) and I (an ethicist) coedited. In our editorial roles, we sought to bring together a diverse range of disciplines and often conflicting perspectives about the American "story" of religion and violence. We sought to foster debate, even to complicate it, not to adjudicate or resolve it. In this way, the work of an editor is different than that of an author. Interestingly, even years after working on an intellectual project, there is a way in which one doesn't always realize what it is really about until well after it has been published. So, I return to this work now, after several more readings and discussions with students, to propose some ambivalent conclusions about the American way of religion and violence. Ambivalence by definition is complicated. But, I first wish to simplify through a review of some different myths about religion, violence, and America. These myths—as well as their limitations—form the palate from which a complex, ambivalent picture can be painted.

The Superman Myth: Covenant, Jeremiad, and American Exceptionalism

I begin by introducing one account of the American way of religion and violence, which lurks in some form in many people's minds. Those who grew up watching the original *Superman* television series starring George Reeves will remember the show's opening lines. Not the part about "[f]aster than a speeding bullet, more powerful than a locomotive" but, rather, Superman's "never-ending battle for truth, justice, and the American way." Interestingly, the "American way" bit was not part of the original *Superman* radio show but was added for television in the early 1950s. This was the era of McCarthyism, when the threat of "godless communism" took on new urgency and the decade in which "under God" became part of the Pledge of Allegiance (1954). Neither Superman nor the announcer ever defined the "American way" with any precision, but its consonance with "truth and justice" was well understood.

In all its vagueness, the "American way" stands in for values that are culturally important yet often unspoken. Scholars Robert Jewett and John Shelton Lawrence, reflecting upon another superhero in their *Captain America and the Crusade against Evil*, describe the latent power and prominence of the American way: "The world-redemptive view of America's destiny prevails especially in such products of popular culture as comic books. In the form of simplified mythic storytelling, they often depict ideals that are widely felt but are no longer explicitly articulated in more sophisticated circles."[3] The myth of the "American way," whether in comic books or the wider culture, connotes a certain affinity with political ideals of equality and democracy, for example as expressed in the Declaration of Independence. Superman, recall, was a great foe of tyrants who thirst after power, glory, and domination of others. The

American Way also represents economic ideals of free enterprise, prosperity, mobility, and innovation as well as social values involving self-reliance, benevolence, and strong moral character. Jewett and Lawrence, again commenting on Captain America, cite a "typical editorial comment" in which an editor writes, "Captain America is not a representative of America itself, but of the American ideal—individual responsibility, moral sensitivity, integrity, and a willingness to fight for right."[4] Of course, the same could be said of Superman. Scholar Will Herberg, writing in 1955—the era of Superman and Eisenhower—described the American way as "a spiritual structure, a structure of ideas and ideals, of aspirations and values, of beliefs and standards; it synthesizes all that commends itself to the American as the right, the good, and the true in actual life."[5] Symbolized by democracy more than anything else, the American way is committed to political and economic ideals that are fueled by a powerful moral energy:

> The American Way of Life is humanitarian, forward looking, optimistic.... But above all, the American is idealistic. Americans cannot go on making money or achieving worldly success simply on its own merits; such "materialistic" things must, in the American mind, be justified in "higher" terms, in terms of "service" or "stewardship" or "general welfare."...And because they are so idealistic, Americans tend to be moralistic.... Every struggle in which they are seriously engaged becomes a "crusade."[6]

Though influenced by traditional religions in America, this unifying mythos operates as a "common faith" for American society. The origins may be Protestant, but as Herberg's title *Protestant-Catholic-Jew* suggests, the ideals evolve and extend to other religious groups, if not to all Americans. This common faith in the "American way" swirls about in secular society, mixing with mundane elements of everyday life such as Coca-Cola, sanitary plumbing, and *Ladies Home Journal.*[7] And, of course, Superman.

Some still may wonder what Superman has to do with religion. On the surface, "truth, justice, and the American way" forms something of a triad, a trinity even. Whether anyone at the time recognized this trinity as religious is probably beside the point. After all, we're talking about an omnipotent superhuman who comes to earth and sets out to save humanity. There is certainly something godlike about that. More importantly, though, the idealism and moralism of the American way that Superman personifies are informed by deeply entrenched religious ideas and idioms. As Herberg notes, "The very expression 'way of life' points to its religious essence, for one's ultimate, over-all way of life is one's religion."[8] Such is the religious backdrop against which the seemingly secular Superman myth takes form.

The earliest religious roots of the American way harken back to John Winthrop's biblical invocation of the "city upon a hill" in which the Massachusetts Bay founder and governor declared that "the eyes of the world shall be upon us." Biblical religion in America, as Robert Bellah and others argue, often coalesced with civic republican strands to form a uniquely American version of civil religion.[9] One clear expression of civil religion is the famous motto of the American Revolution: "Rebellion to tyrants is obedience to God." Proposed by Ben Franklin, championed by Thomas Jefferson (both deists), the refrain accompanied a seal featuring the famous Exodus scene in which Moses and the Israelites flee Egypt as the Red Sea swallows up Pharaoh and his army. Accordingly, American mythology has long found expression in the trope of the "new Israel." One can look to an array of sources, figures, and events in American history to appreciate how religious ideas have shaped how Americans think about themselves, their country, and America's place in the world. What is particularly revealing is how such ideas emerge during crucial moments of conflict, violence, or war. There is, then, something distinctive about the ways that religion and violence converge that is illustrative of America or has helped define the country's history, culture, and identity—for better and for worse.

We can look to other famous Calvinist statesmen—beyond John Winthrop—for examples of such conflicts. Woodrow Wilson and John Foster Dulles, both sons of Presbyterian ministers and both possessing deep Princeton connections (Wilson was professor of government and later president; Dulles was an esteemed graduate and valedictorian), authored foreign policy covenants in their respective eras. These famous Princeton Presbyterians shared certain features with earlier covenant-makers such as Winthrop. To begin with, they all believed that Americans were bound to the terms of a covenant in which God was sovereign—the supreme author and guarantor. They all held that Americans incurred a responsibility to uphold the terms of this covenant as a proper way to acknowledge the special status, mandate, and blessings they enjoyed. Finally, they argued that the failure to live up to the terms of the respective covenants of their day could elicit negative consequences—punishment or retaliation that emanated from the country's connection to a divine moral order.

As Winthrop mused in his "Model of Christian Charity" (1630), "[I]f we shall neglect the observation of these articles...the Lord will surely break out in wrath against us, and be revenged of such a perjured people, and make us know the price of the breach of such a covenant."[10] This is a classic articulation of the American jeremiad, which includes the following features: exemplary ideals and moral norms, often grounded in a covenant; a threat of violence or actual violence that serves as punishment for the failure to live rightly in conformance to such ideals; and, finally, the opportunity to repent and recommit to the founding moral principles when they are breached.[11] This term jeremiad, named after the prophet Jeremiah in the Hebrew Scriptures, recalls the prophet's rebukes of the Israelites for failing to live up to the ideals God established for them, even as God refuses to abandon this favored people for their transgressions.

One sees evidence of jeremiadic thinking in the Americas just a few decades after Winthrop's famous sermon, when, in 1674, New England Puritans found themselves fighting the Wampanoag tribe, led by their chief, King Philip. The Puritan ethic never entailed claiming credit for good fortunes that accrued to them, since all good things emanate from God. But in the case of misfortunes suffered, their sins were entirely to blame. And the results could be quite severe:

> At times God seemed to be punishing New Englanders for their waywardness by inflicting violence upon them at the hands of King Philip's warriors. In one incident, a settler named Wright refused to seek shelter at the garrison with the other inhabitants of his town when the Indians arrived; instead, "he had a strange

confidence or rather conceit, that whilest he held his Bible in his hand, he looked upon himself as secure from all kinde of violence; and that the Enemy finding him in that posture, deriding his groundlesse apprehension or folly therein, ript him open, and put his Bible in his belly."[12]

Wright's prideful approach to scripture provoked God's wrath against him, making him the object of divine violence, and a cautionary example to others. Although the example of Wright's disembowelment made for sensational moral instruction, more typically, and in keeping with the social emphasis of the jeremiad tradition, chastening violence was interpreted by the community as punishment for its collective sins.

It is tempting to think the era of American jeremiads is behind us, but those who listened to rhetoric of the religious right after September 11, 2001, will recall Jerry Falwell and Pat Robertson blaming not foreign terrorists for the attacks but a host of domestic elements—the American Civil Liberties Union (ACLU), abortionists, pagans, gays, and feminists—for subverting the divine ideals to which God called Americans.[13] There were also jeremiads from the religious left. Pastors such as Jeremiah Wright preached sermons that portrayed 9/11 as a case of "chickens coming home to roost" in retaliation for various immoralities of U.S. foreign policy. In Wright's case, he used the attacks as a call for individual and collective introspection, repentance, and reconciliation with God—a central motif of the jeremiad.[14]

Despite this focus on the far right and left, covenantal and jeremiadic thought has been prominent in mainstream politics as well. Historian Jonathan Ebel describes how Woodrow Wilson deployed covenantal language to unite and mobilize the nation to fight the Great War in Europe:

President Wilson invoked the notion of covenant repeatedly in his public pronouncements on war, using it to establish in-group and out-group identities at home and abroad, and to shape understandings of how victory would be achieved and peace maintained. As he used covenant to unite and to pacify, he used it also to divide and to incite. Wilson saw little room in the world and less in the nation for those unwilling, in Puritan terms, to "own the covenant."...In his Second Inaugural Address, delivered on March 5, 1917, less than a month before the United States entered the war, Wilson spoke of war's covenantal benefits: "We are being forged into a new unity amidst the fires that now blaze throughout the world. In their ardent heat we shall, in God's providence, let us hope, be purged of faction and division, purified of the errant humors of party and private interest, and shall stand forth in the days to come with a new dignity of national pride and spirit."[15]

Ebel goes on to chronicle that Wilson was perhaps the most famous—though by no means the only—voice of covenantal idioms in World War I.

Decades later, as the nation was recovering from a second world war, Secretary of State John Foster Dulles delivered similarly styled speeches, in part to unite Americans and renew their commitment to universal moral principles, but also to unite and recommit the world to an international covenant, the terms of which ultimately would be used to pressure the Soviet Union. Ned O'Gorman, a scholar of rhetoric and political thought, demonstrates the religious and political confluence of Dulles's covenantal designs. Dulles had been a drafter and delegated signatory of the newly formed Charter of the United Nations (1945)—a document he saw as a new world covenant that, politically and institutionally speaking, stood the best chance of bringing the world in conformity with the moral order. Make no mistake, this moral order of politics, Dulles believed, was consistent with a divine moral order. The test, O'Gorman shows, was whether the United States and its citizens could generate the "spiritual power" needed to create and sustain the world organization. Dulles no doubt recalled the failures of the League of Nations. His appeal to Christian values sought needed support for creating the UN. O'Gorman comments how, for Dulles, Christianity reinforces "a vision of an expansive, universal covenant, applicable to all humankind." Far from bashing the UN, which has become more faddish in recent years, Dulles repaired to the jeremiad to condemn American skeptics "for their lack of faith in the UN's potential."[16] The United States should be out front exemplifying universal principles of the new international covenant, Dulles maintained. This would not be the last time American statesmen would claim the "exemplarist" mantle for the United States as it implements and models international standards as well as the coercive measures needed to enforce them.[17]

Of course, there was a bleaker side to Dulles's covenantal rhetoric, which appealed to other authorities and recourses besides the United Nations and its pursuit of global peace and international cooperation. Years after the UN Charter was approved, in a famous 1954 speech, Dulles declared the United States' willingness to use "massive retaliation" as a means of deterring Soviet aggression: a right "to retaliate, instantly, and by means and at places of our own choosing."[18] Dulles explicitly raised the specter of nuclear war. Beyond the national security threat the Soviets posed to the United States, Dulles's speech listed several grievances against the Soviets for violating the international covenant that he, the Universal Declaration of Human Rights (UDHR), and the UN charter all envisioned. Such violations included establishing a society premised on a police state and forced labor as well as denying the worship of God, the dictates of reason, and freedom of speech. The Soviet Union's international provocations and its domestic repression were two sides of a common coin—a coin that was not part of the new currency of the U.S.-led international covenant. Dulles's warning of "massive retaliation"—including nuclear strikes against civilian targets—made clear the lengths to which the United States would go to enforce the covenant. This included, O'Gorman notes, "the right to initiate the ultimate end to the remaining solidarity of the international community *in the name of the norms of that community.*"[19]

The approach I've developed in this section considers how violence—real, imagined, or threatened—possesses longstanding, deep-running roots that have been nourished in religious soil. This historical convergence of religion and violence has been central to one iteration of the "American way"—the character, ethos, and place in the world that many Americans and others ascribe to the United States. This view is often associated with an understanding of "American exceptionalism," the notion that the United States has been unusually blessed with certain riches and opportunities (in part due to its geography) as well as certain ideals, principles, and responsibilities (due to its history, its culture, and its political and religious heritage). Some may find more than a hint of a Superman complex in all of this. Or, to invoke another comic book classic, perhaps the Spiderman ethic pertains: "With great power comes great responsibility."[20] The aptness of this refrain for the United States may be realized most when America refuses to act or intervene such as during the Rwandan genocide in 1994, which Bill Clinton called the worst mistake of his presidency.

For many people, this exceptionalist view of the "American way" is nothing to champion. It can mask some rather nefarious elements—including a heavy reliance upon war and a willingness to interpret or justify force in religious terms. The United States was born out of war. The country's independence was secured as a result of violent revolution, and full nationhood only was achieved in and through the Civil War. World War I ushered in modern statehood as Americans from all states converged against a common enemy in Europe. And, of course, the United States emerged from World War II as a great power upon the world stage. This history of warfare would continue to unfold through the Cold War and post–Cold War engagements of the twentieth century and, most recently, military conflicts in Afghanistan, Iraq, Yemen, Syria, Somalia, and other fields of battle in the so-called "war on terror," "struggle against violent extremism," or effort to defeat "radical Islamic terrorism." Is it not accurate, then, to say that the United States has a rather bloody history for such a relatively young nation?

More than a few scholars of religion have argued that violence is a central constituent of Americans' history and collective identity. American theologian Stanley Hauerwas claims that "only war can sustain our belief that we are a covenanted, chosen people worth sacrificing ourselves and others for." Going even further, he affirms, "Wars, American wars especially, must be wars in which the sacrifices of those doing the dying and the killing have redemptive purpose and justification. War is America's altar."[21] Religion scholar John Pahl argues that the simultaneity of exceptional religiosity and exceptional violence found in American culture are hardly coincidental. This lethal cocktail has turned the United States into an "empire of sacrifice" in which the pursuit of seemingly "innocent domination" covertly underwrites "blessed brutalities" against marginalized peoples. This history has included minorities within the United States such as African Americans, Native Americans, and others, but this fetish with violence and conquest also extends to other peoples in distant lands.[22]

There is certainly a place for the critiques these scholarly voices raise. There is nothing noble when a people or their government refuse to think critically about the difficult, painful, and ignoble moments of their past—or worse, ignore them altogether. Recent efforts to rewrite American history in Texas public school textbooks, by downplaying the ugly institutions of slavery and segregation, for example, are deeply alarming.[23] But when critique becomes the only method of reflection and analysis available, we risk oversimplifying the "American Way," reducing it to a kind of deluded moralistic Superman ethic. It becomes too easy to overlook the nobler efforts of Winthrop, Lincoln, Wilson, Dulles, and others, alongside their failings, and to sidestep their efforts to grapple seriously with the real moral and political challenges they faced in their day. Jon Pahl unpacks the religious dimensions of the violence and evil of slavery.[24] Stanley Hauerwas applies a similar approach to the Civil War. The effect is to make all violence per force condemnable, which leaves us with no way to compare the violence of slavery against the violence of the Civil War that would ultimately end it.

Superman may be fiction, but the values to which superheroes draw our attention—good and evil, justice and injustice—are not. Spiderman may dwell in a fantasy world, but pressing questions about moral responsibility, political judgment, and the use of force remain all too real. What is needed is a nimbler approach that admits nuance and provides more refined guidance for ethical reflection, decision-making, and restraint to nations and citizens pursuing truth, justice, and other moral principles by which they hope their societies will be defined. Unfortunately, contemporary scholarship on religion and violence, particularly in the American context, doesn't always afford the moral guidance we need.

The Myth of Religious Violence

The Superman myth is a heuristic device for exploring how religious ideas inform Americans' views of their nation's history, identity, and place in the world. This myth presumes that the United States—its culture and people—are shaped by and reflect a deeply religious, often moralistic character that sees its clearest and most problematic expression in various U.S. wars, particularly against external enemies abroad. Another approach to the American experience of religion and violence focuses on the religions of those who have been on the receiving end of such violence at home within the United States. In many cases, the objects of such violence or force have been deemed internal enemies: either religious "extremists" or religious minorities who somehow threaten Americans or the American way of life. At various points, Catholics, Mormons, Native Americans, and Muslims have been a few of the groups whose beliefs and practices have unsettled Protestant assumptions about American identity. In this Protestant-secular frame, religion is presumed to be a private phenomenon. So when dangerous forms of religion "go public," they threaten or challenge the secular political order. Governments respond to such provocations or crimes through coercion or violence that preserves or restores the dominance of the majority group. In this approach to religion and violence, the United States assumes a strongly secular guise, which becomes a distinctive mark of legitimacy. Secular violence tames dangerous forms of religion either by reconsigning them to the private sphere or eliminating them altogether. William Cavanaugh describes this defining myth of the liberal nation-state as follows:

> The Myth of Religious Violence helps to construct and marginalize a religious Other, prone to fanaticism, to contrast with the rational, peace-making, secular subject. This myth can be and is used in domestic politics to legitimate the marginalization of certain types of practices and groups labeled religious, while underwriting the nation-state's monopoly on its citizens' willingness to sacrifice and kill.[25]

Before considering how this myth applies in the U.S. domestic context, let's consider the backdrop and narrative to which The Myth of Religious Violence responds, including its global dimensions.

There has been great attention paid to the nexus of religion and violence in the last two decades, both within the academy and among broader publics. In the post-9/11 era, especially, a cottage industry of religious violence literature has cropped up. Beyond the events of September

11, 2001, al-Qaeda, and the "war on terror," there has been sustained focus on religiously charged violence in a variety of regions including Africa, Central Asia, Europe, and the Middle East. There have been culture clashes in Denmark, France, and the United States over cartoons and internet films that profane the prophet Muhammad. The rise of the Islamic State in Iraq and Syria and the ISIS-inspired and ISIS-led terrorist attacks in multiple European cities, serve as reminders that religion can be a central justification for significant forms of violence.[26]

Before and throughout these episodes, numerous scholarly works have concentrated on religion's evil, dangerous, or violent propensities.[27] So too with those writing for popular audiences, as Sam Harris argued in 2005: "Indeed, religion is as much a living spring of violence today as it was at any time in the past," and has been "the explicit cause of literally millions of deaths in the last ten years."[28] Other new atheists such as Christopher Hitchens tell us that "religion poisons everything."[29] Within the academy and wider culture alike, we are told, religious violence is somehow especially dangerous. It is absolutist; it imparts cosmic significance to worldly problems; its apocalyptic extremism prematurely seeks to usher in the end-times; and it promotes the demonization of enemies against whom unlimited violence becomes justifiable, if not a duty. Out of a concern to be "equal opportunity" critics of religious fanaticism, many scholars go to great lengths to show that this phenomenon is not unique to Islam or any other religion. Religious violence is found in all faith traditions. We know, for example, that Christians—such as Scott Roeder and others who have killed doctors who perform abortions—have justified their violence with their faith.[30]

The intense focus on religious extremism, however, now has given way to a countermovement led by scholars such as William Cavanaugh who contend that religious violence is not the grave threat we assume it to be and certainly not the greatest purveyor of violence. Cavanaugh and other "demythologizers" of religious violence tell us that we have disproportionately attributed violence to religion or religious people even though most violence is carried out by secular governments. The secular is comparatively more violent than religion, they insist. Scholar Janet Jakobsen claims that "there is plenty of evidence that the modern [secular] state is the origin of, rather than the solution to, most of the contemporary world's violence."[31] Writing for a popular audience, Karen Armstrong assesses that the source of violence and war "lies not in the multifaceted activity that we call 'religion' but in the violence embedded in our human nature and the nature of the state, which from the start required the forcible subjugation of at least 90 percent of the population."[32]

Within the domestic American context, *The Myth of Religious Violence* operates among those who conceive religion in ways that create certain distinctions: between, on one hand, an ostensible secular consensus made up of different citizens (traditionally Protestant majorities) in which believers "safely" practice their religions in private and, on the other, "dangerous," irrational forms of religion that challenge the American consensus because they do not separate religion and politics or privilege this distinction as secular societies claim to do. "Religious minimalism" and "maximalism" are, respectively, the terms that some scholars apply to these two approaches.[33] Religious maximalism includes "other" religions or religions of the "other" that reject or threaten the religiously minimalist, secular character of the American model. When a minimalist mindset takes hold, it becomes possible to distinguish the religious "other" from authentic or true Americans.

Many scholars use these categories to critique the violence the United States government and its agents have carried out against America's religious "others" who have been perceived as threats to the engines of American progress and expansion or have challenged the American consensus established by the rule of law. Think here about coercive actions, violence, and even ethnic cleansing carried out by governments in the American colonies and the United States: against Catholics beginning in the seventeenth century or Mormons in the nineteenth century and Native Americans for much of their history; or against cults such as the Branch Davidians or even enforcement efforts against the Fundamentalist Church of Jesus Christ of Latter Day Saints in Texas in more recent years. In all these cases, the groups in question were threats to Protestant hegemony or the religiously minimalist secular political order (or both). Such minority groups threatened Americans' security, culture, or way of life because their religious beliefs or practices challenged the authority of the state. That many of these incidents have occurred in the American West is no coincidence, religion scholar Todd Kerstetter argues:

The indeterminacy of "the West," its imagined centrality to America's future, and the violent hand of the state all are connected. Religious differences that might otherwise be tolerated are more threatening when they appear on the frontier, calling forth uses of force to expand, to tame and to Americanize maximalist religious minorities.[34]

Kerstetter alerts us to the limitations of prevailing frontier myths of the idyllic American West. One such familiar vision of the Western frontier posits an innocent garden wilderness, abundant with resources for intrepid settlers willing to strike out on their own and pour their labors into the "free land" awaiting them on the western plains, prairies, and mountains. The settler's journey itself represented a turning from Europe and its older way of life based on class and privilege toward the embrace of freedom, egalitarianism, self-reliance, and boundless opportunity that rustic, agrarian life in the "unsettled" territories afforded. The "frontier thesis" goes so far as to propose that American democracy itself was generated out of, and recurrently rejuvenated through, its unfurling sweep across the western frontier. The everyman figures who settled the West—miners and frontiersmen, cowboys and farmers—transcended their status as regional heroes to become quintessentially American icons.[35] But Kerstetter's demythologizing project exposes the dark underside of how the western frontier was settled and civilized. His approach to the American way of religion and violence lays bare the secular violence that was directed at religious minorities (among others) who threatened white settlers, the expansion of the American frontier, and the growing reach of the federal government.

For the demythologizers of religious violence, then, being consumed about the threats of religious violence from "extreme" or maximalist groups, however real, diverts our attention from the primary issue: the American way of religion and violence carried out by secular governments such as the United States. And we come to this insight by critically analyzing and deconstructing The Myth of Religious Violence and the justificatory work to which it is put.

Yet, this approach, too, offers but one side of the interpretive prism. Just as there are problems with the Superman myth, the myth of the western frontier, and The Myth of Religious Violence, there are also hazards to demythologizing the link between religion and violence in American history—a connection that many historians often have overlooked. While demythologizers sharpen our understanding of how religion has been defined and targeted, they offer no comparable guidance for thinking carefully about violence. Alone, these myths and un-myths do not supply the full, multisided approach that is needed for a more capacious understanding of the American experience of religion and violence. To appreciate both the insights and limitations of myth as well as demythification, I wish to consider how fiction opens a revealing window onto the problem of religion and violence—one that can be used to assess and enhance our interpretive prism.

Fiction as Anti-Myth: What Cormac McCarthy Tells Us about Religion, Violence, and America

Reading fiction can be risky; writing about it even more so. For there is always the hazard of reading or writing one's own discoveries into someone else's story. One can do the same with history, of course, and other forms of scholarship and nonfiction. But what is intriguing about fiction are the unexpected uses to which it might be put, the infinite prisms of discovery that can be illuminated, often simultaneously. I found myself reading Cormac McCarthy's novel Blood Meridian; or, The Evening Redness in the West (1985), while completing work on From Jeremiad to Jihad. Only gradually did I come to see how the novel provides several angles for reflecting on themes of religion and violence in the American context, including some that redress the limitations of various myths and scholarly approaches discussed above.

The novel takes place around 1850 and recounts the exploits of a fourteen-year-old Tennessean, known only as "the kid" in whom "broods already a taste for mindless violence."[36] The kid joins up with various posses and outlaw groups—some sanctioned by government officials, some not—to hunt down Apache Indians who are attacking settler towns and communities. His journey takes him to Mexico, Texas, and several territories that would later become states in the American West. It is a work that is striking for its grisliness and gratuitousness. Those who have read McCarthy's other novels or seen movies based on them have tasted this violence before. *Blood Meridian* involves something of a contest in cruelty and savagery over which group can amass the most of its adversaries' scalps. The prose at times is enough to make Quentin Tarantino blush. Particularly disarming is the dispassion with which the gruesome story is told. There is scant semblance of moral sentiment or reaction to the often indiscriminate, seemingly total and senseless violence. With no apparent ethical rhythm to life or nature, the reader is helpless to discern meaning from the violence—to morally evaluate it or make sense of it. Unlike some of McCarthy's other works, one searches in vain for characters with whom to empathize, for anyone not inured to the inhuman brutalities the novel depicts. In *No Country for Old Men*, the kindly Sheriff Bell, however powerless to stop the violence that haunts him, reminds the reader how far the moral compass of American life has turned south. Not so in *Blood Meridian*. Indeed, the indifference with which the speaker narrates the ferocious behavior of the American Indians and American posse alike is unsettling for its equanimity. In one of the tamer passages, the kid and another character have stumbled upon the ruins of an Apache slaughter of Mexicans who had sought a futile refuge:

> There were no pews in the church and the stone floor was heaped with the scalped and naked and partly eaten bodies of some forty souls who'd barricaded themselves in this house of God against the heathen.... The murdered lay in a great pool of communal blood. It had set up into a sort of pudding crossed everywhere with the tracks of wolves or dogs and along the edges it had dried and cracked into a burgundy ceramic. Blood lay in dark tongues on the floor and blood grouted the flagstones and ran in the vestibule... [and] thread[ed] its way down the steps and dripped from the stones among the dark red tracks of the scavengers.... Flies clambered over the peeled and wigless skulls of the dead and flies walked on their shrunken eyeballs.[37]

Not to be outdone, the posse exacts an extravagant viciousness of its own in an Indian camp, "moving on foot among the huts with torches and dragging the victims out, slathered and dripping with blood, hacking at the dying and decapitating those who knelt for mercy." This massacre against women and children accelerates even after everyone has been killed.

> They moved among the dead harvesting the long black locks with their knives and leaving their victims rawskulled and strange in their bloody cauls. . . . [E]very moment on this ground must be contested later in the desert and [the posse leader] rode among the men and urged them on.[38]

Such passages read like medieval chroniclers' accounts of the Crusades—except that chronicles in the Middle Ages, even when exaggerated, were written with moral purpose in mind: to outrage and excite, to champion and condemn, to remember and to forewarn. McCarthy's impassive prose, however, proposes that violence can be described objectively, narrated with almost clinical detachment. It is as if the literary style, despite its incomparable eloquence—a beauty that simultaneously repulses—intentionally suppresses all moral evaluation of violence. For this is, after all, a story of the untamed American West: "Here beyond men's judgments," we are told, "all covenants were brittle."[39] There is no law, natural or human, at least not yet.

There is more to *Blood Meridian*, though, than this amoral wasteland that McCarthy has painted. This is but one feature of a more complex landscape, which the reader gradually comes to see by means of some deft foreshadowing and the novel's final scene of ebullient dancing. The insights so crucial to the novel are actually germane to the study of religion and violence. First, we discover that this apparently amoral chronicle of violence is actually shot through with moral meaning. The clues are hidden, some tracks more visibly left behind than others, but we gradually glean that an overarching reign of putative amoralism is ultimately untenable. No matter how committed one may be to a morally desolate universe where all normative questions about human behavior are bracketed, this is a fool's errand that, pursued by fools a plenty in *Blood Meridian*, only benefits the cleverest character who fully fathoms the depths of evil. This insight bears on the study of religion and violence in that many scholars dodge or dance around ethical questions. Violence is treated descriptively as a fact, a basic yet ubiquitous feature of the landscape, as McCarthy superficially suggests. Many scholars write as if moral questions need not be explicitly or critically raised. Best to keep the study of violence objective, neutral. But, of course, it can never be so. For as McCarthy reminds us, moral concerns persist and slumber beneath the surface. Novelists have the luxury of allowing such unsettling forces to lurk and linger before erupting in clarifying climax or descending in denouement. That's what makes for good storytelling. Scholars, however, have to resort to other ways to paint and elaborate upon the moral backdrops they presume, which they don't always do.

Secondly, by the novel's end we come to see how deeply theological is this otherwise godless universe the speaker narrates. Religion, it turns out, is perhaps most fully present when its absence seems most acute, its enemies most triumphant. The sacred reveals itself marking the ruins of the dead. Putatively secular polities—those that claim to have outgrown religion or scrubbed its traces from public life—do well to recall that religion dies only slowly and violently. It must be killed off in oneself as much as in the other. But this does not mean *God* is dead.

And, finally, perhaps only in the novel's pithy epilogue—suggesting drilling, fence posts, the telegraph, and railroads and symbolizing development, borders, interconnection, and coalescence—do we appreciate fully that this is not just a story that has taken place *in* America. It is, rather, a story about America and the violence on which its expansion and progress, its formation as a nation, and even its very identity has been built. This is not a dime novel that re-inscribes the frontier myth by idealizing its heroes. Rather, *Blood Meridian* is more like anti-myth where the reality it conveys belies all romance.

This brief gloss on McCarthy's novel is offered as a lens for reappraising scholarly studies of religion, violence, and American history. Specifically, the insights of *Blood Meridian* outlined above return our attention to themes and problems in several bodies of scholarly literature. Working backwards, let me take each point in turn, beginning with the final one that the story of America is itself a story of violence. This point responds to the many histories of the United States, especially religious histories, that have neglected or underappreciated how central violence has been to the country's history.[40] While major wars have certainly received their due, until more recently, violence among Americans, or between Americans and the U.S. government (particularly where religious differences and justifications have been involved) has been an underdeveloped theme for many historians of the United States. As well, ignoring or writing over such violence remains a temptation in American history textbooks in some parts of the country. As a correction, Americans remind themselves of the violence of enslaving African Americans, the ethnic cleansing of Native Americans, and the use, sometimes exploitative, of workers of many backgrounds, which were all indispensable to the "progress," growth, and development of the United States, and which were all often justified and underwritten by religious ideas.[41]

Nevertheless, the violence committed by Americans or their government does not provide the full story. Americans' own experience of violence at the hands of others also has been formative, from attacks upon the early Puritans, to Pearl Harbor, to September 11, 2001. Often, as discussed earlier, jeremiads have been crucial to discerning meaning and responding to such violence. From early jeremiads articulated by John Winthrop and Increase Mather interpreting the hardships endured in the early Puritan colonies; to invocations of divine punishment for the blight of slavery by militant John Brown before the Civil War or the recognition in Abraham Lincoln's Second Inaugural in 1865 that God gave "to both North and South this terrible war as the woe due" for the offense of slavery; to contemporary figures such as Jerry Falwell and Jeremiah Wright in the days after September 11, 2001—all have linked various American ideals, aspirations, or expectations of moral uprightness to questions about punishment, suffering, introspection, or redemption when such ideals have been transgressed.[42] The formulations these jeremiads take starkly vary, with some more intolerant and menacing than others. The jeremiad offers religious interpretations of specific violence and affliction that have befallen Americans and their communities, but it is situated within a larger, more enduring covenantal rhetoric that has been indispensable to efforts to enshrine certain American ideals, including, when necessary, decisions to use force or wage war to protect the terms of such covenants.

Other religious tropes also have provided frameworks for interpreting violence that, in turn, helped Americans understand their place in the world. The doctrine of providence, as religion scholar Stephen Webb has shown, has influenced Americans in times of war—from the Revolution to the "war on terror," often contributing to a view of America's special role in history. Yet where religious tropes once guided and united the nation, in more recent decades, notions of providence have vexed and divided American citizens. Webb points to Senator Eugene McCarthy's critique of providential thinking when he called for "a hard and harsh moral judgment on the United States position in Vietnam." Interestingly, even McCarthy's critique possesses an exceptionalist streak, for Webb goes on to ponder, "But why would America warrant such judgment if it was not in some way special—accountable by virtue of its moral calling, unique status, and providential history?"[43] In other words, even the denunciation of using religious ideas to interpret violence and war was itself a product of the very religious traditions being denounced. In total, these examples all show how difficult it is to escape the history of violence on which the United States has been built, including the covenantal, providential, and other religious frames that have given meaning to such violence. Whether Americans affirm or critique this history—or both—we remain in certain ways indebted to it.

The second insight culled from *Blood Meridian* is that religion may be most fully present in its apparent absence. Recall from my discussion above that much post-9/11 scholarship has focused on how religion and its adherents are responsible for significant and spectacular violence. Osama bin Laden comes to mind, though he was hardly the first to ground attacks against the U.S. government in religious ideas. The militant abolitionist John Brown was a violent extremist of his day. But he was not insane, as many assumed, when, in hopes of ending slavery, he led a failed raid on the federal armory at Harper's Ferry, which resulted in the deaths of seventeen people. He justified his actions by the Golden Rule: "I pity the poor in bondage that have none to help them: that is why I am here; not to gratify any personal animosity, revenge, or vindictive spirit. It is my sympathy with the oppressed and wronged, that are as good as you and as precious in the sight of God."[44] He was, it is fair to say, a religious militant. As was bin Laden. They both fit among the numerous works on religion and violence in recent decades that discuss the distinctive flavor if not the particular danger of religious actors who pick up a gun or plan an attack. Still, it must be said, Brown and bin Laden are more aberrations than norms in the American context.

Demythologizers of religious violence argue that most violence is attributable to secular bodies such as nation-states even though much scholarship disproportionately focuses on the dangers of religion. Which is more violent, then—religion or the secular? Recall Kerstetter's discussion above that the U.S. government carried out various acts of violence against religious minorities such as Mormons and Native Americans, which it justified using secular or religiously minimalist rationales. Interestingly, however, historian John Corrigan traces how Protestant Americans drew from the biblical story of Amalek to legitimate attacks against some of the very same groups—Native Americans and Mormons—that Kerstetter describes as victims of secular violence.[45] This suggests that debates about whether a particular act of violence is religious or secular—or whether religion or the secular is more violent—are unlikely to be resolved. Perhaps this is a debate we should move beyond. For as *Blood Meridian* reveals, violence is a human phenomenon. We should not suppose it to be uniquely associated with religious or secular actors or with this group or that group. For that matter, there is no bright line distinguishing religion and secular. These designations can obscure more than they reveal. As in McCarthy's novel, religion never announces itself on the scene. But it never recedes entirely either, even when secular frames dominate or suggest that religion is absent.

A good illustration of the shifting lenses of religious and secular justifications for war can be seen in debates among historians over whether the American Revolution was a just war or holy war. President Obama declared in his Nobel Peace Prize address that "no holy war can ever be a just war."[46] But are the choices really so stark? While many (including Obama) would probably describe the Revolution as a just war—"a secular event, a sober pragmatic struggle against an imperial power," in the words of Karen Armstrong[47]—notable historians of American religion argue it was closer to a holy war given its recourse to religious arguments and justifications. Much depends on what lenses one wears, yet none of these views capture the most important nuances.[48]

To begin with, not every religious invocation in wartime points to holy-war thinking. One Revolutionary-era Congregationalist minister, Josiah Stearns, invoked traditional just-war criteria—legitimate authority, just cause, right intention—in ways comparable to how secular just-war reasoning is used today. But his arguments were interwoven with biblical exegesis and earnest demands that parishioners exhibit holiness, humble themselves, and seek pardon for their sins and reconciliation with the Lord. Within eighteenth-century American thought, it is difficult to disentangle republican theories of governance from biblical references and religious ideas. They are interwoven into the fabric of American civil religion, its advocates argue. For example, as Pastor Stearns claimed, the "voice of reason is the voice of God." (This line echoes the revolutionary refrain "rebellion to tyrants is obedience to God.") Might not the same war be morally justified on both religious and secular grounds, even within the same voice, as Josiah Stearns suggests? Even when citizens today claim the idea that public discourse should be secularized or scrubbed of religious references, that doesn't mean religion goes away. Religion remains present even amidst its apparent absence as McCarthy suggests. Moreover, when we fret too much over "religious" and "secular" designations, we lose sight of what are often more crucial concerns. This brings me to a final point.

Perhaps the most telling lesson from *Blood Meridian* is the false premise of writing about violence from an objective, morally neutral point of view. Yet this is an approach taken by scholars of religion who are suspicious of ethical analysis or reticent to engage in it. Many scholars tend to treat violence as an empirical phenomenon. It's self-evident, perhaps like pornography: we know it when we see it. Both mythologizers and demythologizers of religious violence accept this approach, which reduces violence to its physical context[49] while abjuring normative treatment of moral concepts or reasoning. All violence can be treated equally when reduced to an empirical phenomenon. Moral distinctions fall away. Bruce Lincoln, for example, in his aptly titled *Holy Terrors* (note the "s" at the end), employs a methodology that levels key differences between the violence of Osama bin Laden and George W. Bush. We may critique them both for their moral failings, but they are hardly on the same plane.[50]

While scholars of religion have devoted considerable critical attention in recent years to how religion has been defined and essentialized, there has been no comparable scrutiny of how we use the term *violence* or what it means or the work it performs.[51] The reality that McCarthy shows is that violence is not neutral but, rather, freighted with moral meaning. One cannot "do violence" to another in a morally neutral way. Violence shares Latin roots with *violare*, meaning to violate. The violence that human beings inflict involves not simply physical harm or damage but injury, injustice, and other violations of *right*, the Latin *jus*. Yet not all physical harm or destruction is unjust or morally blameworthy.[52] In sermons during the American Revolution, ministers such as Josiah Stearns employ "violence" to describe British tyranny. By their lights, a just war does not constitute violence in the same way, since the Revolution was defined by the just cause of overthrowing tyranny. *Violence* is derived from *violentus*, meaning vehement or impetuous; the term refers to disordered human passions. By contrast, one of Stearns's sermons proposes how to properly order the emotions in a just revolution: right intention must be preserved, vengeful attitudes suppressed, and restraint observed.[53]

For a range of reasons, then, a broader lexicon is needed that includes terms such as force, coercion, self-defense, and war. As well, associated moral distinctions—justice and injustice, good and evil, legitimate and illegitimate—all further sharpen the precision of moral analysis that becomes available when we distinguish indefensible or unlimited violence from justifiable and limited use of force. It is far better to acknowledge these moral terms of debate and bring them forward—to argue and debate—than to level all such distinctions. Usually, some form of moral critique is operative in the background anyway. As my reading of McCarthy suggests, various forms of moral critique, however oblique or diffuse, inevitably slip through, pervading even ostensibly neutral scholarship about religion and violence in American history and culture. For this reason it's important to integrate ethical analysis into historical study.[54]

It is of course meet and right to subject moral discourses of force and war to critique. This is preferable to what happens in many quarters of the modern academy in which legitimating discourses are deconstructed and dismissed by virtue of their relationship to institutions of power. It is also appropriate to assess moral discourses of violence and force with respect to a larger moral horizon. For unless we hang on to the possibility that an ethical discourse helps us gain purchase on or conform to some ontological reality, that it helps illuminate an ethical order of nature, we consign ourselves to a world devoid of moral law or norms. Indeed, such a world is extolled by the most diabolical character in *Blood Meridian* when he advances the view that might doesn't just make right—might transcends it:

> Moral law is an invention of mankind for the disenfranchisement of the powerful in favor of the weak. Historical law subverts it at every turn. A moral view can never be proven right or wrong by any ultimate test. A man falling dead in a duel is not thought thereby to be proven in error as to his views. His very involvement in such a trial gives evidence of a new and broader view.... Decisions of life and death, of what shall be and what shall not be, beggar all question of right. In elections of these magnitudes are all lesser ones subsumed, moral, spiritual, natural.[55]

We should spurn such a vision of collective life that separates the historical from the moral from the natural. The ethical interpretive dimension remains part of the multisided prism by which we assess problems of religion and violence. For without ethical analysis, we are reduced to a world in which covenants are not only brittle—dependent upon coercion to defend them—but mere contrivance and construction.

The One, the Few, and the Many

The myths by which the American way of religion and violence has been defined focus on the violence carried out by either religious extremists on the fringe of American society or in the main of society and government.

We would do well to move beyond this false choice between focusing on fringe actors, as some scholars do, and violence carried out by the secular state on behalf of majorities and the nation, as others urge. Rather, we can study militant figures and elements on the fringe not simply for what they tell us about the militant few but also for what they tell us about the many and the mainstream. "Violence" in America often has served as the fault line in struggles between majority and minority, including efforts to define or expand consensus about what America represents or who counts as fully American. The case of antislavery militant John Brown offers such an illustration. For the actions of this religious extremist were a prelude to the epic struggle to preserve and define the nation that ultimately would cost six hundred thousand Americans their lives and rip apart the social fabric of the United States. From the embers of the Civil War, a new foundation for American nationhood would be forged, one that, over many generations, would become more inclusive and beholden to the self-evident truths of its birth as expressed in both John Brown's "Declaration of Liberty by the Representatives of the Slave Population of the United States of America" and the Declaration of Independence on which Brown's document was modeled.[56]

Not all efforts to forge consensus in the United States entail such drastic measures as civil war. For example, we might conceive an updated version of Herberg's classic called *Protestant-Catholic-Muslim-Jew.*[57] In the end, American figures as diverse as John Winthrop, John Brown, Abraham Lincoln, John Foster Dulles, and even Martin Luther King all understood that the effort to form consensus and define the principles and values that should represent the American Way necessarily involves conflict, struggle, and not infrequently violence and suffering. The prominence of violence in American history suggests that we ought not to ignore that reality or pretend that it can necessarily be otherwise. Yet it is only by bringing ethical reflection to bear upon that history that we can distinguish national disgraces that must be shunned, on one hand, from the moral struggles that must be fought and great achievements that should be extolled, on the other. In undertaking this task, we should think carefully about what we mean by *religion* and how we assess it; more importantly, though, the moral meanings we assign to and associate with *violence* make all the difference in the world.

Notes

I am grateful to Darius Ansari, who provided excellent research assistance with this essay. I also thank Eva Brumberger, Jonathan Ebel, Michael Stancliff, and two anonymous reviewers for their thoughtful feedback on earlier versions of this chapter.

1. Richard T. Hughes, *Myths America Lives By* (Urbana: University of Illinois Press, 2003).

2. This is not to say religion plays a determinative role. One can affirm the principles behind the Declaration's self-evident truths without necessarily affirming the theological particulars of the Creator who bestows such rights.

3. Robert Jewett and John Shelton Lawrence, *Captain America and the Crusade against Evil: The Dilemma of Zealous Nationalism* (Grand Rapids, MI: Wm. B. Eerdmans Publishing, 2003), 6.

4. Ibid.

5. Will Herberg, *Protestant-Catholic-Jew: An Essay in Religious Sociology* (Garden City, NJ: Doubleday, 1955), 88.

6. Ibid., 92.

7. Ibid., 88–89.

8. Ibid., 89.

9. Robert N. Bellah, "Civil Religion in America," in *Beyond Belief: Essays on Religion in a Post-Traditionalist World* (Berkeley: University of California Press, 1970), 168–89; and Robert N. Bellah et al., *Habits of the Heart: Individualism and Commitment in American Life* (New York: Perennial, 1985).

10. Quoted in Andrew R. Murphy and Elizabeth Hanson, "From King Philip's War to September 11: Religion, Violence, and the American Way," in *From Jeremiad to Jihad: Religion, Violence, and America*, ed. John D. Carlson and Jonathan H. Ebel (Berkeley: University of California Press, 2012), 30.

11. Sacvan Bercovitch's classic, *The American Jeremiad* (Madison: University of Wisconsin Press, 1978), remains a still penetrating examination of this enduring trope.

12. Murphy and Hanson, "From King Philip's War to September 11," 33–34.

13. Laurie Goodstein, "Falwell: blame abortionists, feminists and gays," *The Guardian* (September 19, 2001). http://gu.com/p/xv7c9/stw.

14. Wright did not explicitly state that God was using the terrorist attacks to punish America, though some of his remarks later were interpreted that way, especially following a 2003 sermon featuring a litany of America's violent immoral misdeeds against Indians, blacks, and other minorities that ended with these ominous lines: "The government...wants us to sing 'God Bless America.' No, no, no. Not 'God Bless America'; God Damn America! That's in the Bible, for killing innocent people. God Damn America for treating her citizen[s] as less than human. God Damn America as long as she keeps trying to act like she is God and she is supreme!" See Brian Ross and Rehab El-Buri, "Obama's Pastor: God Damn America, U.S. to Blame for 9/11," *ABC News* (March 13, 2008).

15. Jonathan H. Ebel, "From Covenant to Crusade and Back: American Christianity and the Late Great War," in Carlson and Ebel, *From Jeremiad to Jihad*, 66.

16. Ned O'Gorman, "From Jeremiad to Manifesto: The Rhetorical Evolution of John Foster Dulles's 'Massive Retaliation,'" in Carlson and Ebel, *From Jeremiad to Jihad*, 83–85.

17. In his acceptance speech for the Nobel Peace Prize, President Obama averred, "I am convinced that adhering to standards, international standards, strengthens those who do, and isolates and weakens those who don't.... America—in fact, no nation—can insist that others follow the rules of the road if we refuse to follow them ourselves. For when we don't, our actions appear arbitrary and undercut the legitimacy of future interventions, no matter how justified." Barack Obama, "Nobel Lecture: A Just and Lasting Peace," December 10, 2009, http://www.nobelprize.org/nobel_prizes/peace/laureates/2009/obama-lecture_en.html.

18. Quoted in O'Gorman, "From Jeremiad to Manifesto," 87.

19. Ibid., 87.

20. In a forceful article arguing for humanitarian military intervention, Jean Bethke Elshtain invokes the Spiderman ethic to remind great powers of their special responsibilities to prevent or respond to massive atrocities. See her "International Justice as Equal Regard and the Use of Force," *Ethics & International Affairs* 17, no. 2 (September 2003): 73.

21. Stanley Hauerwas, "Why War Is a Moral Necessity: Realism, Sacrifice, and the Civil War," in Carlson and Ebel, *From Jeremiad to Jihad*, 224, 228.

22. Jon Pahl, *Empire of Sacrifice: The Religious Origins of American Violence* (New York: New York University Press, 2010).

23. Emma Brown, "Texas Officials: Schools Should Teach that Slavery Was 'Side Issue' to Civil War," *Washington Post* (July 5, 2015).

24. Pahl, *Empire of Sacrifice*, 63–102.

25. William T. Cavanaugh, *The Myth of Religious Violence: Secular Ideology and the Roots of Modern Conflict* (New York: Oxford University Press, 2009), 4.

26. See Graeme Wood, "What ISIS Really Wants," *The Atlantic* (March 2015), 78–94.

27. Mark Juergensmeyer, *Terror in the Mind of God: The Global Rise of Religious Violence* (Berkeley: University of California Press, 2003); Charles Kimball, *When Religion Becomes Evil* (New York: HarperCollins, 2008).

28. Sam Harris, *The End of Faith: Religion, Terror, and the Future of Reason* (New York: W.W. Norton and Company, 2005), 26.

29. Christopher Hitchens, *God Is Not Great: How Religion Poisons Everything* (New York: Twelve Books, 2007).

30. Juergensmeyer, *Terror in the Mind of God*, 20–30.

31. Janet R. Jakobsen, "Is Secularism Less Violent than Religion?" in *Interventions: Activists and Academics Respond to Violence*, ed. Elizabeth A. Castelli and Janet R. Jackobsen (New York: Palgrave Macmillan, 2004), 63.

32. Karen Armstrong, *Fields of Blood: Religion and the History of Violence* (New York: Anchor Books, 2015), 394.

33. Bruce Lincoln, *Holy Terrors: Thinking about Religion after September 11*, 2d ed. (Chicago: University of Chicago Press, 2006).

34. Todd M. Kerstetter, "State Violence and the Un-American West: Mormons, American Indians, and Cults," in Carlson and Ebel, *From Jeremiad to Jihad*, 144.

35. Historian Henry Nash Smith argues how deeply American society and identity have been suffused by this frontier myth—the alluring westward "pull of a vacant continent"—in his tellingly titled *Virgin Land: The American West as Symbol and Myth* (Cambridge, MA: Harvard University Press, 1950; 1970), 3. Smith traces this myth back to nineteenth-century historian Frederick Jackson Turner who "believed that the highest social values were to be found in the relatively primitive society just within the agricultural frontier," 256. Like other historians who internalized Turner's thesis, Smith explored how famous icons such as Daniel Boone, Kit Carson, James Fennimore Cooper's fictional Leatherstocking, and the cowboy heroes of dime novels entrenched the potent myth of the western frontier into the American consciousness.

36. Cormac McCarthy, *Blood Meridian; or, The Evening Redness in the West* (New York: Vintage Books, 1985), 3.

37. Ibid., 63–64.

38. Ibid., 162–63.

39. Ibid., 111.

40. Sydney E. Ahlstrom, *A Religious History of the American People* (New Haven, CT: Yale University Press, 1972); Jon Butler, *Awash in a Sea of Faith: Christianizing the American People* (Cambridge, MA: Harvard University Press, 1990); Martin E. Marty, *Pilgrims in Their Own Land: 500 Years of Religion in America* (New York: Little Brown, 1984). Some histories outright glorify violence such as Robert Baird, *Religion in America* (New York: Harper & Brothers, 1844).

41. See Jon Pahl, *Empire of Sacrifice*, as well as chapters by John Corrigan and Todd Kerstetter in Carlson and Ebel, *From Jeremiad to Jihad*.

42. For extended discussions of different jeremiads, see the introduction, "John Brown, Jeremiad, and Jihad: Reflections on Religion, Violence, and America," by Jonathan Ebel and myself, as well as Murphy and Hanson's "From King Philip's War to September 11," in Carlson and Ebel, *From Jeremiad to Jihad*.

43. Stephen H. Webb, "American Providence, American Violence," in Carlson and Ebel, *From Jeremiad to Jihad*, 102–3.

44. Quoted in Carlson and Ebel, "John Brown, Jeremiad, and Jihad," in Carlson and Ebel, *From Jeremiad to Jihad*, 1–2.

45. John Corrigan, "New Israel, New Amalek: Biblical Exhortations to Religious Violence," in Carlson and Ebel, *From Jeremiad to Jihad*, 112–22.

46. Obama, Nobel lecture.

47. Armstrong, *Fields of Blood*, 270.

48. For the full treatment of this problem, see John D. Carlson, "A Just or Holy War of Independence? The Revolution's Legacy for Religion, Violence, and American Exceptionalism," in Carlson and Ebel, *From Jeremiad to Jihad*, 197–219.

49. Cavanaugh notes that of the nine scholarly perpetuators of The Myth of Religious Violence that he studies, only one provides a definition of violence. All describe violence in terms of physical harm and destruction such as war and terrorism. Thus, Cavanaugh, too, accepts and works with this rather limited definition, Myth of Religious Violence, 7.

50. Lincoln, "Symmetric Dualisms: Bush and bin Laden on October 7," in *Holy Terrors*.

51. I explore this problem in John D. Carlson, "Religion and Violence: Coming to Terms with Terms," in *The Blackwell Companion to Religion and Violence*, ed. Andrew R. Murphy (Oxford, UK: Wiley-Blackwell, 2011), 7–22.

52. Think here about a public official who uses deadly force to protect an innocent bystander.

53. Carlson, "A Just or Holy War of Independence?," 204–7.

54. See, for example, Harry S. Stout, *Upon the Altar of the Nation: A Moral History of the Civil War* (New York: Viking, 2006).

55. McCarthy, *Blood Meridian*, 261.

56. Carlson and Ebel, "John Brown, Jeremiad, and Jihad," 13–14.

57. For one articulation of how Islam reflects and contributes to American values, see Imam Feisal Abdul Rauf, *Moving the Mountain: A New Vision of Islam in America* (New York: Free Press, 2012), 179–200.

5

Confronting Historic Injustice
Truth and Reconciliation

ELAINE ENNS AND CHED MYERS

Nothing of the past five hundred years was inevitable. Every raised fist and brandished weapon was a choice.... The decision to censor the native truth was a choice. The decision to manipulate the knowledge of American history was a choice.... With my relations around me, I go into mourning—but I go angry, alive, listening, learning, remembering.... I do not vanish. I do not forget. I will not let you forget.

—Wendy Rose, Hopi/Me-wuk[1]

History, despite its wrenching pain
Cannot be unlived, but if faced
With courage, need not be lived again.

—Maya Angelou[2]

Introduction
How do nonviolent faith and practice deal with historic violation and oppression? This chapter profiles two veteran activist pastors in the United

States who, from very different contexts, have led significant efforts to face and heal the violence of the past.[3] Lawrence Hart's pioneering work to repatriate native remains, and Nelson Johnson's experiment with a grassroots-led truth and reconciliation process around a 1979 massacre in Greensboro, North Carolina, represent the frontier of peacemaking as restorative justice.[4]

Stories of past violence and justice denied reside in the bones of the children of both victims and perpetrators, whether acknowledged or not. For most of us in the dominant culture, the truth of historic crimes is slowly buried under the heavy soil of denial, rationalization, and amnesia. History as told by the victors is usually a devised narrative, full of half-truths, caricatures, and cover-ups. The story of victims, meanwhile, is dismembered from the official history of the body politic. One of the most demanding yet transforming tasks of restorative justice and peacemaking today is to revise and remember the past, uncovering a fuller, more inclusive truth, and listening to the voices of those left out.[5] Healing can come only through the difficult and painful labor of exhuming—literally and figuratively—the bones of these violations.

Here we offer testimonies of two men who help us set our moral and political compass. These elders are giants among us, fierce in their quest to vindicate the suffering of their community, patient in their work to overcome collective amnesia and ambivalence. Like the Apostle Paul, Elder Lawrence, and Pastor Johnson understand well the three key aspects of the divine imperative of reconciliation outlined in 2 Corinthians 5:16ff:

1. All Christians are invited and challenged to act as ambassadors of reconciliation;
2. It is possible for us to "accept the grace of God in vain"[6] by not taking initiative to heal wounds and restore justice; and
3. "The time is now"[7] for the work of reckoning with histories of oppression, exclusion and violation.[8]

As pioneers of two different expressions of truth and reconciliation work in the United States, it is not too much to say that these two ministers are national treasurers of courage, conscience, and compassion.

Lawrence Hart: Return to the Earth

The testimony of Elder Lawrence Hart shows how a deeply entrenched legacy of oppression toward Native Americans can be challenged and changed—but only by not letting us forget. His pioneering efforts to repatriate Native American remains continues to be a compelling and creative expression of contemporary restorative justice. As his biographer Raylene Hinz-Penner puts it, Lawrence "represents a unique bridge to the Cheyenne peace traditions of an earlier time...a dynamic and creative force in the country for mediation, restoration, conciliation and preservation."[9] We interviewed Elder Lawrence on February 12, 2007.

Elder Lawrence was raised by his paternal grandparents, John P. Hart and Corn Stalk, until he was six years old. They taught him to speak Cheyenne and instructed him in traditional ways. John Hart was a missionary of the Native American Church, and Lawrence would often accompany his grandfather on his trips. Lawrence's father, Homer, was baptized as a Mennonite at age seventeen. He worked for the church and the tribe for forty years in Clinton, Oklahoma, where he was a highly respected preacher, farmer, and leader. "I have connections to three religions," says Lawrence: "Our own Cheyenne traditional religion, the Native American church of my grandfather, and my father's...Mennonite faith."[10]

Lawrence married Betty Bartel, a Mennonite with German ancestry, in October 1957. He completed studies at Bethel College in Newton, Kansas, and then at Associated Mennonite Biblical Seminary in Elkhart, Indiana. In 1963, Lawrence and Betty accepted a call to pastor at Koinonia Mennonite church near Clinton, Oklahoma, where they have served for more than forty-five years now. They have worked tirelessly to preserve Cheyenne culture, history, and tradition, establishing the Cheyenne Cultural Center in 1977, which serves as a community center for history, art, language, and interpretation. Betty and Lawrence have three children and four grandchildren.

Over the years Lawrence has garnered a number of honors, including Indian Elder of the Year from the National Indian Education Association; the Oklahoma Heritage Association Distinguished Service Award; and Friend of the Oklahoma Supreme Court. But it is his work as a peace chief that is most significant to him and to our story.

"Everything I Do Is from My Stance as a Peace Chief"

The Cheyenne have an unbroken line of peace chiefs since their cultural hero, Sweet Medicine, institutionalized the "Council of Forty-four" many years ago. Four chiefs were chosen from each of the ten Cheyenne bands, along with four additional principle chiefs. Lawrence's grandfather John was one of these peace chiefs.[11]

Despite being raised Mennonite, Lawrence served in the U.S. Navy and Marines from 1954 to 1958. "He believed he was the first full-blooded Native American to make it as a jet fighter pilot."[12] But Sweet Medicine had said that a great peace chief must have a conversion experience, since most were at one time warriors. John Hart was nearing the end of his life, and approached the council with the unusual request that Lawrence take his place as a principal peace chief, and they agreed. "Being so close emotionally to his grandfather, Lawrence could not say no. He took it as a call. But one cannot be a peace chief and continue to be a warrior.... Four months after he was made a principle peace chief of the Cheyenne people, Lawrence was out of the service."[13]

Over the past fifty years Lawrence has never experienced a full Council of Forty-four, because as older chiefs pass on it is challenging to find replacements. Few are willing to live by the stringent requirements made by Sweet Medicine, such as this:

> Listen to me carefully and truthfully follow my instructions. You Chiefs are peacemakers. Though your son might be killed in front of your tepee, you should take a peace pipe and smoke.... If your men, your soldier societies, should be scared and retreat, you are not to step back but take a stand to protect your land and people. Get out and talk to the people. If strangers come, you are the ones to give presents to them and invitations.... Never refuse.[14]

A peace chief is to be a person of peace no matter what the cost, being available for discernment, encouragement, and intervention. He must recognize what is required for healing his people and land, and use his influence to address those needs, acting as tribal negotiator and spokesperson. It is courageous and demanding work.

Elder Lawrence speaks often of a powerful turning point in his life, in which he was mentored by elder peace chiefs. It occurred at the centenary of the 1868 Washita massacre, the victims of which were his direct ancestors.

In the 1860s the Cheyenne met the most difficult decade in our history. Even though our Peace Chiefs had made great efforts to be at peace with the U.S. Government, it proved futile. In 1864, our village at Sand Creek was attacked; many of our people were killed. Four years later, Lieutenant Colonel George Custer and the 7th Cavalry attacked our people again at the Washita. My great-grandfather, Afraid of Beavers, was fairly young and survived the attack. When the Cavalry left, he came out of hiding and, with other survivors, began to look for people. As they walked over the bodies they called out the names of those who had been killed. They found Chief Black Kettle and his wife, Medicine Woman, in the river. They laid their bodies under a cottonwood tree until the next morning, when they took them away and buried them at an undisclosed location. A few years after the massacre, Afraid of Beavers had a son, John P. Hart, who is my grandfather.[15]

One hundred years later, the white residents of Cheyenne, Oklahoma, near the massacre site, decided to celebrate the "Battle of Washita." They contacted Elder Lawrence, asking for the Cheyenne people to participate. Lawrence responded that they could not celebrate what occurred at Washita.

But the townspeople were persistent. After conversation with other chiefs, Lawrence negotiated that the Cheyenne would participate in the event on one condition. Several years earlier, the remains of one of the victims of the massacre had been unearthed by erosion, and the townspeople had put them on display in a local museum, which was offensive to the Cheyenne. If the chiefs were allowed to take back the remains and re-inter them, the Cheyenne would take part in the commemoration.

So it was set. We would set up our tepees and have a mock village filled with our own children and elders. The townspeople would dress up in blue uniforms and undergo a mock attack on our village. After the attack we would proceed downtown and inter the remains. It was difficult to rehearse the event but we planned that as the fake gunshots rang out, we would pretend to be hit and fall down. On Nov. 29, 1968, the day of the commemoration, I was on the hillside and could see my children in the village. The mock attack began. I saw to my right some young men dressed in blue uniforms with the 7th Cavalry insignia. I had not been told about these young fellows, who called themselves "The Grandsons of the 7th Cavalry," Custer's regiment. They marched towards the village, playing the familiar battle tune of "Gary Owen." With their authentic, carbine weapons, they began to fire blanks into the village. It became so terrifyingly real. I did not want those grandsons to be there, shooting at my children and fellow tribal members. Who invited them? And why were we not told? I began to harbor feelings that I knew I shouldn't have as one of the young Peace Chiefs. There was screaming, chaos, and gunfire until it was over.[16]

The day's closing ceremony at the Black Kettle Museum, where the chiefs had prepared the historic remains for burial, involved four special songs for their recessional. Much to Lawrence's dismay, as they began singing, the grandsons of Colonel Custer's regiment ceremoniously "presented arms."

I thought, "How dare they salute this one!" Intense feelings of hatred surfaced. As we walked through a large group of people, a Cheyenne woman stepped forward and removed a beautiful wool blanket from around her shoulders and draped it over the coffin. This act was unplanned, and it required another ritual to acknowledge this gift, which would need to be given to someone else that day. I was thinking the blanket would go to the Governor or another state dignitary that was present. Then the chiefs told me to call the Captain of the Grandsons of the 7th Cavalry. They handed me the blanket, and told me to give it to him. I complied, because I was not going to question my elders. The Captain came towards us in sharp military fashion, drew his sword and saluted us. I stepped forward and draped the blanket over his shoulders. It was one of the most powerful moments in my life. There was not a dry eye in the audience.

The Chiefs went back into the museum and the Grandsons followed us in—young men in their early 20s, with tears in their eyes. The Captain approached me and we embraced, crying. He took a pin from his uniform and said, "Lawrence, this is the 'Gary Owen' pin worn by original members of the 7th Cavalry. It is the signal to attack. I have taken it off my uniform and I want you to have it on behalf of the Cheyenne people. We are sorry that 'Gary Owen' was played that day 100 years ago, and never again will it be played against your people." I still have that pin. It reminds me less of his words than of the actions of my elders, who showed me that day what it really means to be a Peace Chief.[17]

"Everything I do," says Elder Lawrence, "is from my stance as a Peace Chief." Lawrence was instrumental in establishing Washita as a designated National Historic Site.

Twice I testified in Congress for the National Park at Washita. I believe it is good when the National Park Service manages a site like that because it allows us to tell our side of the story. They are in the process of building an interpretive center. All of the remains associated with the Washita site that have been unearthed by development or by inadvertent discoveries, have been reburied right near those grounds.[18]

It is this work of repatriating Indian remains and giving proper burial that lies at the heart of Elder Lawrence's work.

Laying the Past to Rest with Dignity

Chief Lawrence has also been involved in working towards appropriate commemoration and repatriation of remains from the Sand Creek massacre, as the following narrative explains:

Nov. 29, 1864, Sand Creek, Colorado. It was a time of fiercely proud Cheyenne warriors, broken treaties, gold-greedy whites, bloody Indian raids and civil war. On the morning of the attack, it was cold. Everyone in the peaceful Cheyenne camp was asleep in blankets and buffalo robes. Col. John Chivington and the First Colorado Regiment broke the quiet with rifle fire. Cheyenne chief White Antelope ran to stop the soldiers. He believed the attack was a mistake, because the village had already surrendered to the Army just weeks before and had been promised the army's protection. He cried out in English: "Stop! Stop!" When he saw that it was a deliberate attack, he stood still and began to sing his death song. He was one of the first to be shot down. Desperate to stop the attack, Cheyenne Peace Chief Black Kettle raised an American flag and a white flag of surrender at his tepee. But the guns wouldn't stop. Soldiers shot down women and children, killed babies in their mother's arms. Scalps were taken; private parts like breasts and testicles were cut off to make tobacco pouches. Finally the guns fell silent. More than 150 Cheyenne, mostly women and children, were dead. Ten Cavalrymen were killed. Army and Congressional inquiries would later call the attack a massacre. Chivington resigned his commission in dishonor. The fields of Sand Creek were heavy with the bodies of the dead.

November, 1997, Smithsonian Institute, Washington, D.C. For over 100 years the remains have been in the storage area of the Smithsonian. Back in the 1860s army surgeons had gathered the remains.... The rifle was evolving rapidly on the heels of the Civil War, and surgeons were very interested in studying the effects of the new weapons on the human body. For a century the Cheyenne had grieved the wandering souls of Sand Creek, longing to bring them home to give them rest.

An Indian crier begins his song to call the Cheyenne tribe together. He is a long way from Oklahoma. His song echoes through the vast corridors of the Smithsonian Institute, where, on dusty storage shelves, the remains of the ancient Cheyenne have been kept. The Cheyenne have come to bring them home. Chief Lawrence Hart offers a blessing, asking the Creator to be with them as they prepare the dead for the journey home. Visitors are blessed with sage. "God, look down upon us. Grant us your mercy. Our relatives, we are here. We have come for you. We are taking you back home."

There is a horrible silence as the Cheyenne see, for the first time, remains of their ancestors. Then the drum begins. One can see the pain of a hundred years on the skulls: bullet holes, signs of scalping. Elders ceremonially prepare the dead, marking the bones with paint made from the earth of their sacred mountain. Bones gathered so long ago for "scientific research." For a moment each Cheyenne holds one of the dead in his hands. "There is a lot of pain involved here," says one elder, holding back tears. "What they went through. Some of these here have bullet holes on top of their heads. They were not prepared to defend themselves."

Women gather at the side of an adolescent girl killed that November day. Their emotions are uncontrolled. "Whenever she died or whenever her body was taken, there would have been no one holding her, because of all the chaos and people running for their lives. She never would have had anyone in all these years to hold her like that. She deserved it." With tears and cedar incense the young girl's remains are placed in a small coffin. It is a swirl of emotions: outrage at the massacre, a sense of violation that the remains had been in a museum for these decades. Everyone is straining towards home, where there is rest for the bitter feelings.[19]

In the 1860s the United States Surgeon General and United States Army Medical Museum circulated requests for troops on the frontier to collect Native American skulls. It is estimated that between six hundred thousand and two million skeletal remains were subsequently shipped to public and private museums, societal collections, scientific laboratories, and universities across the country for study and storage. "After each massacre or battle medical personnel would collect the remains," Lawrence told us. "Today decapitating the remains of an enemy and shipping the crania far away for 'scientific study' would be considered a war crime."

Two laws were passed to begin addressing this horrific injustice. The National Museum of the American Indian Act (1989) focused on museums maintained by the Smithsonian Institute, and the Native American Graves Protection and Repatriation Act (NAGPRA, 1990) required museums or universities that have received federal funds to repatriate Native American remains and cultural objects.

> After NAGPRA was passed, the Chiefs gathered and I was asked to serve as liaison and work to repatriate our people's remains. I did museum consultation, repatriation and assisted in burials under both Acts. One repatriation in particular stands out in my memory. When the Northern Cheyenne repatriated the remains of ancestors who had died at Fort Robinson, they invited me, a Southern Cheyenne, to come to the Smithsonian Museum of Natural History where they were stored. During that time, I became acquainted with the Keeper of the Sacred Hat, Joseph Black Wolf. When they were ready to bury the remains at the Two Moon cemetery in Busby, Montana, they invited us to come and take part in the burial ceremony. Mr. Black Wolf was to lead his people as they carried the remains on a one mile walk to the cemetery grounds. He wanted four people to walk beside him, two on his left and two on his right, and asked if I would be one of those four. The other three were Northern Cheyenne. It was an honor I will never forget, and further inspired me to continue my work of repatriation.

In 1995, Lawrence was appointed by then Interior Secretary Bruce Babbitt to serve on the Review Committee of NAGPRA, which included monitoring implementation, resolving disputes, and making annual reports to Congress. He helped tribal groups that could not agree on who should steward remains to resolve their differences in traditional ways, rather than through litigation.

Many remains are now being repatriated by tribes who can lay claim to them. But because of disregard for how remains were collected and stored, and because of poor record keeping, many remains cannot be identified. Scientists are able to determine gender and approximate age, but cannot establish tribal identity. The NAGPRA office at the Department of Interior has been accepting inventories of stored remains from museums and universities around the United States, and their database now lists over 118,000 culturally unidentifiable remains. During the eight years Lawrence served on the Review Committee, he worked on recommendations for the disposition of these remains, which are now being made into rules and regulations.

> One of the recommendations we made was to establish dedicated burial grounds to receive culturally unidentified remains only. These cemeteries will always be a reminder of this part of our history as a nation. The federally recognized tribes should take the lead in determining where these cemeteries will be located. Some wanted to use federal lands controlled by the Bureau of Land Management or the U.S. Forest Service. But others felt that tribes need to be responsible to find a place to bury the remains, and not depend on the U.S. government. I agreed with the latter rationale, recommending that tribes try to establish regional cemeteries throughout the U.S.

The National Congress of American Indians, the largest and oldest Native organization in the United States, is helping organize regional coalitions to establish such cemeteries.

Lawrence committed to help establish the first cemetery in Clinton, Oklahoma, that could serve as a model for other regional sites. On April 3, 2007, at his invitation, thirty-nine federally recognized tribal leaders and designated NAGPRA personnel came to Clinton to dedicate a new building at the Cheyenne Cultural Center, and to walk the proposed grounds for the cemetery. There the Southern Tier High Plains Coalition was formed to be responsible for all the unidentifiable remains and objects in their area, and it will contact museums and universities in Colorado, Kansas, Missouri, Arkansas, Texas, Louisiana, and Oklahoma, which hold an estimated twenty-three thousand unidentifiable remains. The cemetery in Clinton will be large enough to hold all of these remains.

The process has been slow, as tribes concentrate on repatriating culturally identifiable objects and remains. In 2005, Lawrence founded the "Return to the Earth" project (RTE), whose mission is to "support Native Americans in burying unidentifiable ancestral remains now scattered across the United States and enable a process of education and reconciliation between native and nonnative peoples. RTE envisions an ecumenical effort developing regional burial sites throughout Indian country supported by people of faith and governed by diverse, regional Native committees."[20]

The horror of the massacres and the human dismemberment that followed is, Lawrence states, "a gross injustice that needs to be corrected." He is enlisting the help of faith-oriented groups who believe in peace and justice (RTE is fiscally sponsored by Mennonite Central Committee U.S.). In the process of contacting MCC constituents, a couple of church groups offered land for other possible burial grounds, which Hart calls "a gracious and wonderful gift."

> I am glad that faith-based people who believe in restorative justice are coming forward to be a part of Return to the Earth. This whole project operates under the mantra of restorative justice. I approached MCC first because of the Mennonites' strong stance on peace and justice. The U.S. Conference of Religions for Peace includes about seventy different groups, and they have indicated they will participate as well. RTE is a massive, multi-year project that will be expensive, and we are avoiding federal funding. So we are depending on the goodwill of all faith based groups.

Elder Lawrence hopes RTE will become important to churches, which in turn will organize local study programs, facilitate fund-raising efforts, and distribute RTE materials.

A centerpiece of the project is the invitation to congregations to build cedar boxes and sew muslin cloths to be used to transport and bury remains.

As congregants are building boxes they also write litanies and prayers. We ask them to hold a special dedication for these boxes, and to be mindful as they are sent off to the MCC warehouse. The congregation helps cover transportation costs. Not long ago, after I described the cedar boxes to an audience, an art student came up and asked if she could make a hard fired clay box of the same dimensions. I answered positively. Now several students from her class are going to make similar special boxes. Perhaps remains of children or adolescents will be buried in these boxes.

We are asking non-Native congregations throughout the U.S. who build these boxes to also invite descendants of the Native Americans who were displaced from that particular place to participate. Two churches in Beatrice, Nebraska, have researched the tribes that historically occupied that region, and invited descendants to become acquainted. My hope is that through this project, reconciliations between Native and non-native peoples will begin taking place all over the U.S.

Hart has experienced some resistance from fellow Native Christians concerning the use of traditional rituals and ceremonies in the preparation and burial of remains.

Some have admonished me saying, "If you are going to leave Jesus Christ out of this, you are not going to get our support." I have tried to reason with them, explaining that it is fine that they bury their people today with Christian ritual. But the people who were killed in the 1860s had never heard the Good News of Jesus Christ. It is better that we allow the traditional people to use their ceremonies. When we buried the remains of our ancestors killed at Sand Creek, we had to remember that they were killed by *Christians*. We used our traditional ways and that is appropriate. It is disappointing to me that some of our own Native brothers and sisters will not support this project because of that, but I am OK with it.

In the past decade the restorative justice movement has begun to acknowledge and rediscover the many traditions of wisdom that indigenous people were using prior to contact.

> *The Cheyenne Way* is used in conflict resolution classes and some law schools across our nation.[21] It clearly shows that the Cheyenne Peace Chiefs practiced restorative justice. We have many stories in our oral tradition about how we dealt with offenders. For example, during the 1860s, a 300 member tribal group under the leadership of Chief Dull Knife and Chief Little Wolf were fleeing from the U.S. military. They came over a small hill and at the bottom saw white buffalo hunters skinning the animals. The Cheyenne despised the buffalo hunters because they slaughtered the buffalo and took only the hides, leaving the rest of the carcass to rot. The tribal members surrounded the buffalo hunters, who thought their fate was sealed. But the Peace Chiefs sat down, took out a pipe and smoked, talking between themselves. When they had finished the ritual, they told their young men to let the buffalo hunters go. It was the Chiefs way of saying, "We are peacemakers, and no matter the cost we will not harm these buffalo hunters."
>
> I marvel at how our people came to use restorative justice. People who were at one time banished from the tribe were always restored after months or perhaps a few years—much like the prodigal son was restored in the Gospel. So I believe that recovering and giving proper burial to our ancestral remains is a good example of what a contemporary Peace Chief should do.

Nelson Johnson: The Greensboro Truth and Community Reconciliation Project

The spirit and power of prophetic African American Christian faith has animated movements for social change many times throughout U.S. history. The most well-known expression of this tradition was Dr. Martin Luther King's leadership in the Civil Rights movement of the 1950s and 1960s. We believe that Reverend Nelson Johnson of Greensboro,

North Carolina, embodies the character and vision of Dr. King in our generation.

Nelson is deeply grounded in the black freedom movement, and has for five decades been involved in struggles for justice, particularly around issues of race and labor. He is pastor of Faith Community Church, located just across the railroad tracks from downtown Greensboro. His church houses a number of grassroots initiatives in this low-income, African American neighborhood. A powerful preacher and teacher, Nelson interprets the story of Jesus and its relevance to the present struggle for cultural and economic equality each week with his small congregation. Nelson speaks with the moral authority of someone who has been profoundly victimized by racism: stabbed by would-be assassins, jailed on trumped-up charges, targeted by the police, and maligned by the political establishment. Yet his countenance bears none of this; indeed, as a community organizer he is more interested in helping residents find their voice and tell their stories. Most importantly for our focus, Nelson has animated the historic Greensboro Truth and Community Reconciliation Project, the first such effort to take place on U.S. soil.[22]

Nelson has been married since 1969 to Joyce Johnson, a woman of equal courage and commitment. Joyce was among the first African American students to graduate from Duke University in 1968, and has worked for black liberation in the United States and Africa and for quality public education, economic justice, and women's rights. She retired in 2000 after twenty-seven years of service to North Carolina Agricultural and Technical (A&T) State University, where she was director of the Transportation Institute. Joyce now directs the Jubilee Institute, which is part of the Beloved Community Center, the hub of Nelson's work in Greensboro.[23] We interviewed Nelson Johnson in January 2006.

Decoding a "Culture of Civility": From the Sit-ins to the Klan Massacre
Nelson grew up in Littleton, North Carolina, a small southern town of eight hundred people and home town of the great civil rights activist Ella Baker. He listened to his mother tell stories of "the white man," some of which were in the realm of mythology, but some of which were strict accounts of what happened to somebody.

There was a farm on Route 4 out of Littleton where large numbers of black folks worked. It had acres and acres of land and was owned by a white farmer, Bernice West. Black people worked on that land all week, they were pushed hard. On Saturdays they would come into town for a day of relief and release. There was a little juke joint with heavy beat music, and sometimes people got a little too juiced. That's when experiences with the police would occur.

As a child I would go to town on Saturday afternoons and often see a policeman open-hand slap a black man across the face. The police would just pull the man's collar and slap him for some offense, like public drunkenness, and then haul him off to jail. But no matter what Bernice West's workers did, West would come, take some of the black man's money, pay a little to the court, grease a few palms, and get him out of jail, so he could be back to work on his farm on Monday. Anyone who wasn't a part of West's farm would stay in jail and get the book thrown at them. It was a good old boy network, and it deeply enforced the pattern of behavior among all parties.

When a black person went to court, they knew their word would not be taken against that of a white person. The death of a black person only got reasonable adjudication, if it were another black person who killed them. If a white person murdered a black person, justice did not follow. Black farmers who owned their land and tried to get a loan to put in crops got the higher interest rate. These kinds of things were rooted in a way of life, and they only got addressed when they passed a certain point of tolerance. In other words, there was a level of normality to this racial oppression. It was all within a "culture of acceptability."[24]

These experiences anchored Nelson in an understanding of oppression. As a young person he couldn't figure out why people didn't get together and resist this system. His father was president of the local NAACP in a little town called Enfield, and often over meals his parents would talk about the struggle. They were not talking to Nelson, but he was listening. People were doing what they could in those days as the civil rights movement gained energy in the 1950s. But Nelson remembers thinking consciously, "I'm going to do something about this system when I grow up."

Raised in the Baptist church, as a child Nelson embraced the ideals of his family and the church. During the 1960s, he was deeply impacted by the work of Dr. Martin Luther King Jr.

> I had Dr. King's records, and listened to them hundreds of times, feeling the depth of his spirit. I had a friend who ran a sound company in Greensboro, and we would rent a big speaker, put it on top of our truck and play Martin's recordings throughout the community. Even after I came to disagree with what I thought was Martin's flawed logic of nonviolence, I never dismissed him or questioned his integrity.

Nelson was in high school when the famous inaugural sit-in took place at the Greensboro Woolworth's on February 1, 1960.[25] There was a palpable fervor and energy among African American youth, and Nelson felt it.

At age sixteen, with great fear and trembling, Nelson and a friend went to Trevi Fountain Restaurant on Main Street in Littleton. It had wicker chairs and tables, and Nelson and his friends had longed to order a soda and sit in those chairs, like white folks did.

> We were so nervous; it's hard for me to capture the dimension of fear that exists when you move past a certain point in the "normative culture." For us that point was buying a soda and sitting in those wicker chairs at Trevi Fountain. The owner came over, looked at us, and said, "You boys know better than this. Get up and get the hell out of here!" And we did. It was deeply painful to experience that and feel no recourse or capacity to do anything about it because it was all legal and acceptable.

Having seen and experienced this kind of discrimination repeatedly, Nelson became part of the movement of the early 1960s that resisted the culture of Jim Crow, articulating the injustice of that system and engaging its practices, customs, and laws.

In the late 1960s, Nelson attended North Carolina A&T, a black college in Greensboro. In March 1969, he successfully organized A&T students to support striking cafeteria workers in their struggle to win better pay and working conditions. Shortly after, Nelson was elected student government vice president. In May, A&T student leaders became involved in a struggle at nearby Dudley High School.[26]

> Dudley was in the middle of student elections, and the majority of students wanted to elect Claude Barnes as student body President, but his name was not allowed on the ballot. But the students wrote in Claude's name on the ballots, and he won an overwhelming victory. Yet the all-white Board of Education refused to allow Claude to be seated because, they said, he was part of a subversive black organization. Barnes, you see, was raising issues of educational equity and racial justice in his platform.

When Barnes and eight friends began picketing out in front of the school, the police came and beat and arrested them. This occurred during class break, and hundreds of Dudley students saw the violence. A large group went over to the A&T campus, where Nelson and others were holding a national Student Organization for Black Unity conference. The college students immediately dropped what they were doing and went to join their younger brothers and sisters, marching back to Dudley with hundreds of others joining them on the way. There they were joined by other black activists, including some Vietnam veterans. The demonstration eventually moved back over to the A&T campus, where the National Guard, brought in to quell a "riot," stormed the campus with tanks, tear gas, and gunfire, penning the demonstrators in to the dorms. One student was killed and many, including five police officers, were injured.

Nelson called a meeting with all of the black ministers in town to plead with the Dudley High School principal, who was himself black, to meet and resolve the situation. But the principal refused to come because the Board of Education forbade him.

The high school principal became a colonial representative in the school as someone who was subject to the will of the dominant culture rather than to his own community. The whole Greensboro community reacted in the wake of this uprising, which polarized the city. While the Powers demonized me, I was exalted by others in the black community. The public discussion labeled us "Black Panthers"—it was all framed in terms of race, even as people were denying it was a racial incident. A report, written later by the Civil Rights Commission under the leadership of the legendary lawyer Julius Chambers, was scathingly critical of how the City reacted. But Greensboro had this deeply developed "Southern sensibility of civility," where people don't talk plainly but just tip their hats and dip and bow—until dark comes, that is. That's when people get hung.[27]

During these years, Nelson became disillusioned with the church because of the way that so many people did not "live up to Christian standards." He began experimenting with different philosophical groundings.

I went through a period where I tried some other things, Marxism in particular. But after a while that well ran dry, not in its logic, but in its ability to fuel my soul. Marxist beliefs animated good work, and the movements were never without spirit. Whenever we got together in the Communist Workers Party we would sing songs, for example, and people really cared for each other. But there wasn't a theology, or the work of a person who embodied it all.

Meanwhile, the civil rights movement had broken down certain discriminatory employment laws, and by the 1970s it was possible for black people to be hired in local mills.

Nelson became deeply involved in textile factory labor organizing, as well as continuing with community work. It was a familiar reality in the mills: black workers were the last hired, first fired, and worst treated.[28] But in fact, no one in the mills was doing well; white workers had their problems and complaints too. It was the potential for white and black workers to talk and organize together that Nelson hoped to mobilize.

Power is always involved in intersecting layers of oppression, such as race, gender, and class. I talk a lot about race because it is the dominant experience in my life as an African American. We see through the glasses we wear, and that have been imposed on us to wear. But in Greensboro we have constantly had to reckon with the concurrent and overlapping power dimension of economic class.

In 1974, I went to my first union meeting at Proximity Print Works, a textile plant that printed beautiful cloths. There were about seven people at the meeting, all older white males. They were not talking about anything that seemed transformative to me, and there weren't any black people there. Soon afterwards, I developed and circulated a leaflet that compared the salary of the highest paid CEO and the lowest paid worker. It read, "Do you think that what the CEO does is worth so much more than what you do?" This was pretty easy arithmetic, and it invited people into lively discussion. Of course, this brought resentment from management, because we were challenging the particular issues of wage justice *and* the whole culture among the mills. At the same time, the issue of race was also woven into this reality. In some ways the community was beginning to overcome the Jim Crow mentality, but race was being used as a divisive tactic in the mill. Gender issues were also articulated in terms of who got what jobs and how much men and women were paid.

By 1979, they had become relatively successful in organizing textile mills, drawing about ninety people, black and white, to union meetings. They were building a strong, unified base to challenge mill leadership, and hoped to further address unjust labor practices and racism.

On November 3, 1979, Nelson and other labor organizers from the Workers Viewpoint Organization (later renamed the Communist Workers Party) were preparing for a legal rally through a working-class black neighborhood in Greensboro. People slowly gathered to begin the demonstration; children and senior citizens were coming out of the housing projects to join in the singing and preparations for the march. Suddenly, a caravan of nine cars carrying Ku Klux Klan and American Nazi party members drove towards the organizers. The Klansmen stopped, calmly pulled weapons out of the trunks of their cars, and opened fire. In eighty-eight seconds, they killed five labor and community organizers: Cesar Cauce, Dr. Mike Nathan, Bill Sampson, Sandi Smith, and Dr. Jim Waller. Ten others were wounded, including Nelson. The attackers escaped injury and most fled the scene unhindered.

Nelson had obtained a parade permit from the city, but only on the condition that he sign a document stating that none of the demonstrators would carry weapons. He had been assured of police escorts. But all of the police assigned to the parade were sent to lunch early, just before the Klan and Nazis arrived. It was learned later that the Greensboro Police Department was fully aware of the Klan's plans, and their own paid informant, Klansman Eddie Dawson, was a leader in the confrontation.

Despite the fact that four television crews had captured the killings on film, the perpetrators were acquitted by all-white juries in two separate trials. Eventually, a 1985 federal civil suit brought by survivors of the shooting found—for the first time in U.S. history—Klan and Nazi members as well as Greensboro police jointly liable for one of the deaths. The city paid a $351,000 settlement, but has never apologized or acknowledged any wrongdoing.[29]

The aftermath of the events shows how the power of domination works through deception and "spin." The day after the massacre, local newspapers reported that Klansmen had attacked a legally scheduled parade. Within two days, the papers had changed their position, stating that the incident was a "shoot-out" between two extremist groups from outside of Greensboro. The labor organizers were demonized as Communists and Nelson labeled as the "most dangerous man in Greensboro." Jim Melvin, Greensboro's mayor in 1979, asserted that the city had no race-relation problems "except for the ones Nelson Johnson manufactured." Many organizers lost their jobs and were unable to find work for years. The entire city has suffered from the impact of this tragedy, and because there is no common understanding about the events, they continue to serve as a basis for fear, division, and distrust.

From Death to Resurrection: Toward Beloved Community

In the wake of the post-massacre trials, Nelson was isolated, maligned, and thoroughly demonized by those who were still fearful of his organizing, and avoided by people in his own community who were afraid to associate with him. Only two preachers visited him during his time in jail—one black and one white. Their conversations stimulated a new look at his childhood faith.

> This isolation forced me to reflect on what I should do. I went to Mississippi for five months to work with Jesse Jackson's presidential campaign in 1984. But there was something in me that wanted to stay in Greensboro to wrestle this thing out. I started going to church, wandering from congregation to congregation. The first thing that struck me was how warmly I was received in the black churches. People hugged me and asked me how I was doing. Aside from the little network of people within the Communist Workers Party, I wasn't getting a lot of affirmation, and then only very privately. The public acceptance in the churches made me feel good, and it got me reflecting on Jesus.
>
> There was an older black pastor who was deeply spiritual but plain spoken—he'd never be accused of being a powerful preacher in the African American tradition! But his account of the prodigal son impacted me powerfully. I identified with it, and began reading the gospels. I saw dimensions of Jesus I hadn't noticed before: how he confronted people and challenged systems of oppression. Because church talk about crucifixion is overly theologized, I had never realized that the cross was the consequence of Jesus' political resistance.
>
> I wanted to know what sustained Jesus in his ministry, and how his sense of reality transcended the status quo. He had a certain unshakeable confidence that while the things of our world may come and go, there is a greater force at work, and even death cannot bring it to an end. I was comforted by that, and felt called into this way of being.

Nelson moved to Richmond and lived with his in-laws so he could attend Virginia Union School of Theology. On weekends, Nelson traveled back to Greensboro to be with Joyce and their two daughters, who were completing high school. Although challenging for the family, school offered a welcome break.

> Seminary was a very enjoyable three years. I wasn't being called at all hours of the night, I wasn't in court, or having to duck the police. Unlike some students, I focused fairly narrowly on Jesus in my studies (I now recognize that I need to work more on the Hebrew Bible). I was in the library reading stories that I didn't know existed, and in vigorous discussions and even arguments with students and professors in class. They all knew about the 1979 massacre, and asked, "What in the world were you doing that for?" And I had to wrestle with them and explain my motivations.

It was during that period that Nelson went to visit a Klan member in a spirit of reconciliation. "It was one of several times," Joyce told us, "that I kissed Nelson goodbye and wondered if I would ever see him again."

After seminary, Nelson returned home and began again organizing around labor and community issues, now with new convictions about discipleship, nonviolence, and the role of the church. Increasingly he looked to Dr. Martin Luther King as a source of inspiration and direction. In 1991, Nelson and African American community members with whom he was working, together with two white Presbyterian ministers, Barbara Dua and Zee Holler, founded the Beloved Community Center. The BCC has become a remarkable hub for community and regional organizing that is committed to "affirming and realizing the equality, dignity, worth, and potential of every person, and to confronting the systems of domination that prevent us from doing so."[30]

> In 1996, I led a group of ministers to become involved with K-Mart workers in Greensboro in their struggle for a living wage. In that campaign my own growth in, and articulation of, nonviolence matured. We were able to bring together deeply adversarial forces within and outside of the union movement, encouraging them to see each other not as the enemy, but as a beloved community. We persuaded union organizers that they

needed to give priority to building allies in the community, and church leaders to recognize that their congregants were workers too. While it wasn't a perfect collaboration, ultimately the workers won the best first contract in the history of North Carolina.

During this period Nelson also began pastoring Faith Community Church, located in a building shared with the BCC. Members of this small congregation work with homeless folks in the neighborhood, and have recently begun a community garden.

Nelson has developed a keen analysis of how power and privilege is patterned locally, regionally, and nationally, and its relationship to historical spirals of violence.[31]

> Reality is made up of a web of particularities, but when the culture demands that we only acknowledge isolated incidents, our ability to grasp the pattern of a system is diminished. One of the things I discovered early on is that the modus operandi of the Powers is never to concede a general pattern of injustice. When people try to name the pattern, the Powers claim it was just an isolated event. Their mantra is, "This incident has nothing to do with race and nothing to do with justice. This is just one small and anomalous occurrence." The Powers are then able to scapegoat the parties involved, and sometimes that can even be a white person. The whole culture participates and endorses the injustice, but individuals are blamed.
>
> If someone pushes to address the pattern of abuse, the culture and the Powers demonize that person. I used to think of this phenomenon as irrational and evil, and it may be, but I'm not sure that is the best way to think about it. Now I believe that the dominant culture is itself profoundly traumatized, and when we push against it we are inviting the culture to look into its own history of trauma. For European Americans this means looking all the way back to their ancestors—many of whom were prisoners or bond-servants—who came to the New World to escape the abuses in their own countries. Because they didn't face their own displacement and abuse, they could only inflict it

on others, thus embedding trauma in the new culture they were building, even as they were proclaiming their liberation from it.

How else can we explain slavery? How else do we shed light on a people who understand themselves as the cradle of democracy while denying democracy to whole communities, and who then unleash a mountain of brutality to enforce and maintain their privilege? I am increasingly persuaded that our country represents an experience in traumatic mutuality: the traumatized are a mirror for the culture of domination which is, itself, traumatized. I am beginning to understand that this is what we are involved in here.

With this in mind, Nelson recognized that Greensboro could never move forward with racial or economic justice if it did not face the truth of the November 3 massacre. So, despite his full plate of church and organizing commitments, he helped spearhead a community coalition that conceived the idea of the Greensboro Truth and Community Reconciliation Project (GTCRP), which was launched in 2001.

> In retrospect, I question whether we were wise in our explicit challenges to the Klan; we advertised our 1979 protest as a "Death to the Klan" rally, and strongly challenged the Klan's efforts to impede our organizing in the mills. I acknowledge that we made significant errors in both our attitude and some of our actions. Yet the fact is, we did not plan to shoot anyone during that march on Nov. 3rd, nor did we shoot anyone. We did not do any of the violent things that were alleged by the authorities. Yet the perception persists. So the question arises: What does one do to help a community work through this level of confusion? That is what led to our exploration of the possibility of a Greensboro Truth and Community Reconciliation Project.[32]
>
> Initially we had a long struggle over whether the project title should include the word "community." One of my concerns was that the role of institutions, like the media, courts and education system, must be addressed in this process, because these institutions are more basic to the community than the role of

any individual. If we only address interpersonal relationships, we might become convinced that we have accomplished transformation, when in fact the social structures remain unchanged.

For example, as a result of the GTCRP one Nazi member met privately with some of the surviving victims. He felt he was close to death and was seeking a private meeting to clear his conscience. In another instance, I received a phone call from a son of one of the Klan shooters who felt helpless, and I offered him pastoral care. But even if honest healing should transpire between a Klan member and myself, our reconciliation wouldn't necessarily change the community. We might become agents of change, but ultimately the pressing issues of racial and economic justice cannot be eclipsed by personalities. Personalizing the issue is one of the flawed assumptions that have complicated this legacy from the beginning. The project's first task was an organizing one: The idea was actively opposed by governmental structures, and by a significant sector of the white population. We had no state subpoena power, and were publicly ridiculed by the white press for daring to raise the 1979 massacre. Our critics framed the GTCRP as a ploy by survivors to reinject ourselves into the "peace and harmony" of the Greensboro community. In order to move forward we had to build significant consensus around the city.

It was very helpful when Carolyn Allen, who had been city mayor for nine years, threw herself into the process, despite experiencing abuses and demonization. We also had to procure support from the outside, and collaboration with the International Center for Transitional Justice (ICTJ) was key. We also received encouragement and participation from several significant actors in the South Africa TRC process: Anglican archbishop Desmond Tutu, Methodist bishop Peter Storey, and Rev. Bongani Finca.[33]

Despite local opposition, the GTCRP was publicly announced during the Martin Luther King holiday in 2002 with a declaration and a mandate explaining why a TRC was necessary. A broad community consultation process followed. In March 2003, the GTCRP invited seventeen different groups, from city officials to grass roots organizations, to name a representative to a committee that would, in turn, select seven commissioners.[34] The commission was sworn in and empaneled on June 12, 2004, by U.S. Representative Mel Watt (D-NC), former Greensboro mayor Carolyn Allen and District Court Judge Lawrence McSwain, with over five hundred people attending to give support and encouragement. Over the next two years, three public hearings were held, and though there was no court order to appear, more than two hundred people presented testimony. This included the judge that presided over the original criminal case, the lawyer for the Klan and Nazis, the lawyers who won the 1985 civil suit, Klan and Nazi members, survivors, and residents of the traumatized Morningside Community. Hundreds of people gathered at these hearings to listen to riveting testimony.

The seven commissioners had to deal with death threats, evidence that had been tampered, FBI reports that had been changed, and filing cabinets that were mysteriously broken into. Still, they persisted with investigative work and community engagement, researching, and assessing evidence, records, written literature, and personal statements. On May 25, 2006, they released a 529-page report summarizing their findings, conclusions, and recommendations.[35] This then launched a formal year of discussion in the city of Greensboro of the findings.

> We think the GTCRP, despite those who opposed it or wanted it quickly completed and "behind us," represents the most democratic process in the city's history. Of course, the most difficult part of the journey is ahead of us—though, truth be told, *each* part of this process has seemed more difficult than the one before! Will the Greensboro community be able to hold a serious discussion and acknowledge that the massacre and its aftermath is a result of hundreds of years of race and class degradation, abuse, and manipulation? If so, how do we begin a process of healing and restoration? This is where the rubber meets the road, and where something new and beautiful can emerge, even if in a stunted form. These are good seeds being sown.

Will our schools embrace a curriculum that is more rooted in truth and compassion? If the massacre was in fact a result of a system of exploitation, in which some enjoy vast wealth while others strain to make ends meet, how do we reconfigure our collective life in such a way that the possibility of enough-for-all can emerge? No one can do this for us—the community has to do it for itself, out of a conviction that there is a more excellent way, so we are not forever confined to destructive extremities of wealth and poverty.

The commission report must not end up as some moral treatise with no practical effect. I hope that we will wrestle with these matters in a way that impacts our newspaper, our courts, and all of our children in prison. I hope that this challenging process will animate people whose hearts yearn for personal and political change. I believe that there is something inside of people that longs for a measure of truth, for a way of understanding the "other" that holds out hope and possibility.

Archbishop Desmond Tutu, who came to Greensboro on several occasions to support the work of the GTCRP, expressed in a recent meeting with Nelson and Joyce his appreciation for the GTCRP, but also his fears. "Unless Truth and Reconciliation Commissions occur on a mass scale in the U.S.," he confided, "this wonderful nation is on the road to destruction given its international conduct and behavior."[36] Nelson, too, is hopeful for this work, but well aware of the difficulties, and believes that TRCs will not spread in this country unless they are linked to the felt needs of people.

A public discussion about a historic event that focuses only on culpability—who was right, who was wrong, or whether the government was involved—isn't enough. These are important moral questions, and I am fighting to answer them, but at the end of the day the TRC must lead to a *therefore*: If this be true, what shall we do? People will not rush to embrace something that doesn't make any difference for their lives. That would be like having a good discussion in church about the Bible, but when the flood comes everybody drowns anyway. If behavior doesn't change, if people are still starving, if their children are still going to jail, TRCs will not be embraced. In order for TRCs to avoid becoming domesticated, as have so many other great political innovations, they must stay connected to real life.

We are working to build initiatives around the GTCRP so it will not be splintered by the culture of domination. For example, we are currently gathering twenty thousand signatures in support of a living wage for the local public and private sector. We see this as congruent with the GTCRP, part of the "therefore," the feet walking right beside the truth process.

Another example is our work developing a "plan from below" for our city. There is, of course, a plan from above, called Action Greensboro, and it has mapped out the future of the city—what industry is coming, what gentrification will happen and where. But no such thing exists from the perspective of the poor who are trapped in the basement of this dysfunctional house. We would hope that the GTCRP will put questions of economic justice on the table, so that the city planning process will face them. The reality of people being excluded from the current global economy has to be examined. Increasingly most of the available jobs are in the service sector, but these jobs don't pay a living wage. A "truth" that doesn't take these issues into account in the public conversation isn't really worth much. Greensboro needs both truth *and* a fair economy.

Nelson has become increasingly interested in facilitating cooperation between labor organizers and clergy, developing an approach he calls "community unionism," which has animated his current Southern Faith, Labor, and Community Alliance.

Recently I helped mediate between some of the largest unions in the nation who were in conflict over jurisdiction in North Carolina. Trade union leadership does not want to fight the clergy because they recognize they do not have the capacity to win anything by themselves—unlike forty years ago, when labor represented 35 to 40 percent of the work force and had more political clout. As clergy, we recognize we can no longer allow labor organizers to come in and tear up our community over jurisdictional fights. So we met at the Beloved Community Center and reached an agreement: each union signed a document stating that before their organizers move into a city on a campaign, they would submit their plans to a group of clergy for discernment and collaboration. When I shared this result with friends at Interfaith Worker Justice in Chicago, they were pleasantly astounded. We are in an historic moment where Labor wants to cooperate with the community, and we have a set of circumstances that make this more possible.[37]

I have a sense that a weakness in the Civil Rights movement was the fact that Dr. King's disciples were never fully developed because of the overwhelming weight on King as a charismatic leader, as well as the pressure exerted on him by FBI chief J. Edgar Hoover's relentless hounding. Martin was planning to meet with the great Trappist monk Thomas Merton in order to plan a lengthy sabbatical for King to think through how to accomplish training and discipleship. I don't know how King would have accomplished this, since at the time he was deeply involved in the Poor People's Campaign, as well as the Sanitation Worker's strike in Memphis that ultimately took him to the Cross. But one of my mentors, Dr. Vincent Harding, believes King would have realized that training priority.[38]

I believe that what Martin left undone is now ours to do. We need to gather the descendants of slaves who are called to the gospel and rooted in a tradition that can be reclaimed, in order to energize a broader movement. It doesn't necessarily have to become a mammoth movement, but it does have to be rooted in an unshakeable faith. When something is thus grounded, it is not easily destroyed, and has an influence far beyond its numbers. We have seen this in our work in Greensboro; we don't have overwhelming crowds involved, but we are rooted locally, try to do our work with integrity, and it is having an impact.

My faith thus continues to be a growing dimension of my work. I am persuaded that we can't calculate or educate ourselves out of this Domination system. The church has to embody a new way of being that centers on compassion and human equality. With creativity and imagination, the church must join with others in mobilizing to reclaim the nondominating power that transforms society. The direction I see for the future is towards locally owned and managed economies that rely largely on local resources that meet the needs of the community and maintain balance with the environment. We will need new forms of social organization, perhaps more like cells of a living organism which are in constant and mutually supportive interaction with each other, while maintaining their individual integrity and functioning together as part of a larger whole.

I am convinced that only deep movements of faith and justice can hope to redirect this nation, which is so deeply divided over race, crippled by economic exploitation, far down the track of an awful war, and engaged in fierce self-delusion about its place in the world. The price we and the world pay for this hubris is so high. People of faith must rise to the task. Even as things stand, healing will be generations down the road. Yet I believe there are other possibilities for us as a nation. And if I am wrong, I will still do this work, because it is my deepest calling, and informs everything I do.

When Nelson answered our question about where his courage and conviction come from, we thought of the following quote: "I am reminded of the sincere faith that lived first in your grandmother," the Apostle Paul is portrayed writing to Timothy. "So rekindle the gift of God that is within you through the laying on of my hands; for God did not give us a spirit of cowardice, but rather a spirit of power, love and discipline."[39] Nelson looked us straight in the eye and said, "I was born in 1943. Many of the people who held me in their hands had been slaves or were the children of slaves. I do this work because I need to bear witness to that." Maya Angelou is right: "History, despite its wrenching pain, cannot be unlived."

Nelson Johnson echoes the Hebrew prophet Ezekiel's searing indictment of a society in denial of its own contradictions:

Because, in truth, they have misled My people, saying, "Peace!" when there is no peace; and because, when the people build a wall, these prophets smear whitewash on it.... I the Lord will break down the wall that you have smeared with whitewash, and bring it to the ground, so that its foundation will be laid bare.[40]

Yet this "laying bare" led Nelson and his colleagues to an historic truth and reconciliation process that holds the possibility of healing for both victims and perpetrators of deeply rooted historical injustices.

This same Ezekiel, in his famous vision of the valley of dry bones, was asked by God, "Mortal, can these bones live?"[41] Mennonite pastor and Cheyenne peace chief Lawrence Hart's work in repatriation embodies the hope of God's answer to that difficult question of the dismembered past: "I will bring you up from your graves, O my people, and bring you back to your land."[42]

With a moral authority forged through excruciating oppression, Nelson and Lawrence, like Wendy Rose, "will not let us forget." And with a moral vision shaped by deep gospel and cultural commitments, they have become elder statesmen of reconciliation. By heeding their wisdom and learning from their experiments in truth, Angelou's promise will also be realized: If faced with courage, that painful history will not be lived again.

Notes

1.   Wendy Rose, "For Some, It's a Time of Mourning," in *Without Discovery: A Native Response to Columbus*, ed. Ray Gonzalez (Seattle: Broken Moon Press, 1992), 6.

2.   Maya Angelou, *On the Pulse of Morning* (New York: Random House, 1993).

3.   This chapter is an excerpt from Elaine Enns and Ched Myers, "Confronting Historic Injustice: Truth and Reconciliation," in *Ambassadors of Reconciliation: Diverse Christian Practices of Restorative Justice and Peacemaking*, vol. 2 (Maryknoll, NY: Orbis Books, 2009), 121–49.

4.   On the politics of restorative justice, see Andrew Woolford, The Politics of Restorative Justice: A Critical Introduction (Halifax, Nova Scotia: Fernwood Publishing, 2009).

5.   For a theological discussion of this task and its unique North American characteristics, see Ched Myers, *Who Will Roll Away the Stone?: Discipleship Queries for First World Christians* (Maryknoll, NY: Orbis Books, 1994), 111ff.

6.   2 Corinthians 6:1.

7.   Ibid., 6:2.

8.   See Ched Myers and Elaine Enns, "'Ambassadors of Reconciliation': Witnessing to the Restorative Justice of God," in Enns and Myers, *Ambassadors of Reconciliation*, 1–17.

9.   Raylene Hinz-Penner, *Searching for Sacred Ground: The Journey of Chief Lawrence Hart, Mennonite* (Telford, PA: Cascadia Publishing House, 2007), 19.

10.   Ibid., 118.

11.   On the Cheyenne peace chief tradition generally, see Stan Hoig, The Peace Chiefs of the Cheyennes (Norman: University of Oklahoma Press, 1980); on Black Kettle in particular, see Thom Hatch, Black Kettle: The Cheyenne Chief Who Sought Peace but Found War (Hoboken, NJ: John Wiley & Sons, 2004).

12.   Hinz-Penner, *Searching for Sacred Ground*, 109.

13.   Ibid., 117.

14.   Hoig, Peace Chiefs, 7.

15.   Elder Lawrence Hart recounted this story at Fresno Pacific University Center for Peacemaking and Conflict Studies' Seventh Annual Restorative Justice Conference, February 25–26, 2000.

16.   Ibid.

17.   Ibid.

18.   Elder Lawrence Hart, phone interview, February 12, 2007. The unattributed quotes that follow are also from this interview.

19.   Mennonite Central Committee, "The Long Journey Home," slightly edited transcript of video with footage from segments of Jane Brayden, Fox 5 News Tonight, 1997.

20.   For more information, see http://www.rfpusa.org/what-we-do/ return-to-the-earth/.

21.   Karl N. Llewellyn and E. Adamson Hoebel, *The Cheyenne Way: Conflict and Case Law in Primitive Jurisprudence* (Reissue, Buffalo, NY: William. S. Hein & Co., (1941) 2002).

22.   For an overview of the TRC movement, see Kevin Avruch and Beatriz Vejarano, "Truth and Reconciliation Commissions: A Review Essay and Annotated Bibliography," The Online Journal of Peace and Conflict Resolution 4, no. 2 (spring 2002): 37–76.

23.   For more information, see www.belovedcommunitycenter.com.

24.   This and the following quotes are taken from an in-person interview with Nelson Johnson in January 2006.

25.   For history and background on the sit-in movement, the best sources are William H. Chafe, *Civilities and Civil Rights: Greensboro, North Carolina, and the Black Struggle for Freedom*, (New York: Oxford University Press, 1981), and Wesley C. Hogan, *Many Minds, One Heart: SNCC's Dream for a New America* (Chapel Hill: University of North Carolina Press, 2007). See also www.sitins.com.

26.   For background to this and other incidents mentioned in Nelson's testimony, see the accounts of fellow survivors of the 1979 events: Sally A. Bermanzohn, *Through Survivors' Eyes: From the Sixties to the Greensboro Massacre* (Nashville:

Vanderbilt University Press, 2003), and Signe Waller, *Love and Revolution, A Political Memoir: People's History of the Greensboro Massacre, Its Setting and Aftermath* (Lanham, MD: Rowman & Littlefield, 2002). For a compelling personal narrative of parallel events during this period in nearby Oxford, North Carolina—just a few miles from where Nelson grew up—see Timothy B. Tyson, *Blood Done Sign My Name: A True Story* (New York: Three Rivers Press, 2004).

27. Chafe, *Civilities and Civil Rights*, traces the history of Greensboro from 1940 to 1970 and its role in launching several national movements. He shows how the white power structure, while attempting to maintain a progressive mystique, systematically avoided, undercut, or attempted to divide the Greensboro freedom struggle—which continues to the present day.

28. For a comprehensive narrative of the relationship between African American struggles for labor and racial justice throughout this period, see Michael Keith Honey, *Black Workers Remember: An Oral History of Segregation, Unionism, and the Freedom Struggle* (Berkeley: University of California Press, 1999).

29. The settlement became the seed money for the Greensboro Justice Fund, which pursued a mission of keeping the story of the massacre alive. In 2009 the fund donated its assets to resource grassroots social justice organizing in the region (see http://highlandercenter.org/programs/internships-fellowships-and-volunteers/greensboro-justice-fellowships/). For personal accounts of survivors see Bermanzohn, *Through Survivors' Eyes*, and Waller, *Love and Revolution*.

30. For more information on this extraordinary network and its kaleidoscope of creative projects, see www.belovedcommunitycenter.org.

31. On this see Enns and Myers, *Ambassadors of Reconciliation*.

32. For information and documents concerning the Greensboro Truth and Community Reconciliation Project, see http://www.greensborotrc.org. Accounts and analysis can also be found in Ellis Cose, *Bone to Pick: Of Forgiveness, Reconciliation, Reparation, and Revenge* (New York: Simon and Schuster, 2004); Greg Grandin and Thomas Miller Klubock, *Truth Commissions: State Terror, History, and Memory* (Durham, NC: Duke University Press, 2007); and Michael T. Martin and Marilyn Yaquinto, eds., *Redress for Historical Injustices in the United States: On Reparations for Slavery, Jim Crow, and Their Legacies* (Durham, NC: Duke University Press, 2007).

33. The ICTJ has facilitated Truth and Reconciliation Commissions all over the world, and played an important role in helping the GTCRP conceive and organize its work; see www.ictj.org. Each of the three South African clerics visited and consulted with the GTCRP on numerous occasions. We (Elaine and Ched) also had the privilege of serving on the advisory board of the project in its planning stage.

34. Out of those groups, fourteen nominated a representative. The Sons of Confederate Veterans and the United Daughters of the Confederacy immediately declined. The police department and the city Human Relations Committee, after much deliberation, chose not to appoint someone. Any citizen of Greensboro could nominate any person to be a potential commissioner, and over fifty people were nominated before the selection

committee was formed. Commissioners had to be people of integrity and principle, willing to commit themselves to seek the truth amidst all of the data and perspectives, and could not have been directly involved in the events of November 3, 1979.

35. The executive summary is available at http://www.greensborotrc.org/exec_summary.pdf.

36. For his reflections on the South African TRC process and thoughts on related issues, see Desmond Tutu, *No Future without Forgiveness* (New York: Doubleday, 1999); see also Russell Daye, *Political Forgiveness: Lessons from South Africa* (Maryknoll, NY: Orbis Books, 2004).

37. Nelson's vision of community unionism was further developed at two collaborative conferences between the Word and World School and Southern Faith, Labor, and Community Alliance: in Memphis (2006) and Tar Heel, North Carolina (2007). Leaders from throughout the South and beyond discussed problems and possibilities of strategic and Spirit-led collaboration in the work of labor and economic justice; central was the story of King's solidarity with the Memphis Sanitation Workers in 1968 (see www.wordandworld.org/FaithLaborCommunityAlliance.shtml). We (Elaine and Ched) had the pleasure of serving on the board with Nelson of Word and World, a school for faith-based justice and peace activists (see Ched Myers, "Word and World: A People's School," *The Clergy Journal* 78, no. 9 [September 2002]: 8ff).

38. See Vincent Harding, *Martin Luther King: The Inconvenient Hero*, 2d ed. (Maryknoll, NY: Orbis Books, 2008); Harding, *Hope and History: Why We Must Share the Story of the Movement* (Maryknoll, NY: Orbis Books, 1990). Dr. Harding, spiritual advisor to Dr. King and the foremost historian and interpreter of the civil rights movement and its enduring implications, worked closely with Nelson on numerous educational projects. See also Charles Marsh, *The Beloved Community: How Faith Shapes Social Justice, from the Civil Rights Movement to Today* (New York: Basic Books, 2005). On Dr. King's interest in meeting with Merton, see Myers and Enns, "'A House Divided Cannot Stand': Jesus as a Practitioner of Nonviolent Direct Action (Mark 1–3)," *Ambassadors of Reconciliation*, vol. 1, n. 18, and sources cited there; on King's involvement in the Memphis living wage struggle, see ibid., "Introduction," n. 5, and references.

39. 2 Timothy 1:5–7.

40. Ezekiel 13:10,14.

41. Ibid., 37:3.

42. Ibid., 37:12.

PART 3

RELIGION AND THE DEFENSE
OF HUMAN RIGHTS

Faith-based or religious peacemaking is a growing field, gathering activists, practitioners, and scholars.[1] In the literature stemming from the field, attempts are made at identifying the specificities of faith-based or religious peacemaking. Aside from the role of textual references, traditional rituals, interfaith dialogue, or the use of safe zones, the element of nonviolence is often associated with faith-based, religious peacemaking.

This section presents two perspectives on the interaction, on the ground, between religion, human rights, and peacemaking. Chibli Mallat shares his analysis of the Arab Spring based on his involvement in the Middle East; the central question of his essay revolves around the use of nonviolence, its development as a tactic to resist violence, and its success. Kathleen Kern and Tim Nafziger provide, with the work of *Christian Peacemaker Teams*, a concrete example of faith-based peacemaking that is predicated on nonviolence. Both texts complement each other very well. If Mallat interrogates the principle of nonviolence itself on both a practical and a theoretical level[2] and encourages peacemakers to engage in such a practice, Kern and Nafziger illustrate its possible application in some low-intensity conflict zones.

Notes
1. For further reading, see the important collection of essays in David Little, ed., *Peacemakers in Action: Profiles of Religion in Conflict Resolution* (Cambridge: Cambridge University Press, 2007), or the inspiring volume by Harold Coward

and Gordon Smith, eds., *Religion and Peacebuilding* (Albany: State University of New York Press, 2004).

2.   Mallat's latest book, *Philosophy of Nonviolence: Revolution, Constitutionalism, and Justice beyond the Middle East* (New York: Oxford University Press, 2015), offers further development on this matter.

6

From Amnesty International
to Right to Nonviolence

Theory and Practice in the Arab Spring Context

CHIBLI MALLAT

I propose to share in this chapter some theoretical and practical considerations on making nonviolence the dominant philosophy of historical change through the narrow lens of my work in the Middle East over the past three decades, but also with a concern for the increasing universality of the appeal of nonviolence as a philosophical category.[1]

My active involvement with nongovernmental organizations (NGOs) over the past three decades started with the formation of the International Committee for a Free Iraq (ICFI) in London in 1991. In the wake of the fiasco coalition "victory" in the Gulf War of 1990–1991, ICFI brought together leading figures from across the world, such as Senator John McCain and former Iraqi president Jalal Talibani, on a platform for a democratic future in Baghdad.[2] I have also been active in various international NGOs, including Minority Rights Groups, the Iraqi Refugee Assistance Project, and the Sri Lanka Campaign for Peace and Justice. Around 1999, I helped establish the regional office of Amnesty International (AI) in Lebanon. The successful legal battle for the establishment of the Middle East AI office in Beirut, which required a decree issued by the Lebanese Council of Ministers, was a significant turning point for human rights in the region. More recently, in 2009–2010 in Beirut, together with like-minded colleagues, I helped establish Right to Non-violence (RN). A year later, mass nonviolent demonstrations removed dictators in power for decades in Tunisia, Egypt, and Yemen.

This chapter shares some theoretical perspectives associated with this very practical involvement with nonviolence on which the Tanner Center philosophy is built. The confluence is not a coincidence, as non-violence can rely on an intellectual and practical pedigree that appears increasingly effective worldwide.[3] Some of the questions raised in this paper result from the context of the Middle East revolution, a.k.a. the Arab Spring, but they are meant to go well beyond.

I discuss presently three issues of both theoretical and practical importance.

The first concerns the vectors of nonviolent action, and why an NGO is better positioned for this sort of change than a political party. This will be examined primarily through the experience of AI. The second is about priorities and trade-offs, or when "to put citizens on the ground." This will be developed through some of the work of RN in the ongoing Middle East turmoil. The third concerns a central false problem, or "how to shun the white man's burden."

Vectors of Action: Learning from the AI Template

Among several differences between an NGO and a political party is the focus of their respective messages.

Political parties must form responses to every relevant public issue, from foreign policy to taxes to education, from labor to gender and sexual orientation, and from neighborhood watch and criminality to crimes against humanity. A political party requires a constant stream of messages reflecting a comprehensive world vision that spares no issue.

NGOs typically focus their work on one message, even if the message varies and eventually multiplies into others. Focus on a message or a series of messages, rather than the embrace of a full and inchoate platform that a political party is forced to carry, is both more efficient and more purposeful. While the NGO dictates the agenda, the political party is weakened by the vastness of international issues it is ill-equipped to address.

A political party seeks to put its members in government. Its central objective is to get them elected. NGOs do not in principle advocate an official position for any of their members and are not encumbered with "politicking" to get their members in government or in public office. While it is generally reassuring to see former NGO members in governmental decision-making positions, the causal connection is severed by nature—one does not run for public office as the candidate of an NGO. The distance is salutary for the integrity of the NGO's message, and for its intensity.

Amnesty International (AI) is the most recognized human rights organization. In 1961, lawyer Peter Benenson was incensed by the news of the Salazar dictatorship incarcerating students who were simply drinking a toast to liberty in Lisbon. He and similarly outraged friends formed a small pressure group in an "Appeal for Amnesty" for the students and other prisoners of conscience, hence the name. A half-century later, Amnesty International is a great misnomer since one of its most active messages is to reject amnesty for political criminals, in particular perpetrators of atrocities. Still, AI chose to keep its original brand, which is closely tied to the first core mandate of the organization, the defense of freedom of expression, and to its most important agent, the nonviolent dissident known as prisoner of opinion or prisoner of conscience. This is AI's original and most enduring message.

Amnesty never wavered on its core message. Whatever one's opinion—in AI's long-standing fight for freedom of expression further distilled in founding bills and human rights conventions—government shall not be allowed to imprison a person for the public expression of her view. The principle is solid, with a strong bright line that remains as forceful today as it was in 1961.

Then came a slow but real expansion of the mandate, including a steadfast opposition to the death penalty, which eventually developed to articulate the need to arrest mass political murderers and try them for the atrocities they perpetrate. Amnesty's support of the International Criminal Court (ICC) and of various forms of universal jurisdiction, especially the Pinochet case in London, and the Sabra and Chatila case in Belgium, is testimony to a strong and active belief in criminal accountability of political leaders turned mass murderers.[4]

In recent years, AI has pursued other avenues under the theme of equality and campaigned in a number of germane human rights fields. Gender equality was and remains prominent, with massive campaigns to denounce and punish violence against women, publically as in mass rape and domestically for battered wives or abused foreign workers. Before she left the leadership of the organization, then AI secretary general Irene Khan developed another target: the fight against poverty.[5] This is another "new" message for AI's mission. All are important and resonate strongly for people everywhere; yet immense resources are needed for AI to be effective.

Organizationally, AI's founders expressed a dual moment of intuitive genius when they separated members' actions from the work of the International Secretariat in London, especially the work done by "researchers," who continue to provide timely alerts to signal the arrest or torture of a prisoner of opinion, oppose a death sentence, warn against impending massacres, or request accountability for dictators' crimes against humanity. To the extent that London remained secure for free speech, the Secretariat was generally sheltered from the ire and immediate reach of dictators. The division between the Secretariat (including the researchers) and the membership allowed a further, crucial protection: members, when active in a specific campaign for a prisoner of opinion or other delicate matter, typically work outside their own country. Letters will inundate the Chinese leadership from Germany, Brazil, or Canada, never from China. Even if the Chinese government wished to sanction the letter writers, it would find it particularly hard to punish people who are out of territorial reach. In that sense, the information and dissemination of AI's powerful and carefully checked criticism is practically impossible to stem.

This balance between the executive branch of AI, the International Secretariat, and the large membership who represents in a way "the people of Amnesty," hampers AI's work to some extent, as with all successful international NGOs. Bureaucracy inevitably creates friction, but the efficacy of AI's human rights response remains phenomenal thanks to the dedication of researchers at the Secretariat, the understanding and commitment of the members, and the innovative division of labor that keeps membership generally active away from the country whose government they criticize.

The involvement of membership is also important in terms of fund-raising, and in terms of street-level action, which is crucial for a human rights organization that operates on a wide grassroots level. AI, by any standard, offers the most remarkable model for that combination.

How does an organization emulate Amnesty? I don't think one should or can "compete" with AI in any way. The multiplication of impressive human rights NGOs on the international scale—such as Human Rights Watch—as well as on regional and national levels, is a positive factor. It enhances the general AI calling by multiplying human rights voices by so many other vectors.

What is needed are new concepts, new horizons for human rights, that can captivate the world imagination in the way Amnesty has since the action of Peter Benenson and his colleagues over students maltreated by a petty government in Lisbon in the early 1960s. I suggest that non-violence is one such concept, should its theoretical underpinnings sufficiently cohere. This explains the emergence of Right to Nonviolence in 2009–2010.

This much more modest development was made possible by the dedication of dozens of seasoned colleagues and youthful volunteers who have generously given their time to Right to Nonviolence, in the belief that it provides an alternative horizon for the region where violence is most endemic: the Middle East.

RN's message came initially from building on the nonviolent character of the Lebanese Cedar Revolution in 2005 and the Iranian Green Revolution in 2009. It was established from within the arguably most violent region in the world to advocate a view of a world free of physical violence. At the beginning of 2011, that concept was made into a reality by the Middle East Revolution, incorrectly described as the Arab Spring. With millions on the street marching peacefully for the removal of dictatorship, a "right to nonviolence" was no longer wishful thinking. The jury is still out, of course, but the achievements in Yemen, Tunisia, and Egypt are tangible with the fall of three entrenched dictators in early 2011, with practically not a single act of violence by millions of demonstrators against them or their instruments of repression. Nonviolence lasted for weeks—in the case of Yemen for months—before the dictator was forced out. Of course, dictators were violent, for there is no conceivable nonviolent demonstration without the unwarranted and criminal violence exercised against demonstrators by those entrenched in power.

While every single dictator in the Middle East was scared, three were forced out of office without the use of any physical violence against them by the revolutionaries. More tangibly still, the initial revolutionary message was self-conscious in the deafening call across the villages and cities of the Middle East: *silmiyya, silmiyya,* peaceful, peaceful.[6] The central message of RN became tangible after Tunisia's dictator fled and Egypt's modern-time pharaoh was dismissed and arrested. We are now certain that Syria's revolution would have achieved much better results if it had continued on its original path of nonviolence sustained from March through August 2011.

RN carries two other connected messages: new constitutions to provide the legal basis for democracy, and judicial and other accountability structures for the dictators of the fallen repressive systems and for their aides who were complicit in the repression. RN's action is based on the belief that successful constitutions secure an open rule of law that prevents the return to authoritarianism, and that judicial and other direct means of accountability for mass murderers of the ancien régime are an essential component for the nonviolent message to continue beyond the removal of a dictator. RN provides a unique and unprecedented regional comparative focus, and reaches out internationally, including to the opposition in China, to underline the commonality of means and ends.

In a way, the horizons of RN were vindicated a posteriori by the ongoing Middle East revolutions. This, however, does not turn RN into a mass movement. To attain success, that message must be true and consistent. It is hard for nonviolence to endure—witness Yemen, Syria, and Egypt—and it is difficult to be consistent, as countries move after the nonviolent revolution to a rule of law that cannot function without a state monopoly over violence.

This is a central challenge for the coherence of the nonviolent message, and requires the concept to be constantly developed, refined, and sharpened. RN advocates the right to nonviolence as a political way of life. The original concept, in Arabic *al-haqq bil-la`unf*, was devised by Lebanese lawyer Thérèse Aoun when RN was being formed in 2008–2009. It can be criticized as redundant with the original "right to security," which one finds in the very first human rights bills in the world, but the originality of the concept lies in its dual dynamism: a person has a right to be spared violence in her everyday political life, but she also has a right to exercise nonviolence, to the point of active revolution against a sitting order it considers unjust. The founders of nonviolence thought that the concept echoed best the extraordinary legacy of civil resistance/nonviolence embodied in the massive nonviolence of Gandhi's revolt against British colonialism, Martin Luther King's civil rights marches, and on through the 1989 fall of the Berlin Wall, the collapse of the Soviet system, and the Tienanmen Square protests. It had its clear predecessors in the Middle East with the failed nonviolent revolutions in Lebanon in 2005–2006 and in Iran in 2009. Right to Nonviolence sends a message that turns the whole society into the extension of prisoners of conscience when like-minded people, often the mothers, sisters, and relatives of people jailed for the peaceful expression of their opposition to a dictator, find themselves by the millions on the street, while dictatorship continues its systematic and structural repression. If the Middle East revolution is world historical, in Hegelian terms, it is because nonviolence is effective as a breakthrough with an unprecedented spirit. The increasingly articulate message of nonviolence meets the reality of history in motion, and gets refined and reinforced by its spread to a much larger international constituency.

Coherence and the integrity of a full philosophical system based on nonviolence as the nexus of history are important. I tried to articulate this in my recent book.[7] The other horizon for nonviolence is organizational. Absent the objective of a political party to ascend to power, capturing the street imagination requires a different type of mobilization. While remarkable technological innovations transform citizens into real-time journalists, emails, tweets, and Facebook pages are not sufficient for the success of a mass, street movement.[8] Old-fashioned organization is needed "to put citizen boots on the ground," to coin a phrase.

To develop a mass international movement, it is hard to work on street deployment without a meaningful injection of funds needed to sustain any massive organizational mobilization. But even if funds are always needed, including for small NGOs, they are not the central problem. The central challenge is the message of the NGO: its novelty, its truth, its consistency, its capacity to captivate the human imagination and the public space, and to grow.

Trade-offs

Political parties and NGOs both confront trade-offs in terms of capacities. Unlike political parties, NGOs enjoy the luxury of ignoring electoral calendars and the concomitant political bazaars that are inherent to seeking public office and retaining government positions. Still, setting the right priorities on a global level is extremely difficult. The massive Avaaz movement shows the limitations in its emails, distributed across the planet: one day, it is the rainforest of Brazil, on another it is the flow of arms to Syria's repressive machine, and on a third it is anticensorship of U.S. internet legislation. How does one cohere the movement on such disparate, albeit individually important, issues across a wide spectrum?

A balance is needed for personnel, countries, publications, and focused campaigns. At RN, we reacted, with modest means, to a bewildering array of events unfolding sometimes dramatically at the same time in several countries. There are immense constraints. The trial of a dictator is by itself extremely time consuming and requires a high level of legal expertise without which the judicial process is incomprehensible. Correct information and the right level of abstraction are both key. This is also true in constitution making, where details and context are central.[9]

To address the avalanche of approximate information publically available, RN volunteers created its Middle East Constitutional Forum, which provided timelines and documents that are carefully chosen to support further work.[10] And we had to decline several offers to participate in the constitutional processes of several Middle Eastern countries. Each requires an immense amount of careful analysis and a sustained investment, both personal and institutional. Proper, educated legal information, without which constitutional discussions are impossible to conduct, needs to be sifted, sometimes even created from scratch.

So there are trade-offs, per force. The question is to distill the trade-off that is inevitable because of the shortage of expert personnel and the high volume of unclear information, from the trade-off where a substantive decision needs to be made on a matter of high moral ambivalence. Take the issue of self-immolation, also known as "tactical suicide": in close work with colleagues fighting dictatorship in China, RN took a strong position against the risk of a hunger strike being carried to the end—that is, to death—in Bahrain. We opposed that sacrifice and expressed it to our Bahraini colleagues.[11] We took a similar stance towards self-immolation of Tibetan monks as a wrong expression of nonviolent philosophy.[12]

Syria presented another difficult case. Where does one stand on the request of millions of Syrians for international (military) protection without sacrificing the message of nonviolence carried out by the Syrian street for six months before its militarization? Three years after this stark choice should have been made, failing to create a safe haven for the nonviolent revolution for cities like Hama on the occasion of the visit of the U.S. and French ambassadors in July 2011, turned Syria into a mayhem of biblical proportions.[13]

Another example is our work in Bahrain. Before the clampdown, RN worked on a "Constitutional Options" paper with the opposition and some leading governmental figures, in coordination with the U.S. State Department. The effort was stalled a day before the dialogue was due to start by the invasion of Bahrain by Saudi and other Gulf country troops on March 14, 2011.[14]

And so on. Examples of the hard choices to be made every day can be multiplied. One should not agonize over these choices. You do the best you can, with the modesty and the resolve needed to avoid being continuously mugged by a contrarian reality. At one point in the life of the NGO, the core group must decide whether or not to "go public," which is the effective mobilization of people in the street. It can choose not to do so, as much work continues to be carried out behind the scenes and without having citizens demonstrate in the streets. If my reading of Amnesty International as one of the most successful models for a worldwide NGO is correct, that day needs to be carefully chosen. Putting citizens on the ground is not an easy proposition.

Avoiding the "West and the Rest" Mentality

How does one build an anti-atrocity constituency without falling in the "white man's burden" complex? Or the trap of reproducing colonial imperialism? This is an important but ultimately wrong question. If one believes in universal values, of which the rejection of mass murder and of the impunity of their perpetrators is self-evident, then one does not need to be constantly worried about the "West and the rest" conceptual trap.

Let us consider the issue from a more symbiotic angle. A mass international movement to end impunity needs to be conscious of history and form. By history I mean colonial history, which cannot simply be brushed away in a "hearts and minds" campaign carried out by "innocents abroad." One does not erase four hundred years of colonialism and its attendant atrocities by shouting, "HUMAN RIGHTS!" By form I give the example of the intolerable picture of governments and organizations that flaunt gender or minority equality without a single woman or minority member in the group photo. In a similar vein, an international movement where the West is overrepresented is neither universal nor international. A constant, difficult effort is needed. For RN, it was key to establish it from within the Middle East, with a significant number of Arab human rights leaders on board from the outset.

This does not, however, lessen the importance of Western input, not only because Western countries, the United States in particular, continue to be extremely powerful actors across the globe. It is also important because Middle Easterners, in my experience at RN and previously with the International Committee for a Free Iraq, openly seek support from their Western colleagues, are proud of it, and benefit immensely from its activation under a common policy and set of objectives.[15]

There is a lot of hypocrisy in the diffidence of Middle Easterners towards the West. Xenophobia is a dead-end, whether performed in a Western country or in the formerly colonized East. People need each other at a level of international cooperation way beyond the real, but ultimately secondary, legacy of colonialism. In every Western society are thousands of Bartolome de Las Casas standing up against the massacres of the local "Indians."[16] In Eastern societies, most people do not espouse extremism unless they are cornered into isolation. I find little traction in "us" and "them." Among "them" are many of "us," and, more importantly, among "them" are many more ready to be with "us" if we engage. I never hesitated during the formation of RN as an NGO to see the immense value of friends and comrades across the divides whether East-West, Orient-Occident, Islam-West, Christian-Muslim, or Shia-Sunni. Here, religions do not matter as universal policy. The divide between East and West is real historically; so are divisions between religions, mostly the three Abrahamic religions, and within sects, mostly Shias and Sunnis. The commonality of purpose for human rights, on the scale of Amnesty International, down to Right to Nonviolence, is easily discernable and expressed. Work on the details of the language and references to achieve the commonality is a different matter, addressed in other chapters of this work. It does not undermine the overall philosophy of the groups involved.

A healthy, open relation with colleagues from the West within an NGO is an essential part of a worldwide struggle for nonviolence as a guide to the twenty-first century. The proposition is in fact trite. The challenge is in the details of balance of work and representativeness inside the NGO and in its public expression.

Conclusion

If there is a philosophy of nonviolence in the making, it lacks both the theoretical and organizational instruments for its fulfilment. Building on the example of Amnesty International, Right to Nonviolence sought to fill some of the gap in active work—in public and privately—in the Middle East Revolution that offered the template for the reality of nonviolence as the nexus of history. It did so by recognizing that an international NGO is better positioned for impact than a political party. It sought to avoid the trap of the West versus the rest by equally relying on the good will of participants from within the Middle East and international actors, while refining its theoretical reach in several practical interventions. It has not yet reached a stage of organization and maturity to put "citizens for nonviolence on the ground."

This is more needed than ever. Violence continues unabated in the Middle East.

Notes

1. I attempt to draw a system in *Philosophy of Nonviolence: Revolution, Constitutionalism and Justice beyond the Middle East* (New York: Oxford University Press, 2015).

2. Mallat, "Obstacles to Democratization in Iraq: A Reading of Post-Revolutionary Iraqi History through the Gulf War," in *Rules and Rights in the Middle East: Democracy, Law and Society*, ed. Ellis Goldberg, Resat Kasaba, and Joel Migdal (Seattle: University of Washington Press, 1993), 224–47; "Voices of Opposition: The International Committee for a Free Iraq," ibid., 174–87.

3. See Erica Chenoweth and Maria Stephan, *Why Civil Resistance Works: The Strategic Logic of Nonviolent Conflict* (New York: Columbia University Press, 2011), and the work of the International Center on Nonviolent Conflict.

4. The main court decision in several Pinochet cases is Regina v. Bartle and the Commissioner of Police for the Metropolis and Others Ex Parte Pinochet; Regina v. Evans and Another and the Commissioner of Police for the Metropolis and Others Ex Parte Pinochet, UKHL 17 (March 24, 1999). A majority of six judges rejected immunity and considered actionable crimes, acts of torture committed after the 1984 Convention Against Torture came into effect in Britain three years later. For Sabra and Chatila, AI supported the action of the victims from the very first day, and worked unsuccessfully to prevent the retroactive change of legislation in Belgium after the victory of the victims before the Belgian supreme court, Cour de Cassation (February 12, 2003), *Pasicrisie Belge*, vol. 1 (2003): 307, 317–18 (Belgium). In English, "Court of Cassation of Belgium: H.S.A. et al. v. S.A. et al. (decision related to the indictment of Ariel Sharon, Amos Yaron and others)" (February 12, 2003), *International Legal Materials*, 42 (2003): 596–605. In both cases, Amnesty International was continuously supportive of the victims.

5. Irene Khan, *The Unheard Truth: Poverty and Human Rights* (New York: W. W. Norton & Company, 2009).

6. This even struck Barack Obama when Hosni Mubarak was finally forced out of power: "We saw protesters chant 'salmiya, salmiya'—we are peaceful—again and again." Speech at Robert Mackey, "Updates on Day 18 of Egypt Protests," *The Lede, New York Times* (February 11, 2011).

7. See note 1.

8. See the discussion in Chibli Mallat and Edward Mortimer, "The Background to Civil Resistance in the Middle East," in *Civil Resistance in the Arab Spring: Triumphs and Disasters*, ed. Adam Roberts et al. (Oxford: Oxford University Press, 2016).

9. See, e.g., RN work with various groups on constitutional issues in Egypt, Bahrain (2011), the role of Islamic law in the constitutions of Libya and Tunisia (2012), lustration in Libya (2013; written up in Mallat et al., "The Efficacy of Lustration Laws Within the Pyramid of Accountability: Libya Compared," *Yale Journal of International Law* (online) 39 [Spring 2014]: 112–33), national dialogue and constitution in Yemen (2013), in Iraq on the constitutional process in August 2014. Details on papers, interventions, proposals, and wide media coverage are available on RN's site.

10. Middle East Constitutional Forum (MECF) of the section of the Right to Nonviolence site established by Tobias Peyerl and Jolsyn Massengale.

11. E-mail to Mariam al-Khawaja, whose father, ʿAbdel Hadi, had been quickly declining on hunger strike, April 19, 2012.

12. See my lecture, "Nonviolence from Damascus and Manama to Moscow and Beijing: Why the Middle East Revolution Makes Dictatorships Tremble," at Initiatives for China's Seventh Annual Interethnic/Interfaith Leadership Conference, Los Angeles, CA, April 21, 2012. http://www.righttononviolence. org/mallat-addresses-7th-annual-initiatives-for-china-leadership-conference/.

13. For details of the Syrian revolution's turn to violence in summer 2011, see "A Brief History of Nonviolence," in Mallat, *Philosophy of Nonviolence*; in Arabic, Mallat, "Al-suʾal al-falsafi fi thawratina: hal al-ʾunf mumkin fiha ʿalal-itlaq?" (The philosophical question in our revolution: is nonviolence possible in the absolute?), Nahar (Beirut) (July 28, 2012). For work on Syria, see Initiatives for Syria on RN's website.

14. See Bahrain under "Countries" on RN site for a full dossier, including Mallat and Jason Gelbort, "Constitutional Options for Bahrain," *Virginia Journal of International Law* 2 (April 12, 2011): 1–16.

15. In the summer of 1992, a year after the formation of the International Committee for a Free Iraq, the top Iraqi members of ICFI were invited by the U.S. secretary of state to meet with him in Washington over a common strategy for the future of Iraq. I was asked by my Iraqi friends to join the delegation, but I thought that the matter was now in firm hands, that Iraqi leaders had come enough of political age not to be "accompanied," and that they did not need a new version of the "white man" to tag along, in that case non-Iraqis in the committee. Through the travails of the opposition that followed that high moment, and on several other occasions, I realized that people confronting unique hardship caused by dictatorship, and inevitably disagreeing with each another, benefit significantly from nonnational colleagues even for their domestic deliberations. In part, this stems from the trust built over the years of common opposition. It also results from the fact that nonnationals cannot be competitors on the domestic political scene.

16. In his *Brevísima Relación de la Destrucción de las Indias* ("A brief account of the destruction of the Indies," 1542, available in both Spanish and English on the internet), Dominican friar Bartolomé de las Casas (d. 1566) decried the immense brutality meted out upon the native Indians under Spanish colonial rule.

7

Partnering in Nonviolent Resistance

The Evolution of Christian Peacemaker Teams

KATHLEEN KERN AND TIM NAFZIGER

Perhaps nothing better illustrates how *Christian Peacemaker Teams'* approach to peacebuilding has evolved over the last twenty-five years than the change in its slogans. The 1995 training of full-timers and reservists came up with "Getting in the Way,"[1] which, besides being short and snappy, had a double meaning. "The Way" was the earliest name recorded in scripture for the Christian Church. By getting in the way of violence and oppression, CPTers saw themselves as following in the way of the earliest Christians.

Increasingly, however, as people from the Global South whose first language was not English began working with CPT, the motto became problematic. Linguistically, the double meaning worked only in English. More significantly, the motto carried overtones of white missionary saviors coming to protect helpless third-worlders, and CPT's best efforts were happening when it worked in partnership with local communities who had already organized to challenge systemic violence facing their communities. Thus, CPT's shift away from this motto indicated a change within the culture of the organization driven by a commitment to undo oppression and privilege both internally and in relationships with partners. A mission statement that developed out of the three-year

"Mission and Presentation Re-visioning" (MAPR) process perhaps best summarizes this change: "Building partnerships to transform violence and oppression."[2]

This chapter will offer glimpses into how CPT has built partnerships both on the ground and in the digital realm in its recent work with Colombian and North American indigenous communities. However, in order to better understand the shift, it will begin with a review of CPT's origins.

In 1984, Ron Sider challenged the Mennonite World Conference in Strasbourg, France, by asking the question:

> What would happen if we in the Christian church developed a new nonviolent peacekeeping force of 100,000 persons ready to move into violent conflicts and stand peacefully between warring parties in Central America, Northern Ireland, Poland, Southern Africa, the Middle East, and Afghanistan? Frequently we would get killed by the thousands. But everyone assumes that for the sake of peace it is moral and just for soldiers to get killed by the hundreds of thousands, even millions. Do we not have as much courage and faith as soldiers? ...
>
> Even small groups of people practicing what they preach, laying down their lives for what they believe, influence society all out of proportion to their numbers. I believe the Lord of history wants to use the small family of Anabaptists scattered across the globe to help shape history in the next two decades. But to do that, we must not only abandon mistaken ideas and embrace the full biblical conception of shalom. One more thing is needed. We must take up our cross and follow Jesus to Golgotha. We must be prepared to die by the thousands. Those who believed in peace through the sword have not hesitated to die. Proudly, courageously, they gave their lives. Again and again, they sacrificed bright futures to the tragic illusion that one more righteous crusade would bring peace in their time, and they laid down their lives by the millions. Unless comfortable North American and European Mennonites and Brethren in Christ are prepared to risk injury and death in nonviolent

opposition to the injustice our societies foster and assist in Central America, the Philippines, and South Africa, we dare never whisper another word about pacifism to our sisters and brothers in those desperate lands. Unless we are ready to die developing new nonviolent attempts to reduce international conflict, we should confess that we never really meant the cross was an alternative to the sword. Unless the majority of our people in nuclear nations are ready as congregations to risk social disapproval and government harassment in a clear ringing call to live without nuclear weapons, we should sadly acknowledge that we have betrayed our peacemaking heritage. Making peace is as costly as waging war. Unless we are prepared to pay the cost of peacemaking, we have no right to claim the label or preach the message. Unless we . . . are ready to start to die by the thousands in dramatic vigorous new exploits for peace and justice, we should sadly confess that we never really meant what we said, and we dare never whisper another word about pacifism to our sisters and brothers in those desperate lands filled with injustice. Unless we are ready to die developing new nonviolent attempts to reduce conflict, we should confess that we never really meant that the cross was an alternative to the sword.[3]

Although many point to Sider's speech as the "beginning" of *Christian Peacemaker Teams*, in reality, certain members of the historic peace churches had for years discussed developing groups of trained Christian volunteers who would intervene nonviolently in violent situations.[4] According to Gene Stoltzfus, CPT director from 1987 to 2004,

There were those of us in the seventies who were pushing the church to take a more activist position in the areas of peace and social justice. We wanted members of the church to move from focusing on what Jesus could do for them to thinking about what it means to follow Jesus. Sider's speech legitimized this position in the wider church.[5]

Among the activists involved in these discussions were former Mennonite Central Committee (MCC)[6] volunteers in the United States who had been involved in the movements for civil rights in the U.S. South and against the Vietnam War.[7] Other MCC alumni exploring the possibility of nonviolent Christian peace teams had worked in international settings with people systematically oppressed by their governments. Because criticizing these governments and their U.S. sponsors would endanger years of development work, MCC volunteers often could not speak out publicly about the oppression they witnessed. These alumni were thus seeking a venue in which they could speak out against, and even intervene in, systemic violence. They also had an appreciation for the damage that hundreds of naive North Americans without international experience could do if they were suddenly dumped into a violent conflict. The MCCers' participation, and later the participation of those who had worked with Brethren agencies, helped bring a reality check to Sider's vision when a conference was held in Techny, Illinois, in 1986, and the first Christian Peacemaker Team Steering Committee was formed.

Outside of the Mennonite Church, other religious and secular organizations were also exploring active, organized, and risky nonviolent direct action as an alternative to military or police actions. In the 1970s, human rights organizations such as Amnesty International had involved ordinary citizens in advocating on the behalf of unknown political prisoners in remote nations. Such successful advocacy naturally led grassroots networks into exploring ways that international activists could intervene to prevent the torture and massacres committed by totalitarian governments. In the 1980s, the Central American Solidarity movement took this intervention a step further and gave birth to two organizations committed to accompanying civilians targeted by their governments.

Accompaniment as a Peacemaking Tool

In April 1983, a delegation of American Christians, including the future director of CPT, Gene Stoltzfus, went to Nicaragua on a fact-finding tour. During a visit to a small village that U.S.-backed paramilitaries (called "Contras") had just attacked, the U.S. activists asked the people of the village why the Contras were no longer shooting. "Because you're here," the villagers told them. After hearing about the effect of their presence, some considered staying, but instead went home to organize a long-term presence of U.S. citizens in Nicaragua. Those efforts turned into the organization Witness for Peace.

Three years earlier, at an international conference on nonviolence held at Grindstone Island in Ontario, Canada, participants from Europe, Asia, and the Americas met to discuss ways that active nonviolence could become a practical tool for confronting violent conflicts. This meeting led to the founding of Peace Brigades International. A second meeting in the Netherlands in 1982 approved committees to investigate project possibilities in Central America, Sri Lanka, Namibia, Pakistan, and the Middle East. In March 1983, PBI set up its first team in Guatemala, where the government, also with U.S. backing, was pursuing a vicious, genocidal campaign against indigenous people, as well as killing and torturing political dissidents,[8] and since then has expanded into several Latin American and Asian countries.

CPT's Development of Partnerships

When CPT set up its first full-time work in Haiti in 1993–1994,[9] a team moved into the rectory of a parish targeted by rightwing paramilitaries because of its support by the deposed president, Jean-Bertrand Aristide. In the minds of the team members there, the model they were most closely following was that of Peace Brigades, viewing themselves primarily as a violence-deterring presence in communities they accompanied. They consciously used the idea that North American lives were more valuable in order to provide some measure of protection to the people they accompanied. Moreover, they would invoke this principle of privilege as essential to accompaniment (although adding caveats about how sad it was their lives were considered more valuable) during presentations they gave to churches and activist groups in North America.

Colombians joining the Colombia team in 2003, without the passport privilege of North Americans, brought a radical paradigm shift to the entire CPT organization. Initially filling in because the Colombian government had denied North American team members visas, the Colombians who served on the team with international CPTers made the work so much more effective that everyone agreed the benefits of having Colombians on the team far outweighed the possible increased risk to Colombian team members.[10]

The change that Colombian CPTers had wrought in the organization as a whole was evident in a September 2006 antiracism training held in Chicago after the biennial full-timers' retreat. Participants noted that the CPT website was full of references to how North American privilege had protected the people among whom CPT had set up projects. Given the fact that Colombians on the team without this privilege had worked so effectively, that this promotion of protection via privilege was off-putting to marginalized people, and that everyone in the organization wanted CPT to become more multinational and multiethnic, those present agreed that a change in the CPT attitude toward accompaniment was necessary. This decision was not made without a sense of sacrifice. Hearing that one's presence saved a life is a heady, energizing experience. However, most CPTers agreed that it was more important and more effective to accompany communities whose focus was building solidarity among their members as a way of protecting themselves. This emphasis was already happening in CPT's work among the subsistence shepherding villages of the South Hebron Hills and with indigenous communities in Canada. It had been a feature in CPT's support of the movement in the Puerto Rican island of Vieques to stop the U.S. military bombing raids there. And these communities were accomplishing much more on their own than communities whom CPT had "protected."[11]

Thus, even if some benefits could be derived from racism for the people CPT accompanied, the organization decided as a whole that these benefits were fruit from a poison tree, and that tree must be uprooted.

A crucial milestone in CPT's antiracism work came in 2007 when the organization hired Sylvia Morrison as its Undoing Racism coordinator. From May 2008 to February 2009, Morrison gave leadership to an Undoing Racism audit of the organization. She enlisted the services of two outside auditors from Mennonite Central Committee's Anti-Racism Program: Valentina Satvedi and Harley Eagle. The culmination of the audit was a strategic-planning gathering with stakeholders from many different parts of CPT. The resulting seven strategic directions formed the basis for CPT's cultural shift:[12]

Strategic Directions for Shaping an Antiracist Identity for CPT

1. Resourcing the wellbeing of CPT and its members;
2. Cultivating a CPT culture that is antiracist, antioppressive, and anticolonial;
3. Articulating and sharing a transformed mission for CPT;
4. Honoring the voices of our partners throughout CPT communication vehicles;
5. Widening ownership of CPT;
6. Empowering CPTers through clear, accountable processes of decision making and leadership;
7. Making all of CPT accountable to our partners in an open and transparent way.

Morrison's influence and that of other CPTers who have focused on antiracism work within the organization, have helped CPTers to view each other and partners on the ground through a different lens. White CPTers have learned that when CPTers of color confront them on racist behaviors, they have received a gift. CPTers of color are telling them, "I want to work with you in a better way, and to do so you need to know that this behavior is marginalizing me (or marginalizing people with whom the team works)." CPTers have learned that the process of Undoing Racism is never complete, and often painful, but those willing to enter the process have found much richness in the journey.

Below are descriptions of two partnerships CPT as an organization has undertaken recently that illustrate its current methodologies: one with the Colombian community of Las Pavas which included actual physical accompaniment, and one with the #IdleNoMore movement that took place almost entirely in the digital realm.

Las Pavas

In 2008, Daabon, a palm oil company, displaced the community of Las Pavas from land the corporation claimed to have bought, ignoring the fact that the community was in the process of filing for a claim to the land, which it was entitled to do under Colombian law. When the corporation arrived with members of an armed paramilitary group (paramilitaries commit by far the greatest number of atrocities in Colombia), the community fled.

Palm oil is a central part of the vision held by Colombia's elite for an export economy, having multiple uses in cosmetics, food, and biofuel.

In most cases for Colombia's small farming, indigenous, mining, or other disenfranchised communities, the scenario has ended there: corporation wants the land, uses paramilitaries to remove the people in its way, the people join the five million *desplazados* (displaced persons). Colombia has the highest percentage of internally displaced people in the world.

But the 124 families of Las Pavas decided to fight back. CPT first became involved with Las Pavas in 2009, providing physical accompaniment for the community and telling the story of its displacement. When team members found out that The Body Shop, an international chain of cosmetics stores that prides itself on having a social conscience, was buying palm oil from Daabon, they realized they had the handle for an excellent campaign.

In October 2009, as part of CPT's first training in London, CPTers organized protests at fifteen Body Shop stores by teams of CPT trainees and supporters.[13] Managers at the stores met the protesters with letters from their higher-ups about the situation, demonstrating that press releases the trainees had sent out before the protest had caught the corporation's attention. The following day, CPT got a call from The Body Shop's vice president for corporate responsibility.

At first, The Body Shop accepted Daabon's assurances that the people of Las Pavas were squatters. However, after continued protests and actions from CPT and its supporters,[14] and a visit to Colombia with the UK charity Christian Aid, The Body Shop eventually concluded that Daabon had been lying and canceled its contract with Daabon in October 2010.[15]

With the support of CPT and other NGOs, the community on its own initiative decided to return to its land in April 2011, even without guarantees of security by the local police. Over the next three years, its 124 families faced violent attacks and harassment by "security" guards hired by the palm oil company. These acts of violence included setting fire to their homes and community buildings, sabotage of their farming equipment, refusal of access to the road leading to their lands, the slaughter of their animals, and even the shooting of a community member who was documenting this harassment with his video camera. In February 2012, rather than order an investigation into those who were persecuting the community, a constitutional court ordered INCODER, the Colombian Institute for Rural Development, to investigate whether the people of Las Pavas had fabricated the story of their displacement, occupied land that did not belong to them, and had connections to guerrilla insurgents.

CPTer Stewart Vriesinga wrote:

> Attempts to silence victims seeking justice and restitution here in Colombia are generally dealt with primarily through intimidation, death threats, and extrajudicial killings.
>
> But in some cases, like that of Las Pavas, the national and international profiles of the victims are simply too high to kill them with impunity—the resulting scandal would be counterproductive to the interests of those wishing to silence them. In such cases—often based on the testimony of demobilized paramilitaries—the victims are simply redefined and prosecuted as criminals.[16]

The community appealed to the federal prosecutor, Viviane Morales, who paid a visit to the community. When she arrived, CPTers were there, carrying a banner expressing solidarity for the people of Las Pavas that said, "We continue walking with you in faith for your right to the land and life with dignity." Many allies of the community as well as national media were also present to cover the event, as well as hundreds of police and military personnel who provided the visiting officials with security. She heard testimony from the people of Las Pavas themselves—something the state prosecutor from Cartagena never bothered to do.[17]

In November 2012 the Colombian government's rural land authority published a "definitive decision" in the community's favor, ruling that the government should expropriate all remaining properties of the estate known as Las Pavas from oil palm grower Aportes San Isidro. "With the forfeiture process being definitive, [the case] will proceed to material recuperation and titling in favor of the rural population," read a translated portion of the press release from the Colombian Institute for Rural Development (INCODER). The agency said that plots expropriated in prior months, primarily waterways and wetlands, "never should have been allowed to be privately held."[18] In February 2013, the community released a DVD of songs about their displacement and return to their land, which received a nomination for Colombia's Shock Awards in the "Special Recordings" category.[19]

November 2013 was a triumphant month for the people of Las Pavas. The Colombian government formally recognized them as victims of forced displacement, which meant they were entitled to reparations and it awarded them its National Peace Prize, out of a field of eighty-seven contestants.

Even with this national and international spotlight, the Aportes San Isidro Security guards continue to harass the residents of Las Pavas as of this writing in spring 2014,[20] so the partnership with CPT continues. The relationship goes beyond that of one small farming community and one small peace organization, however. The story of Las Pavas resonates with all of the displaced communities of Colombia who hear it and see in its people a model for how to resist the corporate, political, and military actors who view them as disposable.

The people of Las Pavas also provide a model for CPT when it enters into relationships with other small communities around the world who are facing dispossession by large corporations. Most recently, this context has happened in Iraqi Kurdistan as the Kurdish regional government has sold off the land of Kurdish villagers to large oil corporations, and CPTers have been able to tell Kurdish villagers what the people of Las Pavas did when the Colombian authorities gave away their land to palm oil corporations.[21]

#IdleNoMore

In October 2012 four women from Saskatchewan—indigenous and nonindigenous—joined forces to challenge the legislative attack they saw happening on First Nations people as well as rivers, lakes, and land across Canada. Sylvia McAdam, Jess Gordon, Nina Wilson, and Sheelah McLean organized sit-ins and did other mobilizing on Facebook and Twitter using the hashtag #IdleNoMore.

The key piece of legislation that they opposed was C-45, an omnibus bill put together by Canadian prime minister Stephen Harper's government that aimed to make land more easily available for mining and drilling. When the bill went into law on December 5, 2012, the number of Canada's protected rivers and lakes were reduced from 2.5 million to eighty-two. The lands opened up for resource extraction would once again disproportionately affect the traditional lands of First Nations peoples. A delegation of First Nations chiefs attempted to enter the House of Commons in Ottawa on the day that the bill passed to protest the fact that the government had not consulted them, but Parliament Hill security guards kept them out.[22]

On December 11, Chief Theresa Spence, leader of the Attawapiskat nation in far northern Ontario, began a hunger strike calling on Prime Minister Stephen Harper to meet with indigenous leaders and take their concerns seriously.[23] Spence's hunger strike was quickly folded into the #IdleNoMore campaign. Four days later, Bill C-45 passed the Senate.

Christian Peacemaker Teams had a long history working with Indigenous nations who have suffered the effects of mining and logging on their traditional lands, including the Algonquins of Barriere Lake, Rapid Lake, Quebec; Asubpeeschoseewagong Netum Anishnabek–Grassy Narrows, Ontario; and most recently Elsipogtog First Nation. The polluted waterways of Grassy Narrows that produced horrific outbreaks of Minamata disease seemed especially connected to Bill C-45's removal of environmental protections from lakes and rivers.[24] Thus, CPT's Aboriginal Justice Team threw its support wholeheartedly behind the #IdleNoMore campaign in the days leading up to Christmas 2012 as the movement grew.

On Christmas Day 2012, CPTer Chris Sabas launched the most widely seen Facebook campaign in *Christian Peacemaker Teams* history. During the previous forty-eight hours, Sabas solicited nearly fifty photos showing CPTers (and others) holding signs supporting Chief Teresa Spence and #IdleNoMore, which she posted throughout the day on December 25. One of the signs, depicting a Dutch CPTer and his partner, went viral, with over 2,500 people sharing the photo. Later in the week she posted a photo of a Palestinian CPTer holding a sign in support of Chief Spence and it was shared over a thousand times on people's Facebook walls.

In one week, CPT reached over 230,000 people with messages of solidarity and support for #IdleNoMore and Chief Theresa Spence's hunger strike.

CPT's involvement in #IdleNoMore was not isolated to the digital realm. Some CPTers joined indigenous people as they did round dances in their #IdleNoMore flash mobs in the malls and on the highways.[25] But it was primarily through social media that CPT linked people who may never had made connections with those indigenous activists—people in urban areas without significant indigenous populations, people in Europe and other regions where they might never meet people belonging to the First Nations of North America. (These people in turn might have evaluated how their governments treated the indigenous people of their own nations.) For this brief moment, in a digital time and digital space, CPT was learning how to be a different sort of partner.

Issues That Have Arisen as a Result of the Evolution from "Protection" to "Partnership" Models

Vision for Regional Groups and Strategic Planning for Expansion

In 2000, CPTers met in what would become the first biennial retreat. At that retreat they developed their vision for expansion.

In this vision, regional groups would develop all over the world. Priority for development would go to those areas where people of color were the majority. These groups would address the violence in their own communities and provide support for the trained CPTers in their midst. Eventually, CPT would decentralize, with the Chicago and Toronto offices being two of several headquarters for CPT's work around the globe. In the last decade, CPT has held trainings in Colombia, the United Kingdom, and Iraqi Kurdistan, although people of European descent continue to be the majority in CPT.

How to expand has brought up the "wide vs. deep" issue with partner communities. Palestinians, Colombians, and Kurds would like to see CPT set up similar projects within their regions rather than explore work in other countries or on other continents.

Many CPTers believe that they could actually do more good if they expanded within a region, because they would avoid the stumbling and pitfalls that occur when learning to live in a new nation or culture. On the other hand, because CPT expanded into new territories over the years, it has brought wider constituency and media attention to these areas than might have occurred otherwise. CPT has standing invitations to set up projects in the Democratic Republic of Congo (DRC), Uganda, and the Philippines. Delegations to these regions in 2005 and 2006 resulted in the exposure of situations about which the CPT constituency and the rest of the world were relatively ill informed.[26] However, these delegations were expensive and as of this writing might never lead to the establishment of projects in these locations, whereas projects in Palestine, Colombia, and Iraqi Kurdistan could probably be set up swiftly and relatively cheaply and might have more impact on the systems of domination in those regions—as well as build better partner relationships.

Length of Projects
The founders of CPT originally envisioned CPTers as providing short-term crisis interventions into violent situations. When crises proved to be longer term, and projects difficult to shut down, CPT had to reevaluate this strategy. Moving toward a vision of partnerships that transform oppression has caused the organization to focus on dynamics of long-term systematic oppression, not just the more visible symptoms of physical violence. That shift in focus has led to longer-term engagements as CPT accompanies partners in their work to address power imbalance and injustice at their roots. One does not tell a partner, "Sorry, we are only interested in a short-term relationship."

Additionally, since CPT's partners would remain in an area after CPT removed a full-time team, CPT was not fully removed from the conflict. Thus, even after CPTers stopped living in the South Hebron Hills village of At-Tuwani, the CPT Palestine team continued to post releases from the South Hebron Hills Popular Committee and the Italian peace group Operation Dove who continued to live there. The team in Hebron also continues to participate in actions organized by the Popular Committee when it requests a large international presence. After CPT discontinued its full-time Borderlands project, it continued to send delegations that connected with its partners there. The Aboriginal Justice

Team has established relationships with more than a dozen First Nations communities over the years and responds as needed when members of these nations ask team members to be present.

Undoing Oppressions

As noted above, CPT understood that moving into a partnership model required that the organization undertake antiracism work to build strong relationships both within the organization and with partners. Because of the pain caused by racist interactions on teams, and to give CPTers of color a chance to share their common experience, CPT began organizing gatherings for people of color in the organization every two years. Called the Race Relations Council, the group also has two positions on the CPT Steering Committee.

Oppressions, of course, are not the sole purview of race. CPT has incorporated into its training oppressions based on gender and sexual orientation as well. Most recently, they were included in a training held in Iraqi Kurdistan, despite qualms expressed that the culture there would not tolerate it.

This work has also happened at the team level with undoing-oppressions conversations happening regularly on teams as they look at their relationships with each other and with their partners. Sometimes new insights developed at the team level have then worked their way up to the organizational level. For example, the decision to include non-Christians in CPT resulted because of discussions on the Palestine team.

Religious Issues

Although the founders of CPT always thought that the organization would remain firmly rooted in Jesus's gospel message, as the organization evolved, it has in practice accepted workers over the last twenty years with high, low, and most-points-in-between Christologies. In 2011, it began officially accepting CPTers as "associate members" (Muslims had been working as interns on the Palestine and Iraqi Kurdistan teams a couple years prior to this decision).

The Christian faith of CPTers was often more of an asset than a detriment as they worked among devout Muslims in Hebron over the years. Many Muslims understood that CPTers were doing the work they did for reasons of faith, better than they understood doing it for secular principles—and from the beginning the Palestine team and the Iraq teams worked with Muslim and Jewish partner organizations.

But actually having Muslim partners on the teams, adjusting worship times to be inclusive, unlearning the assumptions that were easy to make when CPT was an all-Christian organization, has presented challenges. It has also presented opportunities to connect with partners in more meaningful ways, and almost all CPTers who have worked in Palestine and Iraqi Kurdistan agree that including Muslims on teams is vital in order for the work to expand in Muslim contexts.

Conclusion: From Heroes to Companions

On the twenty-fifth anniversary of Ron Sider's Strasbourg speech, Sandra Milena Rincón, project support coordinator for CPT's Colombia project, delivered an address at the Mennonite World Conference in Asuncion, Paraguay, marking the occasion. Her presentation was one grounded in reality, based on *Christian Peacemaker Teams'* actual experiences in the field with partners and friends, far from Sider's original vision of nonviolent warriors parachuting into battlefields and standing between warring parties, and is thus an appropriate way to conclude this chapter:

> Truly, we would not be where we are now if it were not for the local communities who have given us the opportunity to be present in their struggle and to support their nonviolent resistance to powers that will not allow them to live in their land with dignity. The families of shepherds and farmers and students in Palestine, the indigenous communities of the United States, Canada and Colombia, the displaced communities of Kurdistan and the families of detainees in Baghdad's prison, the communities of miners, farmers and social organizations in Colombia, the women of eastern Democratic Republic of Congo, Mayan indigenous communities in Mexico, the community of Jeremie in Haiti, and many other communities and organizations, have opened their doors to us during these twenty-five years—sometimes with doubts or uneasiness about what

we would do or what we wanted—but they opened the door to us so that we could actively participate in their projects for justice and peace, in their hopes and in the challenges they faced. They have offered us hospitality, warmth and the blessing of considering us their brothers and sisters in the midst of their struggles, companions on the road.[27]

Notes

1. The previous training, in fall 1993, had also been asking to come up with a slogan and submitted "Discovering Christ in Crisis." The personnel running the Chicago office at the time summarily discarded it. Kathleen Kern, *In Harm's Way: A History of Christian Peacemaker Teams* (Eugene, OR: Cascade Books, 2009), 18n35.

2. "CPT INTERNATIONAL: Mission, Vision and Values," *Christian Peacemaker Teams* (June 21, 2012). http://www.cpt.org/cptnet/2012/06/21/cpt-international-mission-vision-and-values.

3. Ronald J. Sider, "God's People Reconciling" (speech, Mennonite World Conference, Strasbourg, France, Summer 1984), http://www.cpt.org/resources/writings/sider. The presentation was later adapted for the book, *Nonviolence: The Invincible Weapon?* (Dallas, TX: W Publishing Group, 1989).

4. The historic peace churches generally include the many branches of the Mennonite and Amish churches, Church of the Brethren, and Friends (Quakers). Certain other related groups, such as the Mennonite Brethren and Brethren in Christ, have historically had pacifism as a part of their theology but currently emphasize evangelism more.

5. Gene Stoltzfus, interview, May 1, 2003.

6. MCC is a relief and development organization sponsored by different branches of the Mennonite and Amish churches. Founded in the 1920s to help Mennonites fleeing persecution and starvation in Russia, it has since expanded to aid sustainable development on every inhabited continent. The breadth of its work has given the small number of Mennonite denominations around the world an influence out of proportion to their size.

7. Edgar Metzler, in a letter to Kathleen Kern, August 5, 2004 (incorrectly dated 2003).

8. Liam Mahoney and Luis Enrique Eguren, *Unarmed Bodyguards: International Accompaniment for the Protection of Human Rights* (West Hartford, CT: Kumarian Press, 1997), 4–5.

9. According to CPT's first director, Gene Stoltzfus, the period between 1987 and 1993 indirectly addressed the question, "Why do we need another peace organization?" The work of CPT during this period mostly involved sponsoring initiatives such as Oil-Free Sunday on the eve of the first Gulf War, delegations, and conferences. Kern, *In Harm's Way*, 11–14.

10. In a May 1, 2013, e-mail to Kathleen Kern commenting on an earlier draft of this chapter, Colombia and Iraqi Kurdistan Project Support Coordinator Sandra Milena Rincón noted that CPT partners agreed that having a mix of nationals and internationals made the team more effective.

11. The importance of allowing communities to do their own work without taking credit for it was highlighted by Lenore Keeshig-Tobias, member of the Chippewas of Nawash First Nation. When asked what CPT needed to do to work effectively in indigenous communities, she listed three objectives for the CPT Ontario training group in 1998: do the work well so it did not need to be repeated, be ready to step back when local people were ready to take leadership, and be ready to leave and be immediately forgotten. Kern, *In Harm's Way*, 556n9.

12. Sylvia Morrison, "Could This Be Our Finest (H)Our?," *Christian Peacemaker Teams* (March 1, 2009), http://www.cpt.org/content/undoing-racism.

13. Christopher Hatton, "LONDON: UK CPT Trainees Call on The Body Shop to Put People Before Palm Oil," *Christian Peacemaker Teams* (November 17, 2009), http://www.cpt.org/cptnet/2009/11/17/london-uk-cpt-trainees-call-body-shop-put-people-palm-oil.

14. UK CPTer Christopher Hatton was involved in some behind-the-scenes conversations with The Body Shop and Christian Aid during the months between the training and the visit to Las Pavas. He writes:

> A basis for what I perceive as a successful behind-the-scenes partnering/ relationship-building with The Body Shop, was that I already worked in an industrial background, understood a little about supply chain management. I have an idea about how long it takes to physically implement changes in suppliers/check impact on quality of product, so I spoke her language (manufacturing supply chain not English). However, I also added the social justice context and reminded her of the Body Shops early Quaker Business values (and I as a Quaker) which jointly reassured her but also challenged her.
>
> A valuable 6 months were gained, in that the Body Shop were able to: meet Daabon at an International Round Table on "responsible" palm oil, organise an audit/inspection (with Christian Aid), and try and work with Daabon (and its subsidiary). The director of values, told me that she soon realised after the November 2009 round table meeting in Malaysia that Daabon didn't like the "semi-public" criticism The Body Shop raised during that meeting, and the situation became tense quite quickly and not conducive to a working relationship. So she recommended to senior management to try and work with Daabon but consider the cancellation of the contract (by invoking a clause about supplier non-compliance with the Body Shops ethical code of conduct).
>
> Over the 6 months, I had 1 longer off-the-record chat with her on progress/business ethics in general, and 1 short chat that was on-the-record, which I then sent a summary of to CPT Colombia. I also followed up with her after the press release where they publicly cancelled the contract, . . . I

heard on the grapevine from another Quaker in Business colleague who works in Corporate Social Responsibility, that she left the Body Shop shortly after, alas reasons unknown.... I got the feeling and agreed with her, that there was little positive encouragement/engagement from CPT (that I saw or heard), and more an aggressive anti-business activist stance. Although we were a good partner to the community in Las Pavas, I wonder if we would be more credible/successful if more of us had experience of the corporate world. Maybe it doesn't matter as we are mainly answerable to our partners who tell us what they want from us in terms of advocacy. Christopher Hatton, e-mail to Kathleen Kern, April 20, 2014

15. "COLOMBIA: The Body Shop Terminates Trading Relationship with Daabon—a Great Step Forward for the People of Las Pavas," *Christian Peacemaker Teams* (October 4, 2010), http://www.cpt.org/cptnet/2010/10/04/colombia-body-shop-terminates-trading-relationship-daabon%E2%80%94-great-step-forward-peop.

16. Steward Vriesinga, "COLOMBIA ANALYSIS: Las Pavas—The Criminalization of Victims," *Christian Peacemaker Teams* (February 14, 2012), http://www.cpt.org/cptnet/2012/02/14/colombia-analysis-las-pavas%E2%80%94-criminalization-victims. Note that the high profile of Las Pavas was a direct result of its partnership with CPT, the Body Shop witnesses, etc.

17. Ibid.

18. "COLOMBIA: Rural Families Celebrate Ruling on Las Pavas," *Christian Peacemaker Teams* (November 26, 2012), http://www.cpt.org/cptnet/2012/11/26/colombia-rural-families-celebrate-ruling-las-pavas.

19. "Grabación especial en CD y/o DVD (Poll Closed)" (Special recording CD and/or DVD [Poll Closed]) *Shock* (accessed May 7, 2014), http://www.shock.co/grabacion-especial-en-cd-yo-dvd.

20. "Las Pavas writes to President Santos regarding continued attacks on their community," *Christian Peacemaker Teams* (March 20, 2014), http://www.cpt.org/cptnet/2014/03/20las-pavas-writes-president-santos-regarding-continued-attacks-their-community.

21. See "IRAQI KURDISTAN: CPT Releases Video about Exxon Mobil's Confiscation of Kurdish Villagers' Land," *Christian Peacemaker Teams* (November 25, 2013), http://www.cpt.org/cptnet/2013/11/25/iraqi-kurdistan-cpt-releases-video-about-exxon-mobil%E2%80%99s-confiscation-kurdish-villag. See also the CPTnet reflection written by Parwen Aziz, who went through the CPT Iraqi Kurdistan in February 2014 and was inspired by the struggles of Las Pavas: "Damn Tree: A Reflection about Colombian Oil Palm Trees," *ECAP Columbia* (March 20, 2014), http://www.cpt.org/cptnet/2014/03/20/iraqi-kurdistan-reflection-damn-tree.

22. Jorge Barrera and Kenneth Jackson, "Chiefs Take Fight to House of Commons' Doorstep," *APTN National News* (December 4, 2012), http://aptn.ca/news/2012/12/04/chiefs-take-fight-to-house-of-commons-doorstep/.

23. This community first made the news in October 2011 when they declared a state of emergency due to health and safety concerns and inadequate housing.

CBC News, "Chief Theresa Spence to End Hunger Strike Today," posted January 23, 2013, updated January 24, 2013.

24. Masazumi Harada et al., "Mercury Poisoning in First Nations Groups in Ontario, Canada: 35 Years of Canadian Minamata Disease," trans. from Japanese, *Journal of Minamata Studies* 3 (2011): 3–30.

25. Kathy Moorhead Thiessen, "Aboriginal Justice: Welcome to Idle No More," *Christian Peacemaker Teams* (March 31, 2013), http://www.cpt.org/news/sott/articles/2013/aboriginal-justice-welcome-idle-no-more.

26. For example, Kathleen Kern, after a delegation to the Democratic Republic of Congo in 2005 was asked to write articles for *The Christian Century* and *Tikkun* magazine. The *Tikkun* article, in turn, resulted in an invitation to write a chapter for a book that was a follow-up to John Perkins's bestseller, Confessions of an Economic Hit Man ("Victims as Pariahs," Christian Century 123, no. 2 (January 24, 2006): 9; "Corporate Complicity in Congo's War," *Tikkun* (March/April 2006): 38–44; "The Human Cost of Cheap Cellphones," in *A Game As Old As Empire: The Secret World of Economic Hit Men and the Web of Global Corruption*, ed. Steven Hiatt (San Francisco, CA: Berrett-Koehler, 2007), 93–112.

27. Sandra Milena Rincón, "The Challenge Continues," trans. Carol Rose (address, Mennonite World Conference, Asunción, Paraguay, July 2009), http://www.cpt.org/resources/writings/rincon-challenge-continues.

PART 4

CHRISTIAN AND MUSLIM DISCUSSIONS

This section provides three essays that dialogue with specific religious traditions, in this case Christian and Muslim. James Heft discusses Pope John Paul II's stand on justice and forgiveness, demonstrating that his interpretation of the traditional just war theory is challenged by his unique commitment to nonviolence.

Abbas Aroua walks us through various Qur'ānic texts and carefully analyzes concepts that can help sustain peacemaking in the Islamic tradition.

In his contribution, John Paul Lederach revisits the Creation story in the Hebrew Bible and its ramification on our understanding of conflict.

These three essays represent a perfect sample of the scholarship that has emerged over the last fifteen years, rereading traditional texts and concepts in light of religiously motivated violence. The Just War theory was certainly at the center of many debates around President Bush's decision to invade Iraq in response to the 9/11 events; Heft retraces some elements of the debate. Seeking for textual evidence[1] to support peacemaking has become part of an important conversation in faith-based peacemaking; again in response to 9/11, scholars of Islam have been under a lot of pressure to do so, and Aroua's chapter is a good example of such exegetical work; he navigates for us what has become an immense body of literature. John Paul Lederach is a prominent voice in the scholarship that discusses the conditions of conflict transformation; as a Mennonite, his vision is deeply rooted in biblical interpretation inspiring not only his understanding of nonviolence and justice, but also of conflict management like in the chapter published here.[2]

Notes

1. See, for instance, John Renard, ed., *Fighting Words: Religion, Violence, and the Interpretation of Sacred Texts* (Berkeley: University of California Press, 2012).
2. In the traditional peace churches (Mennonite, Quaker, Brethren), facing conflict may sometimes be challenging; for further discussion, see for instance Susan Robson, *Living with Conflict: A Challenge to a Peace Churc*h (Plymouth, UK: Scarecrow Press, 2013).

8

John Paul II and the Just War Doctrine

"Make Peace through Justice and Forgiveness: Not War"

JAMES L. HEFT

Christianity has taken many positions on the legitimacy of war from its founding to the present.[1] No one, however, has done more to rethink the traditional Just War theory than John Paul II (1978–2005). Having lived the better part of his life in Poland under a Communist regime, he was acutely aware of the destructive power of atheistic socialism. In his own teaching, especially toward the end of his pontificate, he developed an understanding of the just war teaching that not only made it more difficult to justify war, but also placed the theory within a larger normative theological and ethical framework that underscored the crucial importance of nonviolent means for the resolution of conflict.

Introduction

The chief rabbi of Israel since 2003, Yona Metzger, told a Jewish parable about a young Jew who was on a long hike.[2] It was the custom then to mark one's progress by looking at signposts which appeared regularly at crossroads. The signposts showed various destinations and the direction to them. At one crossroads, the sign had fallen to the ground and the young man had no idea in what direction he should continue.

An old man who was passing by gave him some advice: "If you want to know in which direction to continue, stand the signpost up with the name of the place you have come from pointing in the direction from which you have come."

In other words, there is a real value, as it is sometimes said, in knowing where one is coming from. And on the subject of the Catholic Church's practice and teaching on war, the Church has come, since the time of Jesus, from some very different places. This article will describe the pacifist position of the earliest Christians, draw a very different picture of the church at the end of the first millennium, and then turn to the extraordinary papacy of John Paul II. His attention to the aftermath of war and the Gospel imperatives to establish justice and offer forgiveness have made the traditional criteria for meeting the standards of a just war harder to meet. The significance of his various statements throughout his long pontificate will be made clearer by placing them in their historical contexts.

Christians started out as a persecuted minority almost invisible in the greatest empire of the time. The earliest Christians emphasized the nonviolent nature of the teachings and example of Jesus. In fact, there is no evidence before about the year 170 that any Christians participated in the military. According to an early Church code of laws called the *Apostolic Tradition*, those baptized Christians or persons preparing for baptism, known as catechumens, who joined the military were to "be dismissed [from the Church], for they have despised God." If a man already in the military converted to Christianity, he was to refuse all orders to kill anyone. Origen (254+), a great theologian and interpreter of scripture, wrote that "we [Christians] no longer take up the sword against nations, nor do we learn war anymore, having become children of peace for the sake of Jesus, who is our leader."[3] But in the fourth and fifth centuries, when the Roman Empire first allowed Christianity to exist and then made it the official religion of the empire, church thinkers effected huge changes in its teaching on the legitimacy of war. This change has sometimes been called the "Constantinian Revolution," a period lasting about one hundred years during which the just war theory, developed by Augustine (354–430) and other great Christian thinkers after him, replaced the nonviolent message of the early Christian church. By the middle ages, popes helped to launch crusades.

In order to place in stark relief the contribution of John Paul II, whose long papacy led the Church into the twenty-first century, it is instructive to go back about a thousand years when a certain John XVIII was pope (1004–1009). He owed his appointment to Crescentius, the most powerful political figure in Rome at that time.[4] When John learned that some bishops wanted the abbot of a monastery in their region to burn papal documents that insured the monastery's independence from the local bishops, he "peremptorily summoned [the bishops] to Rome on pain of excommunication, and even threatened King Robert II of France that he would place his entire kingdom under a ban if they failed to appear." One of John's successors, Benedict VIII (1012–1024) not only used armed forces to crush some political leadership in Rome which he opposed, but himself participated in a sea battle in northern Italy to defeat Muslim invaders. Obviously, the times were different then. It was only a little later in that same century that the College of Cardinals was created, in part to wrest from powerful politicians their control of papal appointments.

Nevertheless, popes continued to exercise the use of force to protect their interests and enforce their policies, both spiritual and temporal, until they were no longer able to do so—that is, until Italian nationalists stripped Pius IX (1846–1878) of the use of military force in 1870. Before 1870, the Papal States divided Italy in half. A good case can be made that after 1870, more and more popes began to exercise their spiritual authority, and to exercise it over an ever-widening arena of concerns. In speaking to the General Assembly of the United Nations in 1982, John Paul II described himself in these words: "This is the voice of one who has no interests nor political power, nor, even less, military force."[5]

To return to this brief history of where the Catholic Church has come from on matters of war and peace, the papacy, no longer able to defend by force its own political rights, actually found itself more free to defend the rights of others. At about that same time, a little more than a decade after the U.S. Civil War, one of the first modern wars, the popes began to see more clearly that it made more and more sense to oppose war. We know that Benedict XV (1914–1922) made a valiant but unsuccessful effort to end the First World War, and by 1920 had already called for the creation of an international alliance among the nations of the world.[6] In 1944, the influential American Jesuit moral theologian John Ford condemned obliteration bombing. But it was especially with Pope

John XXIII's (1958–1963) encyclical, *Pacem in terris*, published in 1963, that seeds were sown for a new way to bring about peace in the international order: namely, the vigorous defense of human rights.

On October 4, 1965, his successor, Pope Paul VI (1963–1978), gave a famous speech at the United Nations in which he declared, "No more war, war never again!" The very next day, twenty-five hundred Catholic bishops gathered in Rome for the fourth and last session of the Second Vatican Council (1962–1965) in order to begin their discussion of war and peace. The conclusions of that discussion would be included in the documents of the Council, *Gaudium et spes*,[7] which two months later they finally approved. That document flatly condemned total war (the only condemnation solemnly uttered in all sixteen of Vatican II's documents) and called all people of good will, especially political leaders, to approach war "with a whole new attitude." Paragraph 80 of *Gaudium et spes* states forthrightly: "[A]ny act of war aimed indiscriminately at the destruction of entire cities or of extensive areas along with their population is a crime against God and man himself. It merits unequivocal and unhesitating condemnation." That encyclical also endorsed nonviolent resistance.

These signposts indicate, as it were, a long and circuitous journey that the Catholic Church took over the past two thousand years. Over the last sixty years, and especially during the papacy of John Paul II, significant changes have been introduced into the Catholic Church's teaching on just war. John Paul II's erected new signposts for the Church's official understanding of the just war doctrine.

Enter John Paul II

Mainly on account of his speeches at the Second Vatican Council on key council documents dealing with the church *(Lumen gentium)*, the church in the modern world *(Gaudium et spes)*, and especially religious freedom *(Dignitatis humanae)*, Archbishop Karol Wojtyla, who enjoyed a fine command of Latin, came to the attention of Pope Paul VI. In 1967, Pope Paul made Wojtyla, then age forty-seven, a cardinal. In 1968, when the pope rejected the majority vote on contraception, Cardinal Wojtyla was one of his strongest supporters. In 1976, Pope Paul chose him to give the papal Lenten retreat which Wojtyla devoted to the theme of Christ as a "sign of contradiction." Two years later, after the thirty-three–day pontificate of John Paul I, Wojtyla at the age of fifty-eight was elected the first non-Italian pope in 450 years. He showed extraordinary vigor, both as a writer of encyclicals and as a global spiritual leader who defended human rights and opposed war. At the time of his death in April 2005, some twenty-seven years later, the third longest term of service for any pope in history, a *Time* magazine editorial gave a stirring summary of his extraordinary achievements:

> He was the first pope ever to visit a mosque, or launch a web-site, or commemorate the Holocaust at Auschwitz or find in a broken world so many saints of the Church—more saints, in fact, than all his predecessors combined. Master of a dozen languages, he was the first modern pope to visit Egypt, Spain, Canada, Cuba, Ireland or Brazil, the equivalent of circling the globe 31 times. To half the world's people, he was the only pope they have ever known, or mourned. Thus the prayers came not just from the Catholic faithful but also from Muslims in France and Jews at Jerusalem's Western Wall and from believers across Eastern Europe who before his crusade against tyranny would have had to mourn him in secret. Even those who disagreed with his goals were touched by his goodness and came out to honor the man who made history itself kneel down.[8]

The Liberation of Eastern Europe

This chapter focuses on John Paul II's impact on Catholicism's understanding of the legitimacy of war, his impact on Eastern Europe and the Middle East, and especially his opposition to the Persian Gulf and Iraq wars, and finally, his understanding of the importance of humanitarian intervention. Again, the focus is on John Paul's teaching on war, not on issues mainly internal to the Catholic Church, issues such as the role of women, matters of sexual morality and sexual abuse, the appointment of bishops, or the exercise of papal authority. As important and as interesting as such matters are, their discussion belongs to another essay. However, the late Jesuit moral theologian Richard McCormick contrasted John Paul II's impact on internal Church life with those he made on the world scene:

> In the eyes of millions of people, John Paul II was the most credible and powerful moral voice of the second half of the twentieth century. This is most evident in the areas of peace, human rights, international relations and economic justice. His impact on the world was incalculable. When we turn to the more "domestic" dimensions of his moral teaching, the record seems far more ambiguous. The pope was unable to persuade large numbers of Catholics on key issues. When persuasion failed, various forms of enforcement followed. This led in the Catholic Church to a severe problem of authority that makes one question whether the pope was a true *pontifex* (bridge-builder) within his own believing community.[9]

All of John Paul's teachings on the social order, especially as they evolved over the length of his unusually long papacy, have reshaped the way in which the traditional just war doctrine is now officially understood in the Catholic Church. The core of his international vision rested on a set of theological and philosophical affirmations about human freedom and the dignity of the human person. When John Paul addressed political issues directly, he exercised a certain restraint and emphasized first and foremost a fundamentally religious and Gospel-based approach— an approach that nonetheless had political ramifications. Already in 1968, having lived under the oppression of the communist government for much of his adult life, Wojtyla wrote to the great Jesuit theologian Henri de Lubac:

> I devote my very rare free moments to a work that is close to my heart and devoted to the metaphysical sense and mystery of the PERSON. It seems to be that the debate today is being played on that level. The evil of our times consists in the first place in a kind of degradation, indeed in a pulverization, of the fundamental uniqueness of each human person. This evil is even

much more of the metaphysical order than of the moral order. To this disintegration, planned at times by atheistic ideologies, we must oppose, rather than sterile polemics, a kind of "reca- pitulation" of the inviolable mystery of the person.[10]

There can be little doubt that he wrote his 1981 encyclical, *Laborem exercens*, released on the ninetieth anniversary of Pope Leo XIII's (1878–1903) first social encyclical, *Rerum novarum*, in defense of labor rights. While *Laborem exercens* clearly supported the solidarity movement of his native Poland, it also endorsed all movements that supported the rights of laborers. In that sense, it was nonpartisan. In essence, he sup- ported paragraph 41 of *Gaudium et spes*, which declared "by virtue of the Gospel committed to her, the Church proclaims the rights of man. She acknowledges and greatly esteems the dynamic movements of today by which these rights are everywhere fostered."[11] For John Paul, philosoph- ical and theological affirmations grounded his vision of human rights.

A critically important part of John Paul's legacy includes the promo- tion of nonviolent methods to bring about political and social change. Some of his conservative American Catholic critics, such as Michael Novak and George Weigel, wondered aloud whether John Paul had "gone pacifist." Actually, the pope had not gone pacifist since he still allowed for the use of force, but in very limited and carefully circum- scribed ways. At the same time, however, he increasingly endorsed the use of nonviolent methods. Political observers do not dispute the claim that John Paul played a key role in the fall of communism in Poland. But just what role he played is not clear.

Jesuit Drew Christiansen, the editor of *America* magazine, a national publication of the American Jesuits, relates how Tad Sulcz, a former *New York Times* correspondent and a biographer of John Paul, believed that on account of a relationship with Polish president Wojciech Jaruzelski, John Paul was able to become friends with Soviet president Mikhail Gorbachev.[12] Sulcz argued that when the Soviets decided in the sum- mer of 1989 not to invade the countries of Eastern Europe which then appeared to be breaking away, the three-way friendship paid great div- idends. In the midst of this unraveling of the Soviet Union, Gorbachev wrote to the pope at the end of August that same year saying, "I know what you have written," and asked for a visit with the pope. On December 1, 1989, John Paul welcomed Gorbachev and his wife, Raissa, to the Vatican for a visit. In 1992 Gorbachev acknowledged that "everything that happened in Eastern Europe in these last few years would have been impossible without this pope."

More specifically, Sulzc claimed that the three-way friendship among Jaruzelski, Gorbachev, and John Paul prevented the Soviet Union from invading Eastern Europe in the way that it invaded Hungary in 1956 and Czechoslovakia in 1968. Sulzc believed that the combination of broad popular support for change in Poland and the lack of any military threat were the main contributors to the peaceful revolution of 1989. It would seem that John Paul saw the situation in much the same way as Sulzc when, two years later, in his 1991 encyclical *Centesimus annus*, he suggested in paragraph 23 that the use of nonviolent methods made the "velvet revolution" possible, not only in Poland, but also in the rest of Eastern Europe.[13] Again, Drew Christiansen drew my attention to the following texts of John Paul II:

> It seemed that the European order resulting from the Second World War... could only be overturned by another war. Instead it has been overcome by the nonviolent commitment of people who, while always refusing to yield to the force of power, succeeded time after time in bearing effective witness to truth. They disarmed the adversary, since violence always needs to justify itself through deceit, and to appear, however falsely, to be defending a right or responding to a threat posed by others.

Two paragraphs later, John Paul rejected the so-called realist view of international affairs:

> The events of 1989 are an example of the success of willingness to negotiate and of the Gospel spirit in the face of an adversary determined not to be bound by moral principles. These events are a warning to those who, in the name of political realism, wish to banish law and morality from the political arena.

Having rejected the political realist approach, he made clear in that same paragraph 25 his theological, and especially Christological, foundation for doing so:

Undoubtedly, the struggle which led to the changes of 1989 called for clarity, moderation, suffering and sacrifice. In a certain sense, it was a struggle born of prayer, and it would have been unthinkable without immense trust in God, the Lord of history, who carries the human heart in his hand. It is by uniting his own sufferings for the sake of truth and freedom to the sufferings of Christ on the cross that man is able to accomplish the miracle of peace.

In *Centesimus annus*, published on the one-hundredth anniversary of Leo XIII's *Rerum novarum*, John Paul presents his own Christ-centered spirituality as an alternative to the so-called realist approach that has typified his thinking about international affairs. Many realists would assume that such a Christ-centered spirituality would have little, if any, relevance to the brutal realities of military power and international conflict. But John Paul's spirituality forms the foundation for a whole host of practical decisions about the use of force. At the end of the passage just quoted, John Paul wrote:

[The person who unites his own suffering... to the suffering of Christ on the cross] is in a position to discern the often narrow path between the cowardice which gives in to evil and the violence, which, under the illusion of fighting evil, only makes it worse.[14]

This last quotation captures precisely the meaning of Christian courage in defending rights as opposed to the violence of the warrior. The Christian, who is committed to nonviolence, opposes any violation of human rights and actively, but nonviolently, opposes all such evil, but does not use coercion or force. The warrior, on the other hand, also opposes evil, but in using force and creating violence runs the risk of leaving things in an even worse state than before. In the United States, the statements about war and peace that appear in *Centesimus annus* have been largely ignored, in favor of debates led by liberals and neoconservatives about the legitimacy of capitalism. To overlook what the pope wrote about war and peace is especially unfortunate since this encyclical gives more attention to those issues than any since *Pacem in terris*, published in 1963.[15]

Middle East and the Process of Reconciliation

The last fifteen years of John Paul's papacy were especially important for the development of his views on war and nonviolence. After 1989, he did not have to deal with the tensions created by two superpowers with two different economic and political systems squaring off against each other on the world stage. Instead, he was confronted with the tragedies of genocide, the rights of minorities, and the use of military power by the only remaining superpower, the United States. It is in facing these events that the pope most directly developed new ways to interpret the traditional just war doctrine. As mentioned earlier, the pope had already stressed in 1981, as did the American bishops in their 1983 pastoral letter on war, *The Challenge of Peace*, the importance of nonviolence. He firmly opposed the 1991 Gulf War and the 2003 invasion of Iraq. It is obvious that during this period the pope supported and developed further what in 1983 the U.S. bishops had called the "presumption against the use of force" in matters of war and peace.

That the pope found himself in opposition to U.S. foreign policy should be obvious. Nothing makes this opposition clearer than the effort of the Vatican to prevent an invasion of Iraq. Weeks before that invasion, the pope sent Cardinal Pio Laghi to the White House for a conversation with the president that turned out to be a "dialogue of the deaf." Christiansen describes that meeting in this way.

> Laghi, a friend and tennis partner of the elder President Bush, reported with dismay that the president did not even open the pope's personal letter of appeal. Later the White House denied Laghi the usual privilege of meeting reporters on the White

House lawn. In the meantime, the assiduous U.S. ambassador to the Vatican, James Nicholson, a former Republican national chairman, invited Michael Novak to offer a defense of preventive war in the very shadow of the Vatican. It is very evident that most Americans, including American Catholics, know the White House hermeneutic and view the world through it. Fewer know the papal stand and fewer view the world through its prism.[16]

Given the pope's emphasis on nonviolence and the importance of learning how to build a lasting and just peace, a number of concerned Catholics, as stated earlier, have worried, especially some conservative American Catholics, that the pope had become a pacifist. Between August 2, 1990, and March 4, 1991, John Paul II spoke publicly fifty-six times on the crisis in the Middle East. The then president George H. W. Bush regularly used just war language to defend his administration's conduct of the Gulf War. Especially troubling to Catholic conservatives was a widely reported prayer that John Paul II uttered when he said, echoing Paul VI's dramatic call at the United Nations for an end of all war: "Never again war, adventure without return, spiral of struggle and violence, never this war in the Persian Gulf...threat to your creatures in the sky, on earth and in the sea.... No war ever again."[17] Had John Paul II become a pacifist? No, or not quite. On February 17, 1991, at a church in Rome, he remarked to the congregation, mainly composed of youth, that "we are not pacifists; we do not want peace at any price." It might have been more helpful had the pope recognized in his remark the fact that pacifists do not desire peace at any price, since they are willing to die, but not to kill, so that justice, the only lasting basis for peace, might prevail.

Nearly a decade before, in his January 1, 1982, World Day of Peace message, a tradition established by Paul VI of devoting the beginning of the New Year to reflections on world peace, John Paul II stated that "peoples have a right and even a duty to protect their existence and freedom by proportionate means, against an unjust aggressor." Such proportionate means could include the use of force. But John Paul continued immediately to qualify this statement in an important way. He explained that "in the view of the difference between classical warfare and nuclear or bacteriological war, a difference so to speak of nature, and in view of the scandal of the arms race seen against the backdrop of the needs of the Third World, this right [of armed self-defense], which is very real in principle, only underlines the urgency" of finding alternatives to war. He stated, finally, that "war is the most barbarous and least effective way of resolving conflicts."[18]

The pope's emphasis on nonviolence and peacemaking brought him to interpret in a much stricter fashion than ever before the criteria that must be met for a particular war to be considered just. After reading John Paul's 1991 encyclical, *Centesimus annus*, Bryan Hehir, the main advisor to the U.S. bishops in drawing up their 1983 peace pastoral letter, concluded that "one surely comes away from the Gulf debate and this encyclical with a sense that the moral barriers against the use of force are now drawn more tightly by this pope."[19] In fact, John Paul rarely used the language of the traditional "just war" doctrine. It would be no exaggeration to describe John Paul's position towards the end of his papacy as a theology of peace of which the theory of a just war is only a part.

Taking all the above into consideration, it would still be incorrect to describe John Paul simply as a pacifist. He cautiously supported the toppling of the Taliban government in Afghanistan. After the 9/11 terrorist attacks, he stated that "there exists therefore a right to defend oneself against terrorism, a right which, as always, must be exercised with respect for moral and legal limits in the choice of ends and means."[20] He added that a response to terrorists required that those responsible be clearly identified, and that efforts be made to eliminate the contributing causes of terror. He also saw a role for the use of force for humanitarian purposes, that is, to protect "whole populations" that might be at risk, as in the case of genocide. He was among the first international figures to advocate humanitarian intervention in the former Yugoslavia. His calls for similar interventions in the cases of Rwanda and the Congo were ignored. John Paul understood legitimate intervention in a broad way, a way that includes, for example, the use of international monitors. Actual military intervention, mounted preferably by international coalitions, remained in his thinking as only a last resort.

One of the clearest examples of John Paul's rethinking of the just war theory can be found in his 2002 World Day of Peace message, entitled "No Peace without Justice, No Justice without Forgiveness." At the opening of this important statement, he located the events of 9/11 in the light of Christian hope:

> The enormous suffering of peoples and individuals, even among my own friends and acquaintances, caused by Nazi and communist totalitarianism, has never been far from my thoughts and prayers. I have often paused to reflect on the persistent questions: *how do we restore the moral and social order subjected to such horrific violence?* My reasoned conviction, confirmed in turn by biblical revelation, is that the shattered order cannot be fully restored except by a response that combines justice with forgiveness. *The pillars of true peace are justice and that form of love which is forgiveness.*

Already in 1994, in an apostolic letter, *Tertio adveniente millennio*, the pope called upon the whole church to prepare for the millennium by entering a period of self-examination and repentance. Against the advice of a number of the members of the Vatican curia, the pope called for the public expression of repentance for the failures and sins of the members of the church, present and past. A 1997 book written by the Italian Luigi Accatolli lists some ninety-four texts in which John Paul II either acknowledged the historical faults of the church or, at least, of Christians, and asked pardon for them.[21] The chapter headings under which Accatolli gathers these texts reveals the gamut of concerns: the Crusades, dictatorships, divisions among the churches, women, Jews, Galileo, war and peace, the wars of religion, burning of Jan Hus, the excommunication of Calvin and Zwingli, the enslavement of Indians, multiple injustices, the Inquisition, integralism, Islam, Luther, the Mafia, racism, Rwanda, the schism with the East, the history of the papacy, and the slave trade. On the first Sunday of Lent of the year 2000, the pope had many Church leaders confess such faults, including Cardinal Joseph Ratzinger, who then served as head of the Vatican congregation that monitors orthodoxy, and whom John Paul II directed publicly to ask forgiveness for the sins committed in the service of truth. Nor should it be forgotten that twice (in 1986 and 2002) the pope invited all the leaders of the world's religions to gather with him in Assisi to pray for peace; it was at those gatherings that the pope emphasized that religion should be a force for peace and justice, and never be a pretext for violence. He asked forgiveness for the many times in history when religion has been used to promote violence. Whatever reservations then-Cardinal Joseph Ratzinger had about syncretism at the Assisi meetings, after being elected pope himself in 2005 he strongly reinforced John Paul's teaching that religion and violence should have nothing to do with each other.

More could be said, for example, about Pope John Paul's commitment to improved relationships with the Jews and his dramatic visit to Israel in 2000, where he visited the Holocaust museum, Yad Vashem, and prayed and asked forgiveness at the sacred Western Wall. On the slip of paper he inserted into the space between the great stones of the Western Wall he wrote these words: "Lord of our fathers, you chose Abraham and his descendants to bring your name to the nations. We are deeply saddened by the behavior of those who in the course of history have caused these children of yours to suffer and, asking your forgiveness, we wish to commit ourselves to genuine brotherhood with the people of the Covenant." Or about his tentative outreach to the Muslims, which his successor, Benedict XVI (2005–2013), initially aggravated through his September 2006 Regensberg address, but subsequently made good on with his visit two months later to Turkey, and then his extended discussion with representatives of an international group of Muslim religious leaders who in the fall of 2007 sent a lengthy statement, "A Common Word," inviting the West to consider the common ground that Christianity and Islam occupies. Or we could describe John Paul's largely unsuccessful outreach to the Orthodox Church, made difficult by the unraveling of the Soviet Union in 1989, and the subsequent aggressive proselytizing by mostly evangelical Christian missionaries of the largely religiously illiterate Russian people. Or finally, we could consider John Paul's many statements about capitalism. Martin Marty, the American Lutheran historian of Christianity, remarked that the pope "said just enough to inspire free market ideologues to make him sound like St. Adam Smith... [b]ut no sooner would they quote such lines than their critics would counter with paragraphs in which the pope issued cautions, made criticisms, and prophesied: the market does not automatically produce activity congruent with human need."[22]

All of these other topics more or less affect John Paul II's reinterpretation of the just war theory—but they are best left to another article.

Conclusion

By way of conclusion, three remarks should be made. First, it may be asked whether the official teaching of the Church developed under John Paul II in a way similar to the way it developed on the death penalty. The first English edition of the *Catechism of the Catholic Church* appeared in 1994. Its statements on the death penalty were not precise. Commentators who support the death penalty seized upon these ambiguities to continue to argue that the death penalty is necessary. The next year, 1995, John Paul published his encyclical *Evangelium vitae*, in which he acknowledged a person's right to self-defense, but said that "in the context of a system of penal justice ever more in line with human dignity and thus, in the end, with God's plan for man and society," the death penalty should be strictly limited to cases of "absolute necessity."[23] By that phrase the pope meant that without the death penalty, we would have to have a situation where "it would not be possible otherwise to defend society." He judged that such situations would be "very rare, if not practically non-existent." A few weeks later, Cardinal Joseph Ratzinger explained that the pope's reservations about the use of the death penalty were stronger than those mentioned in the *Catechism*, and that the *Catechism* would therefore need to be revised.[24] And it was. The American Sister Helen Prejean and other opponents of the death penalty had effectively underscored how some Catholics were interpreting the ambiguous phrases in the first edition of the *Catechism* to argue for its continued use.

The question then arises: was John Paul's thinking on the just war theory moving in the same direction as his teaching on the death penalty—for all practical purposes, opposing it flatly?[25] The answer has to be a qualified "no." The pope's ever-stricter restrictions have not completely excluded a very limited use for force under very carefully circumscribed conditions. However, Catholic restrictions on the death penalty are now nearly absolute.

Second, John Paul's views on war may perhaps be best understood as a recasting of the traditional just war doctrine within a more comprehensive theology of peace and reconciliation. Traditional just war theory distinguished *jus ad bellum* and *jus in bello*. The first describes the conditions which make entering a war morally defensible; the second describes how to fight a war justly. A growing number of theologians and ethicists now point to a third dimension that needs to be included as an essential part of the moral evaluation of a war. That dimension might be named the *jus post bellum*, or the consideration of the consequences of a war and the obligations all participants in a war have for rebuilding and for forgiveness. John Paul's commitment to nonviolence was a principled one, but his acute awareness of the consequences of war, the primary one being the making of the evil worse, made him very reluctant to endorse the traditional just war theory without considerable revision. As mentioned earlier, John Paul wrote in paragraph 42 of *Centesimus annus* that wars leave "a trail of resentment and hatred, thus making it even more difficult to find a just solution of the very problems which provoked the war." Jack Miles argues that the moral evaluation of a war must include not just a moral evaluation of *jus ad bellum* and jus in bello, but also of the *jus post bellum*, that is, the destruction of a society's social order, its medical facilities and supply of clean water, and all the illnesses and diseases that take the lives of innocent civilians for months after the war has ended.[26]

And third, it should by now be obvious how opposed John Paul's view of the use of military force is to the Bush/Cheney policy of preemptive war. In an article about *The Compendium of the Social Doctrine of the Church*, published in 2005 by the Pontifical Council for Justice and Peace, one commentator argued that the Catholic Church's body of social doctrine, deeply influenced as is now evident by the writings of John Paul II, challenges some of the major directions of current American foreign policy:

> On point after point—the document's deep respect for the United Nations and international law; its call for a universal public authority that will banish war; its conviction that poverty is the one contemporary issue that challenges the Christian conscience; its praise for unarmed prophets of conscience; the very strict restrictions it places on the just war doctrine; its call to end indiscriminate trading in arms; its conviction

that preventive war cannot be waged without clear proof that an attack is imminent; its strong support for the International Criminal court; and its call to fight the war on terrorism with respect for human rights and the principles of a state ruled by law—Catholic social thought is clearly at odds with the neo-conservative philosophy that has been embraced by many in the Bush administration.[27]

The American bishops have been consistently more vocal about abortion and same-sex marriage than they have been about the Iraq war. Unfortunately, many Catholics seem to be simply unaware of recent papal teaching on the morality of war.

When John Paul II was elected pope, a fellow Pole, Cardinal Stefan Wyszynski, told him: "If the Lord has called you, you must lead the Church into the third millennium." And as he did, he significantly reshaped the just war doctrine, leaving behind a rich and challenging reflection on what needs to be done if the world is ever to establish a just international order. Scott Appleby stated that John Paul engaged "world leaders with a more explicitly geopolitical analysis" and that he spoke "more openly about power and how it should be directed and contained" than any of his predecessors.[28] It is almost as though the position of the Church on war has, since its beginnings, come full circle. More than any pope before him, John Paul II has erected important signposts for the creation of a more peaceful and just new millennium. Would that his teachings were more widely known and embraced.

Notes

1. This chapter is reprinted from *Religion, Identity, and Global Governance: Ideas, Evidence, and Practice*, edited by Patrick James, 203–19, © University of Toronto Press, 2011. Reprinted with permission of the publisher.
2. Yona Metzger, "Yesterday, Today and Tomorrow," *America* 193, no. 12 (October 24, 2005).
3. John Sniegocki, "Catholic Teaching on War, Peace, and Nonviolence since Vatican II," in *Vatican II: Forty Years Later*, ed. William Madges (Maryknoll, NY: Orbis Books, 2006): 224–44.
4. J. N. D. Kelly, *The Oxford Dictionary of the Popes* (New York: Oxford University Press, 1986).

5. William L. Portier, "Are We Really Serious When We Ask God to Deliver Us from War? The Catechism and the Challenge of Pope John Paul II," *Communio* 23, no. 1 (spring 1996): 47–63.

6. One of the last documents approved in 1965 by the Second Vatican Council was entitled *Gaudium et spes*, or, *The Church in the Modern World*. It stated clearly the need for an international authority to ensure justice and respect for human rights: "It is our clear duty to spare no effort to achieve the complete outlawing of war by international agreement. This goal, of course, requires the establishment of a universally acknowledged public authority vested with the effective power to ensure security for all, regard for justice, and respect for law," Austin Flannery, ed., *Vatican Council II: Constitutions, Decrees, Declarations* (Northport, NY: Costello Publishing, 1996), 268–69.

7. Flannery, *Vatican Council II.*

8. "Pope John Paul II," *Time* 165, no. 15 (April 3, 2005): 27.

9. Richard McCormick, "Deeds Not Words," in *John Paul II: Reflections from The Tablet*, ed. Catherine Pepinster (London: Burns & Oates, 2005), 31.

10. Henri de Lubac, *At the Service of the Church: Henri De Lubac Reflects on the Circumstances That Occasioned His Writings* (San Francisco, CA: Ignatius Press, 1993), 171–72.

11. Flannery, *Vatican Council II.*

12. Drew Christiansen, "John Paul II Peacemaker: A Nonviolent Pope in a Time of Terror" (unpublished paper, 2005).

13. Pope John Paul II, *Centesimus annus* (Boston: St. Paul Books and Media, 1991).

14. Ibid., par. 25.

15. Portier, "Are We Really Serious When We Ask God to Deliver Us from War?"

16. Christiansen, "John Paul II Peacemaker."

17. Portier, "Are We Really Serious When We Ask God to Deliver Us from War?"

18. In another World Day of Peace message (1993), the pope stated: "War worsens the sufferings of the poor; indeed, it creates new poor by destroying means of subsistence, homes and property, and by eating away at the very fabric of the social environment.... After so many unnecessary massacres, it is in the final analysis of fundamental importance to recognize, once and for all, that *war never helps the human community*, that violence destroys and never builds up, that the wounds it causes remain long unhealed, and that as a result of conflicts the already grim condition of the poor deteriorates still further, and new forms of poverty appear." See Sniegocki, "Catholic Teaching on War, Peace, and Nonviolence since Vatican II," for these and other key quotations of John Paul II.

19. J. Bryan Hehir, "Reordering the World: John Paul II's *Centesimus annus*," *Commonweal* 118 (June 14, 1991): 393–4.

20. Pope John Paul II, "If You Want Peace, Reach Out to the Poor" (message, XXVI Annual World Day of Prayer for Peace, January 1, 1993).

21. Luigi Accattoli, *Quand le pape demande pardon* (Paris: Albin Michel, 1997).

22. Martin E. Marty, "Insights of a Family Friend," *America* 192, no. 13 (April 18, 2005): 32.

23. Pope John Paul II, *Evangelium vitae* (Boston: St. Paul Books and Media, 1995).

24. See Portier, "Are We Really Serious When We Ask God to Deliver Us from War?," especially 49–51.

25. Ibid.

26. Jack Miles, "The Iraqi Dead: Respect Must Be Paid," *Commonweal* (July 18, 2003).

27. Joseph J. Fahey, "On Peace and War," *America* 193, no. 11 (October 17, 2005): 19.

28. Scott Appleby, "Pope John Paul II," *Foreign Policy* 119 (Summer 2000): 14.

9

Peace, Conflict, and Conflict Transformation in the Islamic Tradition

ABBAS AROUA

The foundational texts of the Islamic religion and the practices of the Prophet of Islam and the early Muslim community provide enough teachings to elaborate a comprehensive theory of conflict and peace. But the historical events the Muslim community went through and particularly the major political conflicts in the first decades of Islamic history prevented the emergence of a healthy approach to conflict. Today there is an increasing awareness for the need in the Muslim world to master the techniques of conflict analysis and transformation. The aim of this contribution is to provide peacebuilders with a few resources from the Islamic tradition that can be used when addressing a conflict rooted in an Islamic context.

Peace and War in Islam

Salām: The Imperative of Peace

There is no peaceful or violent religion, culture, race, or nation. All religions call for peace and, at the same time, authorize the use of violence when justified and well controlled. But the followers of religions, the communities which belong to them, are all human beings, complex entities sharing the same inclination to violence and the ideal of peace.

The Arabic word *Islām* comes from the same root as *silm* and *salām*, meaning "peace." Therefore Islām may be translated as "seeking peace near or with God." In fact, *As-Salām* is one of the names/attributes of God. According to the Qur'ān, he is the "Source of Peace"[1] and "invites unto the abode of peace."[2] The believers are called to peace: "O you who believe! Enter all of you into peace and do not follow the steps of Satan."[3] Some Muslim scholars interpret "enter into peace" as "enter into Islam" making therefore a strong association between Islam and peace.

Peace is three-dimensional. In the Islamic perception, life has three dimensions: one vertical, between the individual and his or her Creator; and two horizontal, one between the individual and his or her inner self, and one between self and other creatures. So, although the vertical planes are distinct and share only the reference to the Creator (vertical axis), the horizontal plane is common to all (self and other creatures); it offers plenty of space for cooperation and allows for cohabitation in this life. This has an implication on how peace is viewed in the Islamic tradition: it is projected on the three axes leading to inner and outer peace. You therefore have peace with self (inner peace), peace with the Creator, and peace with other creatures (humans, animals, and the whole environment). The three dimensions of peace are interlinked. As pointed out by Algerian academic Omar Benaïssa, "The divine name *As-Salām* is the one by which all the other opposed names are reconciled. One must make peace within self to be able to make peace around. Moses first learned to control his inner 'pharaoh' before triumphing on the external Pharaoh."[4] To be in peace with God implies necessarily peace with the others, and to be in peace with the others is a requirement for peace with God. For Sheherazade Jafari and Abdul Aziz Said,

> [W]ithin an Islamic peacemaking framework, inner personal transformation is connected to societal conflict transformation; peace within oneself and peace in relation to others is linked not only with each other, but to a relationship with God. In particular, *Tasawwuf*, the Sufi branch of knowledge and mysticism in Islam, understands the purification of one's inner self as a way to peace, which is defined as harmony or equilibrium.... The Islamic framework provides a conceptualization of

transformation that works from the inside out, addressing what is deeply rooted at the personal level in order to come closer to God's love and, ultimately, peace.[5]

Peace is a basic need. It is a prerequisite to the realization of human rights. Two basic needs are mentioned in the Qur'ān in the same verse: food and peace, "Let them worship the Lord of this House (Ka'ba), who fed them from hunger and secured them from fear."[6] Being considered as a trustee of God (*khalīfa*), the duty of the human being is to guarantee these basic needs around him or her to his or her fellow men and women. The duty of the state is to guarantee them at a larger scale to the whole community.

Peace is the greeting of Islam. "Peace be upon you!" (*as-Salāmu alaykum*) is the greeting used by Muslims. The Prophet said, "You will not enter into Paradise until you believe and you will not believe until you love each other. Shall I tell you of something if you do it you will love one another? Spread the greeting of peace amongst yourselves."[7] "Peace be upon you!" is also the formula that closes the formal prayer.

Peace is a continuously reiterated wish of the Muslim. After every prayer it is recommended to follow the prophetic tradition and say the following invocation, "Ô my God, You are Peace, the Source of Peace, blessed is the Lord of Majesty and Bounty."[8] Some believers may add, "You are the Origin of Peace, make us live in Peace, and ultimately let us enter the Abode of Peace (Paradise)."

Peace is the language of the righteous. "The true devotees of *Ar-Rahmān* (God, the Loving) are those who walk on the earth with humility, and when the ignorant address them [harshly], they say: Peace!"[9] Peace is also the salutation of God to the righteous: "Their greeting on the day they meet Him will be: 'Peace!' and he has prepared for them a generous reward."[10]

Peace is the name and the language of Paradise. "For them will be a home of peace (*Darussalam*) in the presence of their Lord."[11] "They shall enter the eternal Gardens of Eden, along with the righteous from among their fathers, wives and descendants. From every gate the angels will come to them, saying: "Peace be upon you for all what you have steadfastly endured. How excellent is the final abode!"[12] "They will hear no vain talk there (in the Gardens of Eden), but only peace."[13]

Peace must be the attitude and behavior of the Muslim. The Prophet said: "The true Muslim is the one with whom the others feel in peace and do not fear his tongue and hand,"[14] and "the true believer is the one who is trusted by others for their wealth and life."[15]

Jihād: An Effort In/Out

Jihād is a common word at the international level, regularly used and largely misused by the media, most politicians and academics, and in the public discourse in general, particularly in the West and by many Muslims. Let us begin by clarifying what jihād is not. Jihād is not aggression. Aggression is forbidden in Islam. Jihād is not a "holy war," a concept that does not exist in the Islamic tradition. It is not about forcing people to change their faith and to convert to Islam, which is forbidden, too.

After this negative definition, let us define jihād positively. Jihād originates from the root verb *jahada*, meaning "to make an effort." Two derivative verbs are *jāhada*, meaning "to engage in a mutual effort," and *ijtahada*, meaning "to exert an (intellectual) effort for a specific goal such as solving a problem, answering a question, passing an exam," and so on. From this comes the word *ijtihād*, which refers to interpreting Islamic foundational texts and inferring jurisprudential rules in a specific context.

Jihād may be defined as an effort, of any kind (of the heart, the tongue, or the hand) that is permissible, made in the way of God (intention), in order to fight against (goal): (1) all forms of evil inside oneself (greater jihād), and (2) all forms of injustice outside oneself (smaller jihād).

Some Muslim scholars distinguish between two types of smaller jihād: (1) reactive (*jihād ad-daf'*) to resist an aggression on one's land, and (2) (pro)active (*jihād at-talab*) to lift religious persecution (*fitna*) in another land.

'Udwān: On Aggression and Terrorism

Terrorism is about aggression and oppression. To commit a terrorist act is to inflict harm on innocent people, to destroy their property, to spoil their rights, particularly their right to physical integrity and even their right to life, with the aim of provoking fear and inducing a desired behavior that helps achieve some predefined goals. Terrorism consists therefore of an action (violent, harmful, deadly), committed by an individual, a group or a state, with a given intention. The intention covers

TABLE 9.1. SITUATIONS WHERE PROVOKING FEAR
IS AN IMMEDIATE OBJECTIVE.

	Type	Means
(a) Aggression	Offensive	Harmful (violent, deadly)
(b) Counter aggression	Defensive	Harmful (violent, deadly)
(c) Counter aggression	Punitive	Harmful (violent, deadly)
(d) Deterrence or Dissuasion	Defensive	Nonharmful (capacity)

an immediate objective (to provoke fear), an intermediate objective (to induce a behavior), and an ultimate goal (legitimate or not).

The Qur'ānic words for aggression and oppression are *'udwān* and *bagh'i* respectively; they are absolutely forbidden, as seen in the following verses: "Fight in the way of God those who fight you, but do not commit aggression. God does not like the aggressors."[16] "O you who believe! Do not usurp unjustly the wealth of each other, except it be a trade by mutual consent; and do not kill one another. God is most merciful to you. And whoever does that through aggression and injustice, then We will drive him into Hell; and this is easy for God."[17] "Cooperate in goodness and piety and do not cooperate in sin and aggression"[18] In this verse, goodness is associated with piety and aggression with sin. "Tell them (O Muhammad): 'My Lord has forbidden indecent acts committed in public or in secret, all kinds of sin, unjust oppression; that you associate with God that for which he has given no authority, and that you say things about Him without knowledge.'"[19] "God bids you to fairness (*iḥsān*)[20] and the doing of good to kith and kin, and forbids indecency, evil and oppression. He advises you so that you may be mindful."[21]

In the Arab world the term commonly used for terrorism is *irhāb*. But irhāb does not convey the full meaning of terrorism. In fact, irhāb literally means "provoking fear" or "frightening," regardless of the action used to achieve it or the intention behind it. Irhāb is also a Qur'ānic word used sometimes with a positive connotation: "Mobilize your force

Immediate objective	Intermediate objective	Ultimate goal
Provoke fear (irhāb)	Weaken other's defense	Spoil other's rights
Provoke fear (irhāb)	Make the other stop an aggression	Recover own or other's rights
Provoke fear (irhāb)	Make the other regret an aggression	Revenge/vengeance
Provoke fear (irhāb)	Discourage the other from committing an aggression	Peace & security

as much as you can, including cavalry, to frighten (*turhibūna*) the enemies of God, your own enemies, and others who are besides them you
may not know but whom God does know. Whatever you spend in the
way of God will be fully repaid to you, and you will not be wronged."[22]
Irhāb is used here in the context of dissuasion or deterrence; it is about
defensive attitude and behavior, contrary to aggression which is about
offensive attitude and behavior. Irhāb in the dissuasive context is achieved
by nonharmful means; it aims at discouraging the other side from engaging in an act of aggression. Table 9.1 gives four situations where irhāb is
sought as an immediate objective.

In Islam, case (a), aggression, is forbidden; case (c), punitive, is highly
disliked, because the Muslim is enjoined to get rid of the spirit of ven-
geance and encouraged to pardon; case (d), defensive, is recommended
to guarantee peace and avoid war; and case (b), defensive, is allowed
under certain conditions.

Harb: The Recourse to War
If Islam may be considered a religion of peace, as shown previously, it
certainly does not advocate pacifism. That is because even if war is considered a disliked enterprise, it is authorized in certain circumstances and
under certain conditions. "You have been enjoined to go to war, and you
dislike it."[23] Therefore a war cannot be holy and there is neither such a
concept as "holy war" in the Islamic tradition, nor such a thing as a war

of religion aiming to convert people to Islam; this is simply because in matters of faith no constraint or coercion is acceptable. "There shall be no compulsion in religion," states the Qur'ān.[24] Prophet Muhammad was ordered by God to "say: 'This is the truth from your Lord. Let whosoever will, believe, and whosoever will, disbelieve.'"[25] Jihād, defined previously, has nothing to do with a "holy war" as it is often mistranslated in Western languages. Even the Crusades were called by Muslims the "Wars of the Franks" (*Hurūb al-Firinja*), since they were perceived more as wars of occupation than as wars of religion.

The first time the early Muslims were allowed to take arms to defend themselves was when the following Qur'ānic verses were revealed: "Permission to fight is given to those against whom war is being wrongfully waged; God has indeed the power to grant them victory. Those who have been expelled from their homes unjustly, only because they said: 'Our Lord is God.' If God did not repel the aggression of some people by means of others, monasteries, churches, synagogues and mosques, wherein the name of God is much invoked, would surely have been demolished."[26]

Muslims are also enjoined to defend others' rights when they are spoiled by an aggressor or an oppressor. This is all about smaller jihād: to fight against all forms of injustice. The context here is related to case (b) in table 9.1.

Other Qur'ānic verses set the conditions and limits of war:

Fight in the way of God those who fight you, but do not commit aggression. God does not like the aggressors. Kill them wherever you may catch them and expel them from the place from which they expelled you. Fitna (religious persecution) is worse than killing. Do not fight them at the Sacred Mosque unless they fight you there. If they do fight you, slay them, this is the due punishment for such disbelievers. But if they desist, then verily God is Forgiving, Merciful. Fight them until there is no more fitna and religion belongs to God alone. If they desist, then let there be no hostility, except towards aggressors. [Fighting in] the sacred month is for [aggression committed in] the sacred month, and for [all] violations is legal retribution. Thus you may exact retribution from whoever aggresses you, in proportion to his aggression, and fear God, and know that God is with the pious.[27]

Once Muslims are engaged in the disliked enterprise of war to fight aggression, oppression, or religious persecution, they are ordered by the Qur'ān to be firm and steady in applying violence. And since war at that time was about crossing swords, several Qur'ānic verses address the behavior at the battlefield and are about smiting the necks of those who fight for the sake of aggression, oppression, and persecution.[28]

From these verses the following principles may be extracted:

1. It is forbidden to commit aggression;
2. You are allowed to fight against aggression;
3. The retribution must be proportional to the aggression;
4. You are allowed to fight against religious persecution that you or others suffer;[29]
5. You are not allowed to fight in order to impose a religion;
6. The fight must end as soon as the aggression and religious persecution end.

Like invasive therapy procedures, war may bring some benefit to social health, but it also brings a lot of harm. War is therefore viewed as a last resort and must be both justified and optimized.

Justification means that war must aim towards a just end when there are no other means to achieve this end. Optimization means to maximize the benefit and to minimize the harm. This implies to comply with a code of conduct, which enjoins proportionality, avoidance of noncombatants, ban of nondiscriminating weapons, etc. Justification and optimization principles, when combined, mean "doing the right thing and doing it right." They may be translated in the following formula: as low occurrence and as low harm as reasonably achievable.

The first Caliph, Abu Bakr, addressed his army before leaving for a battle in 632 CE, advising them with a number of rules for guidance in the battlefield and asking them to keep them in mind.

Do not betray;
Do not misappropriate any part of the booty,

Do not commit treachery,
Do not mutilate dead bodies,
Do not kill a child, an old man, or a woman,
Do not uproot or burn palm trees,
Do not cut fruitful trees,
Do not slaughter a sheep, a cow or a camel, except for food,
   You will pass by people who have devoted their lives to
monastic services; leave them alone.[30]

It is worth noting that in those days, the principle of target discrimination could evidently be followed; however, today's war practices often do not comply with this principle. Not only nonconventional
weaponry, be it atomic, biological, or chemical, but also some conven-
tional arms such as strategic bombers, drones, and long-range missiles
kill massively and indiscriminately. Moreover, the warrior in ancient
times had at least one quality: the necessary courage to confront death
in a one-to-one fight. Today, the operator of an unmanned aerial vehi-
cle or an intercontinental ballistic missile is in a control room thousands of miles far from the target, the pilot of a military aircraft sits
comfortably in his cockpit and shells thousands of people from an alti-
tude of ten miles. No courage, no chivalry in that. This distance creates an emotional shield that prevents the contemporary warrior from
feeling what it is to kill. For these reasons, if for no other, contemporary war must be banned.

Silm: Back to Peace

Even in times of violent conflict, the preference must be for peace. This
is clearly stated in the following Qur'ānic verse: "If they incline to peace
(silm), then you too incline to it and rely upon God. He is the All-Hearing, the All-Knowing. If they seek to cheat you, God is All-Sufficient for
you. It is he who supported you with his help and with the believers."[31]

From what precedes one can conclude that peace is the norm in the
Islamic tradition. The Muslim community has the duty to protect it,
basically by building capacity in order to face any aggression/oppression
that could compromise and undermine it. This is dissuasion or deterrence. In the case of aggression/oppression, the community is enjoined

to react, even by violent means, respecting specific conditions, in order to reestablish the norm: peace. If the aggressor shows a desire to make peace, then it becomes mandatory to accept it, even if there are doubts about the sincerity of his approach and a suspicion that his intention may be only tactical. At the end, the Muslim must rely upon God, who will deal with the cheater.

Conflict, a Human Phenomenon

Definition of Conflict

One way of defining conflict is to consider it as a dynamic relation between two or more parties (individuals, groups, states, civilizations) with (apparently) contradictory goals. The goals may be at the level of positions (what you say you want), interests (what you really want), needs (what you must have), or values (what you believe in).

In his theory of conflict presented in his work *The Unrestricted Thunderbolts*, Muslim scholar Ibn Qayyim al-Jawziyya (1292–1350) distinguished between the origin (reference, input, or value system/world view), the way (methodology, process, or attitude/behavior), and the goal (result, output, or need/interest).[32]

Ibn Qayyim al-Jawziyya considered the absence of conflict as the configuration where the origin is one, the way is one, and the goal is one. Conflict is therefore defined by this fourteenth-century Muslim scholar as the situation where the origins are incompatible, the ways are divergent, or the goals are contradictory.

Conflict in Arabic Terminology

Conflict originates from the Latin *confligere* (*fligere*, "to strike" and *con*, "together"). The Arabic equivalent of *conflict* would therefore be *tadhārub* (from *dharaba*, "to strike," and *ta*, "together or mutually") or *dhirāb* "common participation in the action of striking." In reality, several terms are often used interchangeably to name a conflict in Arabic, although they mean different things.

1. *Khilāf* or *Shijār*, these words mean "difference, dissimilarity, distinction, divergence, disagreement, dispute, discordance." They

designate a neutral attitude focusing on the object (an idea, an opinion, a good, a right, etc.).

2. *Khisām*, "to make an adversary, an enemy, a foe, antagonizing, producing hostility." This word describes a negative attitude focusing on the subject (an individual, a group, etc.).

3. *Dhirāb*, "striking, beating, hitting, knocking, punching, slapping, flapping, tapping." This is a violent behavior focusing on the subject.

4. *Sirā'*, "knocking down, flooring, cutting down, pushing down, toppling, stunning, pole axing, tossing, hitting, picking off, reversing, overthrowing, overturning." This is a violent behavior focusing on the subject.

5. *Qitāl*, "mutual killing, slaying, executing, putting to death, shooting, firing, putting down, finishing (usually involves two or a small number of people)." This is a deadly behavior focusing on the subject.

6. *Hirāb*, "warring (involves a large number of people)." This is a deadly behavior focusing on the subject.

7. *Fitna*, a word which has two meanings according to the context: (a) "trial, ordeal, test, crucible, temptation; to make fitna is to

arouse and provoke discord and division," or (b) "tumult, turmoil, persecution, oppression, dissension, killing of each other,
schism, civil war, and chaos." In the Qur'ān fitna is sometimes
used to mean religious persecution. It is therefore a negative (or
deadly) behavior focusing on the subject.

The seven terms go from a neutral attitude (khilāf and its synony-
mous shijār) to an extremely deadly behavior (fitna). They could be dis-
played as a vicious cycle of violence, as shown in Figure 9.1, that may
start with fitna (fueling discord) and may end up with fitna (chaotic
violence). Fitna is forbidden in Islam. The Qur'ān asserts that "fitna is
worse than killing."[33]

The way to break this vicious cycle is to intervene at the first stage
of khilāf (conflict) and deal with it peacefully. At the stage of khisām
(antagonizing) one should be moderate and avoid violence of any type
against the adversary. Prophet Muhammad said: "Four vices if they meet
in somebody then he is a real hypocrite, and whoever has one of them
has a trait of hypocrisy until he gives it up: when he is entrusted with
something he betrays, when he speaks he lies, when he pledges he cheats,
and when he engages in an antagonism with another one (*khāsama*) he
lets his resentment explode (*fajara*)."[34]

Conflict: Positive or Negative?
If making fitna is forbidden, as mentioned earlier, disputing is recognized
as a human phenomenon. But it should be dealt with in a proper manner.
In the Islamic tradition, conflict is recognized as a normal social phenomenon and a sign of God who could have created all human beings
according to the same "blueprint," but instead preferred to make every
human being a singular entity with a unique intellectual and emotional
character and personal goals and aspirations in life. Similarly, the cultural specificity of communities is not viewed negatively and is recognized as an attractive prerequisite for communication, exchange, and
mutual knowledge: "O you mankind! We have created you of a male
and a female, and made you nations and tribes so that you may know
each other."[35]

To have different opinions and views is in human nature. According
to the Qur'ān, this characteristic came late in the evolution of humanity:

"All mankind were once one single community, and only later did they begin to hold divergent views."[36]

Dispute, difference, and disagreement are acknowledged and the Qur'ān orders Muslims to handle them by referring to the orders of God and his Prophet: "Whatever you differ/disagree upon, its ruling is to be referred to God."[37] The word used here is *ikhtalaftum* (related to khilāf). "By your Lord (addressing Prophet Muhammad), they will not have faith, until they let you arbitrate their disputes."[38] In this verse the word *shajara* (related to shijār) is used.

Ibn Qayyim al-Jawziyya stated that "ikhtilāf (conflict) occurs necessarily and unavoidably between people due to the disparity in their wills, understandings, and sharpness of mind. What is disliked is aggression and hostility to each other. Otherwise... ikhtilāf does not hurt; it is unavoidable since it is constitutive of the human creation."[39]

It is reported that the caliph Ali said, "The excess of agreement is a form of hypocrisy and the excess of disagreement leads to strife." If difference, disagreement, and conflict between individuals and groups are a fact of human life that should be acknowledged, and if it is recognized that they may contribute to reestablishing the balance in human relations and interests and tend in general to improve the situation of the parties involved, they should not be dealt with in a violent way. According to conflictologists, peace is not the absence of conflict but rather its good management. In fact, what should be prevented is for a conflict to end up in a violent (sometimes bloody) form, violence being defined as "actions, words, attitudes, structures, or systems that cause physical, psychological, social or environmental damage and/or prevent people from reaching their full human potential."[40]

Expelling/Repelling Dialectics

Nizā' is another word commonly used in Arabic for conflict. But this term does not convey literally the meaning of conflict. In fact, nizā' (or *naz'*) means removing, stripping, taking off, tearing out, sloughing, extracting, plucking out, eviscerating, expropriating, spoiling other's rights. It refers to an offensive behavior focusing on the object (an idea, an opinion, a good, a right, etc.). To engage in nizā' is to engage in a conflict with an illegitimate goal. Nizā' is disliked in the Islamic tradition: "Obey

God and his Messenger, and do not engage in niza' one with another, for you will lose courage and strength, and be patient and persevering, for God is with those who patiently persevere."[41]

In opposition to niza', there is the concept of *difa'* or *daf'* which means pushing, boosting, pressing, giving, repelling, repulsing, protecting, defending one's own or others' rights. It is a defensive behavior focusing on the object. Difa' is recommended in the Islamic tradition:

> By the will of God they defeated them, and David killed Goliath, and God gave him kingship and wisdom, and taught him whatsoever he willed. Had God not repelled the people, some by the means of others, the earth would have surely been corrupted; but God is most bounteous towards the entire creation.[42]

and

> Permission to fight is given to those against whom war is being wrongfully waged; God has indeed the power to grant them victory. Those who have been expelled from their homes unjustly, only because they said: "Our Lord is God." If God did not repel the aggression of some people by means of others, monasteries, churches, synagogues and mosques, wherein the name of God is much invoked, would surely have been demolished. God will certainly aid those who aid his cause; for verily God is Strong, Almighty.[43]

The Duty of Conflict Transformation
Dealing with Conflict
A conflict may either be dealt with violently or transformed by peaceful means. An attempt to transform the conflict may follow one of the nine processes presented in table 9.2.[44] These are approaches that may involve only one conflict party (unilateral), all conflict parties (bilateral/multilateral), or a third party.

Good concession. Ideally the conflict parties should take the initiative to give rights back to the owner, or to concede some of their own rights

TABLE 9.2. NINE TYPES OF CONFLICT RESOLUTION IN ISLAM

Unilateral	Bilateral/Multilateral	Third Party
Good concession	Dialogue/diapraxis	Facilitation
Nonviolent resistance/ advocacy	Negotiation	Mediation
		Arbitration
		Law enforcement
		Good intervention

for the sake of peace. This should come from a profound conviction that peace is worth it and not a form of conflict avoidance because of a lack of the necessary power to restore the rights, thus keeping a feeling of discomfort, bitterness, or even hatred. This scenario is possible but rare.

More common is the approach that involves all conflict parties through informal talks or formal dialogue and negotiation.

Dialogue/Diapraxis. An exchange between the conflict parties, by words or by actions, agreed by them, for interknowing and in order to reach a shared understanding.

Negotiation. A discussion agreed by conflict parties that seeks an agreement between them. When dialogue and negotiation are difficult to reach by the initiative of the conflict parties, a third party may (should) intervene to help them transform the conflict. This could take one of the following forms:

Facilitation. A nonstructured support—usually limited to logistical assistance—to negotiation, by a third party, with the consent of the conflict parties.

Mediation. A structured support to negotiation, by a third party, intervening in the process and the content, with the consent of the conflict parties.

Arbitration. An arbiter decides after listening to the conflict parties, with their consent. The conflict parties agree to comply with the arbiter's decision.

Law enforcement. The conflict is settled by legal means even if one party does not consent. A court of justice issues a ruling after hearing a case. The decision is applied by a law enforcement authority/mechanism.

Good intervention. Intervention of a third party in order to convince the party refusing negotiation to engage in talks, and to reestablish the balance of power between the parties.

Nonviolent resistance/advocacy. In case of high power asymmetry and the absence of a third party involvement, nonviolent resistance aims at reestablishing a power balance using internal resources, while advocacy is about mobilizing external support for the cause of the weakest party.

The Value of Bond Mending

The intervention of "third party" external actors aiming at transforming a conflict is qualified as being relationship restoring; the Islamic Arabic expression used by the Prophet is *islāhu thātil-bayn*, which means "bond mending." This formulation recognizes that conflict is a relation, and could occur between good people. In a conflict the parties are not necessarily bad, while the relation between them is. This idea is supported by the Qur'ānic verse that mentions mediation of a conflict between believers: "If two groups of believers come to fight one another, then amend (*aslihū*) the relation between them."[45]

Several Qur'ānic verses encourage Muslims to engage in mediation:

"There is no good in most of their secret talk, except in the case of those who enjoin charity and kindness, or *islāh* (bond mending) between people. If anyone does that, seeking the pleasure of God, We will give him an immense reward."[46]

"Do not swear by God to avoid doing good, being righteous and bond mending. God is All-Hearing and All-Knowing."[47]

"Fulfill your duty to God and mend (*aslihū*) the relation between yourselves."[48]

"*Solh* (conflict settlement) is better."[49]

There are also hadiths of the Prophet, which praise the merit of mediation:

"Making peace justly between two parties is an act of charity."[50]

"Do you want to know what is more valuable than fasting, praying, and almsgiving?" asked the Prophet. His companions answered, "Yes." He then said, "It is to restore the bonds between conflicting parties."[51]

The Prophet himself has proven to be an excellent mediator between individuals and tribes both in Mecca and Medina.[52]

The Good Intervention

In the case where bond mending is hampered by one side considering that power asymmetry plays to his advantage, the community should then engage in a good intervention (*at-tadakhul al-hassan*) for bond mending. The verse mentioned earlier on continues like this: "If two groups of believers come to fight one another, then amend (aslihū) the relation between them. But if one of them oppresses the other, fight the oppressor until it submits to the command of God. If it complies, then amend (aslihū) the relation between them with fairness and be just. God loves those who are just."[53]

This verse sets the successive steps of a process:

1. Try mediation between the two fighting groups;
2. If one group refuses mediation, rejects conflict settlement, and persists in oppressing the other group, taking advantage of power asymmetry, you (the community) have the duty to intervene until the oppressor reconsiders his position;
3. If the oppressor gives up oppression and inclines to peace, then you (the community) must cease the intervention;
4. Resume the mediation with fairness and do not be unjust with the group who ceased oppression.

In conflicts occurring in the Muslim world, good intervention should be the duty of the Muslim community, through its organizations such as the Organization of Islamic Cooperation and the League of Arab States. These institutions must endeavor to convince conflicting parties to negotiate, and exert pressure on the party that resists a peaceful solution. Unfortunately, in the absence of such an active role of these Arab and Muslim organizations, the void is filled by others such as the United Nations Security Council (UNSC) and North Atlantic Treaty Organization (NATO) who intervene, by and large militarily, in conflicts related to the Muslim world.

The Virtue of Nonviolence

If difā' is recommended, then, as shown previously, it must be constrained by the principles of rahma[54] and ihsān.[55] Therefore violence, being antagonistic with rahma, must be avoided.

The Qur'ān orders the believer to "repel with that [manner] which is best (*billati hya ahsan*)."[56] Ihsān is here the overarching principle. In another Qur'ānic verse it is explained that "the good deed and the evil deed cannot be equal. Repel with that [manner] which is best (billati hya ahsan), then verily he, of whom you are an enemy, will become as though he was a close friend."[57] This is about the transforming power of *ad-daf' al-hassan* (nonviolence)!

But engaging in nonviolence is not obvious; it is not an easy task and requires a great deal of patience, perseverance, and steadfastness (*sabr* in the Qur'ānic wording). The previous verse is followed by another one indicating that "none attains that [power of nonviolence] except those who are patient; and none attains that except those who are truly fortunate."[58]

Conclusion

The mainstream media discourse often associates Islam with extremism and violence, the Muslim region being today one of the regions with the highest densities of violent conflict in the world (intra- and interstate) with a low capacity in conflict transformation. This impression is reinforced by the fact that some groups in the Muslim world resort to violent means to face foreign aggression and occupation and/or domestic oppression and tyranny. The foundational texts of the Islamic religion and the practices of the Prophet of Islam and the early Muslim community provide enough teachings to elaborate a comprehensive theory of conflict and peace. This contribution attempts to provide peacebuilders with a few resources from the Islamic tradition that can be used when addressing a conflict rooted in an Islamic context. It provides the norms that limit and regulate the use of violence. It views conflict as a human phenomenon and a corrupted relation between individuals and groups. It favors nonviolent means to deal with conflict and considers "bond mending" a religious duty and a work of goodness.

Notes
1. Qur'ān, Al-Hashr 59:23.
2. Qur'ān, Yūnus 10:25.
3. Qur'ān, Al-Baqara 2:208.

4. Omar Benaïssa, personal communication, March 2013.
5   Sheherazade Jafari and Abdul Aziz Said, "Islam and Peacemaking," in *Peacemaking: From Practice to Theory*, ed. Susan Allen Nan, Zachariah Cherian Mampilly, and Andrea Bartoli (Santa Barbara, CA: Praeger, 2012).
6. Qur'ān, Quraysh 106:3–4.
7. Reported by Muslim.
8. Reported by Muslim.
9. Qur'ān, Al-Furqān 25:63.
10. Qur'ān, Al-Ahzāb 33:44.
11. Qur'ān, Al-An'ām 6:127.
12. Qur'ān, Ar-Ra'd 13:23–24.
13. Qur'ān, Maryam 19:61–62.
14. Reported by Bukhāri and Muslim.
15. Reported by Ibn Māja.
16. Qur'ān, Al-Baqara 2:190.
17. Qur'ān, An-Nisā 4:29–30.
18. Qur'ān, Al-Mā'ida 5:2.
19. Qur'ān, Al-A'rāf 7:33.
20. On ihsān see "The Virtue of Nonviolence" above.
21. Qur'ān, An-Nahl 16:90.
22. Qur'ān, Al-Anfāl 8:60.
23. Qur'ān, Al-Baqara 2:216.
24. Ibid., 2:256.
25. Qur'ān, Al-Kahf 18:29.
26. Qur'ān, Al-Hajj 22:39–40.
27. Qur'ān, Al-Baqara 2:190–4.
28. See, in particular, Qur'an, An-Nisā 4:56,89; Al-Anfāl 8:39,60; Muhammad 47:4.
29. Religious persecution occurs when a group or a state represses an individual and violates his or her rights because of his or her set of beliefs.
30. Reported by at-Tabari and others.
31. Qur'ān, Al-Anfāl 8:61–2.
32. Ibn Qayyim al-Jawziyya, al-Sawā'iq al-Mursala 23:7.
33. Qur'ān, Al-Baqara 2:191.
34. Reported by Bukhāri and Muslim.
35. Qur'ān, Al-Hujurāt 49:13.
36. Qur'ān, Yūnus 10:19.
37. Qur'ān, Ash-Shūra 42:10.
38. Qur'ān, An-Nisā 4:65.
39. Ibn Qayyim al-Jawziyya.
40 Simon Fisher et al., *Working with Conflict: Skills and Strategies for Action* (New York: Zed Books, 2000).
41. Qur'ān, Al-Anfāl 8:46.
42. Qur'ān, Al-Baqara 2:251.
43. Qur'ān, Al-Hajj 22:39–40.

44. Partly adapted from Christopher W. Moore, *The Mediation Process: Practical Strategies for Resolving Conflict* (San Francisco, CA: Jossey-Bass, 2003).

45. Qur'ān, Al-Hujurāt 49:9.

46. Qur'ān, An-Nisā 4:114.

47. Qur'ān, Al-Baqara 2:224.

48. Qur'ān, Al-Anfāl 8:1.

49. Qur'ān, An-Nisā 4:128.

50. Reported by Bukhāri and Muslim.

51. Reported by Ahmad, Tirmidhi, and Ibn Hibban.

52. Before the revelation, the Prophet mediated a conflict between the heads of tribes and families of Mecca caused by the desire of each one of them to be granted the honor to set the Black Stone in place in the wall of the Kaaba. In Medina, the Prophet succeeded in transforming the long-standing conflict between the two main Medinian tribes, the Aws and the Khazraj. (See the various biographies of the Prophet, particularly Ibn Ishaq's *Sira*.)

53. Qur'ān, Al-Hujurāt 49:9.

54. Rahma is a key concept in Islam. God tells Prophet Muhammad in the Qur'ān, "And We have not sent you but as a rahma to the entire universe" (Al-Anbiyā 21:107). Rahma has been translated by Muslim classical and contemporary scholars into the words mercy, beneficence, benevolence, compassion, grace, or care. It has also been translated into a word that encompasses all these qualities and that is simply true love.

55. Ihsān is the highest rank of faith and worship and represents the state of human perfection. It may be considered as the sum of virtues since it covers five of them: the good, the fair, the true, the right, and the beautiful.

56. Qur'ān, Al-Mu'minūn 23:96.

57. Qur'ān, Fussilat 41:34.

58. Ibid., 41:35.

10

In the Beginning Was Conflict

Creation

JOHN PAUL LEDERACH

In the beginning God created, Genesis tells us. From a formless void, the winds of the Creator gave shape to the earth. God separated light from darkness, marking the start of time and history.[1] God separated land from water. The dome of the sky separated upper and lower waters. Plants, animals, birds, and fish of every kind were brought forth. Then the miracle of human presence emerged; we were created in the image of God.[2]

Volumes have been written about this marvelous act of God. I do not propose to undertake a scholarly exegesis of Genesis 1. Yet I am always struck with the centrality of this event as related to how we understand who we are, how we live and interact, and the original intention of God in creating human history. I also believe this creation story has much to do with developing a theology of conflict. Let me make several observations about this theology embedded in Genesis 1.

We are created in the image of God. There is "that of God" in each of us. How can we begin to fathom this idea that we, fragile and finite beings, somehow are like the God of history? There are many ways to approach the "image" dilemma. It is instructive to start with the more self-evident question: what, literally, is God doing in Genesis? This is better than trying to answer the far more complex question: who is God?

If we see what God is doing, we will have at least some idea of the nature of God in whose image we have been created. The immediate answer is quite simple: God is creating. This then begs another question: what does it take to create? I believe that the process of creation is built on several different levels of activity and meaning.

Idea. Creation starts with an idea, an image. It calls for the capacity to think, reflect, and plan. In other words, this involves projecting an idea beyond oneself.

Feeling. Creation is also connected to feeling. It is not simply an "idea" in the mind. The image we have relates to a feeling at a deeper gut level. We are "moved" to do something. We feel the idea. In other words, creation is rooted in passion and caring. I cannot help but note here that the word compassion rises from this "gut" feeling and image. Theologians note that, in the many instances that the term *compassion* emerges in Jesus's ministry, it is translated from a Greek phrase meaning "he was moved in the gut."

Action. At another level, creation calls for action. "Let's move on that idea," we say, with some passion. For an artist, the image felt moves toward expression. Action has movement, reaching out, and expression. It purposefully carries forward activity to struggle with and realize the idea. Like the process of birth, it takes something that was envisioned but not physically seen, heard, or felt, and brings it out into the world of sight, sound, and touch. Creation is an act.

When we look at the Genesis story, we see these same basic elements. God envisions and projects, reflects and plans. God feels and cares with passion. And God moves and acts in history. We too have these basic abilities. We are endowed with the capacities of thinking, reflecting, projecting, and acting. We act in history. In fact, we create the very history that we ourselves experience as real. We are ongoing cocreators of our own history, some of it for good and some of it that creates harm for ourselves and others. Nonetheless, we are participants.

Creation Commitments

In Genesis we find that God makes a series of creation commitments. These are specific characteristics or dynamics in the way God has envisioned and built our world. Here are three creation commitments that can inform our understanding of conflict and, ultimately, of reconciliation.

God is present within each of us. In the most significant act of creation, we were created in the image of God. In this act, we find the fundamental commitment that there will be that of God in each of us. We see this through the characteristics present within us that reflect the Creator: we are each provided with the capacity to think, reflect, feel, care, and act.

We can, in a most profound way, affirm what Jacob says in his encounter with his brother: "To see your face is like seeing the face of God."[3] Humanity and each of us as persons are given the gift of life, a gift that carries within it the presence and touch of God. There is that of God within each of us. As early Quakers taught, in peacemaking we need to speak to that of God in every person.

God values diversity. The second affirmation lies in the profound understatement that God created us "male and female." "Aha!" some will say. "Now we see the connection between Genesis 1 and conflict." There is a useful and important body of literature and research on gender differences and conflict. However, I am more interested here in the basic truth present in the creation story: that God brought forth diversity.

Differences and distinctions permeate the creation account. In the first chapter of Genesis, the phrase "of every kind" appears ten times, referring to seeds, plants, birds, fish, and animals. I am left with the overall picture of a rainforest, full of almost infinite varieties of life, or of a coral reef teeming with diverse creatures.

At another level are the careful distinctions to provide order and meaning. Light brings day and night. Earth is separated from the sky. The sky separates upper and lower waters. Water and land are moved apart. Each element is distinct from the other and yet only has identity and meaning as connected to each other in relationship.

The culmination of this process is the creation of humankind as male and female. This simple beginning becomes one of God's firm and consistent commitments. If you look around your family and blood relatives, those closest to you, you cannot find another person that is exactly like you. If you search your community and even your nation, still you will be unique.

Creation Commitments

1. God is present within each of us.
2. God values diversity.
3. God gives us Godlike freedom.

More than seven billion people inhabit the earth, and yet not one is exactly like the other. You can turn your sights back across history to the beginning of time, only to realize that there has never been one person created and living completely like another. Fraternal twins, for all their similarities, have distinctions and unique features. Identical twins are soon shaped by varied experiences. God has valued and continues to value diversity.

God gives us Godlike freedom. The third affirmation is found in the tree of the knowledge of good and evil.[4] This tree is often seen as the precursor to the Fall and the entry of sin into the Garden of Eden.[5] Humans were not satisfied with what God had given them and sought to be "like God."[6] We usually jump to the consequences of Adam and Eve's decisions. If we do so, we overlook the profound insight that God, in creating them, was committed to providing them with freedom of choice.

Perhaps more than any other characteristic, this commitment defines the very nature of God and the image in which we have been created. God is free: free to do, to choose, and to act. In this sense, the tree was necessary in order to provide the choice. This is the reality of freedom. Without opportunity, without choice, without freedom, humankind loses its unique place in the creation. We are created in the image of God to the degree that God was committed to giving us a Godlike freedom.

Humankind: A Dynamic Mix

On the surface, each of these creation commitments seems self-evident and rather simple. Combined, however, they make for quite a mix. Each human was created in the image of God with the capacity to think, reflect, project, feel, and act. And yet each was created as a unique individual, and each had the freedom to choose. All of this was built into the creation before the Fall.

Let us take a step back for a moment and consider the significance of this aspect of creation. With purpose and for fun, I have approached this issue in seminar formats with two illustrations, each involving a question.

First I ask the audience to compare a colony of ants and a colony of Christians like the ones at their church. I want them to identify what distinguishes humans from animals. At first, with laughter, they respond with similarities: "We work hard." "We live in communities." "We are pragmatic and want to get things done." "We all look similar."

Next come the distinctions. "We think and feel, but ants act by instinct." "We have choices and dreams." "We are quite diverse within our own species." "Each of us is a unique person with a soul and a mind and a Godlikeness." We note how much more dynamic and rich our life and experience are than those of ants, because we have this Godlikeness, and we are individuals with minds, hearts, and souls.

Then I add, "Oh, by the way, within their colony, ants don't fight." (A number of times I've had entomologists in the group, who have clarified the scientific facts around such a sweeping comment. With good humor, we usually agree that ants do not experience conflict like humans do.) Then as a second step, I ask them to use their imaginations. "Imagine for a moment," I say, "that you have been asked by the national government to build the perfect factory. You will be given all the natural and human resources you need. There will be no impediment to whatever you wish to try. How would you construct the perfect factory?"

The question is probing the issue of our natural inclinations as we think about building the perfect world. What regularly emerges is our temptation to put robot workers in the ideal factory. The place would work mechanically and without a hitch. People would be asked to do a particular job but not to think, dream, or make many choices. All the choices are already made. People are asked to follow instructions and make the product.

How interesting and ironic that such a place is set up to eliminate diversity and choice! It also eliminates conflict. When you read major novels about the future such as George Orwell's *1984* or Aldous Huxley's *Brave New World*, you see how those who were in control of the supposedly perfect world where everything works without a hitch conceived paradise as a place where conflict did not exist. To achieve such a condition in these worlds, the controllers of the world wiped out diversity and individuality, controlled information, and restricted imagination and choice. In other words, it is the exact opposite of God's creation commitments: Godlikeness in each, unique diversity for all, and freedom throughout.

On the sixth day, God looked over this creation and said, "It is very good." Quite frankly, it was a mess: a dynamic, rich, and wonderful mess. In my view, this is the central point of the creation commitments. The very elements that make human experience rich and dynamic, the characteristics missing in the experience of ants, are the elements that make conflict inevitable. By way of God-commitments in creation, conflict was, is, and will be a natural part of human experience. By the very way we are created, conflict will be a part of the human family.

Let us push this a bit further. Most of us recognize that conflict is a part of our lives and relationships today. However, there tends to be a common and rather strong perspective within Christian circles that conflict represents the presence of sin. Recognition of our fallen nature leads to the general perspective that conflict is in fact sin. On the other hand, God's creation commitments provide a different viewpoint. Built into God's original plan before the Fall, humankind was conceived in such a way that made differences and conflict normal and inevitable.

Adam and Eve were naming the animals and plants, feeding themselves, filling the earth, and being fruitful and multiplying. Can you imagine that they went about their tasks without disagreement and argument? Both were created in the image of God. Each was an individual, and each had freedom. Can you really imagine that they never argued or disagreed? How utterly boring, if that were the case!

The Genesis story sets the stage for conflict as a natural part of our relationships because of who we are, as God created us. Conflict in itself is not sin. But sin may enter into the situation, depending on how we approach conflict, how we deal with it, and especially how we treat each other. Sin is a feature of the quality of our relationships.

The signs of sin entering conflict appear when we want to be God, when we assume superiority, when we oppress, when we try to lord it over others, when we refuse to listen, when we discount and exclude others, when we hold back deep feelings, when we avoid, when we hate, and when we project blame with no self-reflection.

In sum, a Christian understanding of conflict is built on these basic creation commitments: God is present in each of us because we are created in the likeness of God. God values diversity. God is committed to give us freedom. These elements make our lives rich, ever-renewing, and interesting. They also make conflict a natural part of our relationships.

Notes

1. This essay is reprinted from John Paul Lederach, *Reconcile: Conflict Transformation for Ordinary Christians*, pp. 61–68, © 2014 by Herald Press, Harrisonburg, VA. Used with permission.
2. Genesis 1:27.
3. Genesis 33:10b.
4. Genesis 2:9,17.
5. Genesis 3.
6. Genesis 3:5.

PART 5

RELIGION AND PERSONAL CONFLICT

This last section contains one chapter; it ends this volume on the role of religious beliefs and identities in the experience of trauma. Laura M. Bennett-Murphy is a therapist who works extensively with refugees who have come to the United States from conflict zones. Her experience sheds light on how religious beliefs can contribute to the healing of trauma and violence. Based on her practice, Bennett-Murphy shares her observations and findings on the other side of religious force, the one that is powerful in providing stability and meaning in the recovery process of victims of trauma and violence.

This last contribution brings the volume full circle to the personal and internal relationship between religion, conflict, and the art of making peace; this art often starts with oneself. More than ever, the reality of entire populations displaced by conflict is entering our own reality. The ability to heal and to find meaning is therefore crucial for all of us; religious traditions and communities may be instrumental in this process. Bennett-Murphy provides an excellent frame to reflect on this question; furthermore, her bibliographical references allow for a full overview of the current research on the topic.

Contact, Connection, and Community

Religion and Peacemaking

LAURA M. BENNETT-MURPHY

With widespread global violence, many scholars have examined sociopolitical factors leading to war, terrorism, and intrastate violence.[1] There also
exists a rich exigent literature on the evolution of human aggression and
commission of atrocities.[2] In some cases, religion is identified as a cause
of acts of human victimization, especially when religion is connected
with the state.[3] Certainly, as a powerful human organizer, religion and
religious rhetoric have been deeply and insidiously involved in the commission of cultural and structural violence and oppression.[4] As Galtung
describes, aspects of culture, including religion, can be used to legitimize
direct structural violence as it "preaches, teaches, admonishes, eggs on,
and dulls us into seeing exploitation and/or repression as normal and
natural, or into not seeing them at all."[5] Yet, other scholars suggest that
religious rhetoric among violent offenders is merely a psychological tool,
not an index or reflection of religion.[6] Thus, many activists, individuals,
and communities experience religion as a formal, cultural call to peace.
While figures like the Dalai Lama or Mother Teresa are recognized as
peace advocates, relatively less is known about how ordinary communities and people draw upon religious faith to resist oppression and violence. Further, there has been relatively little systematic examination of

the myriad ways in which religions may promote social recovery from the chaos and horror of sociopolitical violence to restore peace.

In the circles in which I move (largely intellectual, humanistic, secular groups), I often encounter an unspoken ideology that faith is fine as long as it remains private. Religion is not private.[7] Religion is a communal expression and thus a social structure vulnerable to the vagaries and possibilities of human striving. Further, as a social ecology guiding interpersonal interactions, religion becomes internalized by individuals creating a filter through which they apprehend the world.[8] Whatever one's conscious belief system, those who develop within a religious community will be formed by it. Thus religion is not purely "transcendent." It is a social, interpersonal, and intrapersonal phenomenon. Consequently, understanding the relationship between religion and peace requires a multileveled, multilayered, systemic exploration. My esteemed colleagues in this edition have reflected on the role of liberation theology, politics, resistance movements, education, economics, and systemic interventions to promote peace and global stability. They thoughtfully consider issues of religion and peacebuilding in the broad, global theater. My stage is much smaller. I will examine the ways in which religion promotes adaptation and recovery among relocated refugees.

> Where, after all, do human rights begin? In small places close to home—so close and so small that they cannot be seen on any map of the world. Yet they are the world of the individual person.... Such are the places where every man, woman, and child seeks equal justice, equal opportunity, equal dignity.

> —Eleanor Roosevelt, Remarks at the United Nations, March 27, 1958

My work, though "global," transpires in the "small places." I meet my clients within the confines of the therapy consulting room, school classrooms, shelters, doctors' offices, and homes. In this essay, I reflect on the role of religion in the psychological healing of children, adults, families, and communities touched by violence. By definition, refugees have been persecuted due to the social groups, including, but not limited to, the religious groups to which they belong.[9] Further, they have been unprotected by the state. This triad of persecution, betrayal, and abandonment is a psychological centerpiece for refugees and refugee communities. All of my clients have survived severe war trauma and torture. At times, their victimization came at the hands of neighbors, social leaders, or kin. All experienced extreme and tremendous loss. For many, their histories are unspeakable. As Scarry and Hamber poignantly point out, there is "no language of pain."[10] The lived experiences of the refugees I serve are often beyond words, and in what Hamber and Gampel call the realm of "the unthinkable, the unspeakable, and 'the uncanny.'"[11] Yet amid the suffering, I am privileged to witness men, women, and children struggle to create communities of peace.

It is commonly accepted that violence begets violence, hatred leads to hatred.[12] Indeed, those who have suffered interpersonal violence are at increased risk for committing violent acts. For example, children who have been abused are more likely to victimize someone else in their lifetimes.[13] Further, when compared to those from civilian populations, former U.S. soldiers may be more likely to act violently toward family members and themselves.[14] Finally, refugees who have survived sociopolitical violence have relatively high rates of domestic violence.[15] Yet the vast majority of individuals who have survived terrible and horrific events do not go on to perpetrate such acts. Theirs is the quiet and heroic peace through which healing occurs. Theirs is the practice of respecting human rights in the smallest of places. Theirs are the stories of peace created in a shared meal, in the marketplace, at a funeral, huddled under a blanket, or over a cup of tea. Theirs are the stories of peace created by the faithful in mosques, temples, churches, and tents. Theirs are the stories of individuals and communities who resist violence, opting instead for the courageous journey of building peace from the rubble.

How do we understand such heroism? In the field of trauma studies, there is growing interest in the phenomenon of *resilience*. Understanding how individuals, communities, and societies not only survive war and trauma, but learn to recover, grow, and thrive is commanding the attention of scholars, educators, policymakers, and clinicians. The studies of resilience are wide-ranging, although most still focus on individual, not group, resilience. The lives of soldiers, Holocaust survivors, refugees, orphans of war, survivors of genocide, child soldiers, torture survivors, victims of interpersonal violence, and survivors of natural disasters, all have been examined.[16] Results suggest that resilience is not a trait, but rather, a lifelong, active process in the service of self-reintegration. Resilience may ebb and flow over a lifespan. And for the severely traumatized, resilience requires both good fortune and hard work. In a self-analysis, Holocaust survivor Henri Parens describes it such:

> Healing… has required active, vigorous, continuous, indeed lifelong efforts, conscious and unconscious. It has required efforts to cope with pain and loss of family, even uprooting from one's ongoing life and home; to mediate and sublimate one's omnipresent reactive rage; to accept the Kafkaesque reality and have a sustainable explanation for what happened, all in order to repair, to regenerate, and to prevent maladaptive defects and sequelae of this specific trauma. The will to live, to overcome, must prevail over passive surrender to brutally sadistic traumatization.[17]

The findings are clear. Even amid the horror and devastation of unspeakable violence can be found "the unbroken soul."[18]

Cyrulnik and Causa eloquently and succinctly remind us that resilience involves "making sense out of chaos."[19] At its heart, resilience is an act of resistance against adversity and creative action toward recovery. Resilience results from the interplay of constitutional, familial, and societal factors (known as the "Garmezy-Luthar triadic processes")[20] which dynamically interact in service of three functions. They promote *relatedness, agency,* and *reflectiveness.*[21] Almost all studies of resilience identify spirituality, faith, and/or religion as societal cornerstones of resilience.[22] In individuals, religiosity has been linked to better physical health, greater psychological well-being, and recovery from trauma.[23] Religions can serve not only as a wellspring of hope, but also as a source of coherence and connection. For survivors of extreme violence, restoration of and reconnection with community is essential to recovery. Religion may serve as a bridge from the isolation of personal horror and loss, to the common ground of human suffering and companionship. By creating pathways for relatedness (to God and others), agency (religious service and action), and reflection (prayer or meditation), religion serves two critical functions of healing: providing a meaningful and flexible narrative of suffering ("the uncanny"), and creating connection with community (both present and past). In order to better understand these functions, we must first apprehend what is threatened and lost when individuals, families, and communities experience trauma and sociopolitical violence.

The Refugee Experience

What is madness but nobility of soul
At odds with circumstance? The day is on fire!
I know the purity of pure despair.

—Theodore Roethke[24]

More than a decade ago, the United Nations issued a crisis call. Considering the horrific nature of contemporary violent conflicts, a UN Report (2002) noted that wars are "increasingly being fought in homes, communities, and on women's bodies." This disturbing trend was reflected in a United Nations Children's Fund report which indicated that the proportion of civilian, noncombatant war casualties, the majority of whom are women and children, increased over twenty years from 5 percent to 90 percent.[25] In many conflicts, winning the "hearts of the people" is no longer a strategic goal. Rather the installation of chaos, terror, suspicion, and isolation allow for the consolidation of power.[26]

Thus attacks on women, families, children, and communities are particularly useful because they serve to disrupt and destroy community and resistance. Refugees are targeted because of the social groups to which they belong. These may be "racial" or ethnic groups. They may be social or political groups, or they may be religious groups or sects. Armed groups, then, purposefully and systematically cut individuals off from the communities, families, and faith in which they lived. Survivors of sociopolitical violence must eventually come to terms with the abuse they experienced. They face added challenges, however. Survivors must create meaning out of atrocity. They also must grapple with the personal and social implications of persecution based on group membership. Many must find ways to reconcile the knowledge that the perpetrators were neighbors or colleagues. Some must come to terms with the acts of violence they perpetrated during conflict, or acknowledge their failure to assist others in dire circumstances. This recovery is not a private event. It occurs in a social context laden with betrayals, failures of protection, shared pain, and a "tidal wave of emotion."[27]

Stages of the Refugee Experience

The refugee experience typically occurs in stages that may last for weeks, months, or years. First, refugees experience a period of escalating threat, known as "preflight." In this period, antilocution escalates, as in Rwanda when radio stations broadcast warnings about the Tutsi people, calling them "cockroaches." Social structures may begin to erode or function poorly. The breakdown of the social ecology is particularly toxic for children's development. Disappearances occur. Gunshots may be heard in neighboring areas. Threats are made. Businesses may be vandalized or looted. Often it becomes less safe for children to attend school. Rumors and fear abound.

The second stage is the period of "disaster and flight." During this stage, violence erupts. Perhaps soldiers enter one's community. A family member may be murdered, a home invaded. Individuals and families realize that they are in serious and mortal danger. They can no longer remain at home. The flight period may last days or years. There is a global trend for protracted refugee status, with some people living in refugee camps for years or their lifetime.[28] This period is characterized by chaos, instability, and danger.

The third, final, and longest stage involves relocation and acculturation. This stage begins when refugee status is granted and the individual or family is relocated out of societal danger. The relocation stage may include accompanying feelings of relief, disbelief, hope, and disorientation. While physical safety now has been addressed, the refugee must confront living as a stranger in a strange land. For many, the terrors of the past "catch up." Grief and loss may be profound, as "home" loses meaning.[29] A drawing of a recently relocated child of war powerfully presents the disorientation and destabilization of the early period in the relocation phase. When I asked this ten-year-old child to draw "home," she replied, "I don't have one." I asked her to imagine what "home" might look like.

Although one cannot see it clearly, the ground is drawn with brown and green colored pencil. It is half dead. The home floats in space, foundationless and far above the ground. When I asked the child to describe her drawing, she responded, "No one can live there." Then she elaborated. "I don't know where this is. Maybe Syria or Turkey because of the fig tree. But we don't have roofs like that in Syria, so maybe Turkey or the U.S. I don't know. No one can live there." She went on to describe that in her home one could see the curtains and kitchen table. Her walls, her protection, were permeable; the boundaries could not hold. The internal and external worlds were colliding in ways that felt uninhabitable. Yet there were suggestions of resilience. Flowers, ripening figs, and a smiling sun trying to emerge from behind the clouds were in evidence. Life continued.

In addition to disorientation, acculturation brings a host of stresses including learning a new language, understanding new customs, trying to make a living, and encountering poverty, racism, xenophobia, and marginalization. Children often acculturate at a faster rate than parents, bringing more tension into the family. Children may struggle with feelings of inferiority, parentification, or shame. Individuals within the family may be coping with shared and private trauma and their recoveries may proceed at differing paces. As cultures and religions clash, parents frequently report to me that they saved their child's life by coming to the United States, only to lose his or her soul. Further, extended families often are separated in a global diaspora. Some research indicates that psychological and emotional distress are greatest in this third stage.[30]

Yet, the third stage often offers people the first chance to try to make meaning of the horror they have experienced. With relative safety at hand, individuals and families are challenged to understand and heal from the suffering and loss brought about by war. They must learn to tolerate extreme levels of distress. They must grieve and mourn. They must cope with memories of what was done and what was witnessed. At the same time, they must try to build a new and meaningful life. Religion may promote healing, especially during this stage.

Telling the Story

A critical process in recovery from massive trauma lies in telling the story. This can be terrifying for survivors, for as the individual begins to structure her story, the self comes once again into contact with overwhelming events. Yet the silence of not speaking is devastatingly and profoundly harmful. It leaves one forever alone, bound in the presence of violence which cannot be understood. Locked in silence, stories tend to become rigidified, deadened. Consider for a moment, the picture drawn by an eight-year-old child. Aaqil[31] moved with his family to the United States from his war-torn homeland. The United States had a strong military presence in his country of origin. Aaqil's uncle had been murdered. His father had been threatened and beaten unconscious. Aaqil's only explanation for the violence was that "they" were killing people based on their names. Aaqil was uncertain who the perpetrators were and there was much confusion about who was a "good guy" and who was a "bad guy." Aaqil's entire family was highly traumatized. No one spoke of the violence they had witnessed or of their ambivalence about the United States. In our first session, I invited Aaqil to draw a picture of his home.

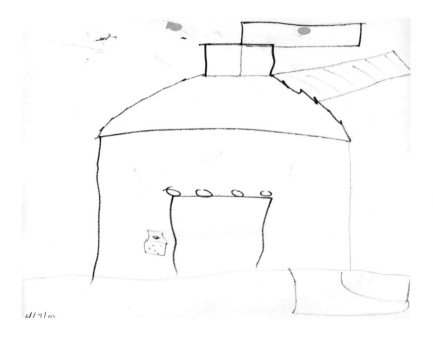

Aaqil described his home as having steel bulletproof walls, more than a foot thick (explained by gesture). There were no windows and only one door. The door was monitored by sensors and motion detectors above. It also was thick and made of steel. To the left of the door was the entry keypad. It had a retinal scanner and fingerprint reader. The only two humans allowed entrance were Aaqil and the "mad scientist" with whom he lived. Aaqil described that while the mad scientist occasionally left home to purchase food and building supplies, Aaqil himself did not leave. In this "safe house" the two developed weapons, machines, and inventions. While the roof was impenetrable, it contained a giant telescope which allowed Aaqil to gaze at the stars and heavens.

In his drawing we witness the desperate isolation, the need for protection, the barren inner world, the companionship of "madness," and the terror of a child exposed to violence. But within it, we also view kernels of resilience. We hear of Aaqil's agency in his description of constructing weapons and inventions. We also see attempts at reflection. Cut off from the living world, Aaqil holds on to a vision of a universe beyond, the light of the heavens. In the heavens lie possibilities.

It is important to realize that trauma does not reside within horrific events, not even the assault on Aaqil's family. Rather, trauma lies in the mental representation of those events. For a child like Aaqil, there was no way to incorporate and represent massive trauma. All he could do was creatively build a fortress. His story, his representation of the trauma, became rigid and static. It did not allow for relatedness, nor did it offer much in the way of meaning making. While protective, it also reified a traumatic world view. In order for healing to occur, the story needed to shift. Others needed to be allowed entry. Aaqil needed freedom of movement from the home. Further, his relationship to the heavens needed to be understood, developed, and supported.

For a story to be healing, and not retraumatizing, several things must occur. First is the recognition that the story is not about the "facts." A verbal repetition of the violence that was perpetrated is not, in and of itself, healing and may be harmful.[32] However, saying that, I recognize that I enter into dangerous waters. As Danieli described, there is often a powerful collusion between perpetrators and victims, therapists and clients, and survivors and bystanders toward a "conspiracy of silence."[33] Many of my clients express significant hesitancy in sharing their stories. In addition to their own fear of reconnecting with past events, they believe that those unaffected (i.e., residents of the United States) will not want to hear or should be protected from the horrific realities of the world. They do not want to blemish innocence. In addition, there is fear of retraumatizing others from their home culture. When everyone has been touched by violence, there is a sense of inescapability. Further, this shared trauma magnifies its impact, overwhelming and fragmenting social groups.

Shame is a third powerful inhibiting factor in sharing one's story. Many survivors feel shame over their experiences (torture, rape, abandoning others along a roadside) or shame about their emotional responses to terrible events. Kauffman suggests that shame is a "common and pervasive feature of the human response to death and other loss."[34] The ubiquity and multiplicity of shame make it particularly challenging to work with in traumatized refugees. Refugees have been targeted not for what they have done, but for who they are. This violence based on identity may serve to magnify shame.

In spite of the many barriers, what appears to be healing in "telling the story" is the sharing of one's experience with an attentive and compassionate other. Meaning is created in a social context or, as Cyrulnik and Causa describe, "the starting point is in someone else's mind."[35] This clearly requires the presence of a listener. In the storytelling, the self has the potential to come into contact more deeply with his or her own experiences, feelings, and thoughts. Yet, the act of telling a story also brings the self into relationship with an "other." The privileged listener becomes a witness as the self bears witness to her experiences. This intersubjectivity becomes the foundation for the new related and resilient self to develop. So fundamental is this process that without it individuals may experience a sense of annihilation. Our very existence, our subjectivity, is always in relation to another. Thus the danger when one's story is silenced and unshared. If one is fortunate, these "others" become internalized so that throughout our lives, we may remain engaged in dialogue with an internal witness.[36] Felman and Laub suggest that the inner witness is necessary for a sense of one's self as a subjective agent.[37] Torture destroys the inner witness and thus threatens one's very subjectivity, fostering a sense of annihilation of the self. In their studies of Holocaust survivors, Felman and Laub see this destruction of the inner witness as being central to the psychological experience of survivors. As witnesses were quite literally destroyed, reality became unreal, the self, unknowable. They argue that this experience explains some of the spontaneous deaths in concentration camps that seemed to result from "loss of hope," while also accounting for the difficulty of some survivors to adjust in the postwar years.

Philosopher and ethicist Kelly Oliver argues that "witnessing," to conceive of oneself as a subject who can address and respond to another, is the key to survival and healing. She also argues that bearing witness to the lives of others is the cornerstone of peace. Recognition of a struggle is not enough. We must be able to bear witness to "oppression, domination, subordination, enslavement, and torture in ways that open up the possibility of a more humane and ethical future beyond violence."[38]

Religion and Bearing Witness

So what is the role of religion in transformative storytelling and witnessing? How might religion serve recovery from violence and trauma? First, we must be clear that religions don't act, people do. Yet, religions offer ideals, and religions offer rituals for human striving.[39] Thus religions may serve as mechanisms by which individuals reconnect and reconcile with themselves, others, and a creative life source which offers meaning. Again, these very mechanisms act in service of resilience by promoting relatedness, agency, and reflection.

With respect to storytelling, religions offer narratives, parables, and role models for suffering and redemption.[40] Religious leaders may support healing stories through rituals and practices of reconciliation, pastoral counseling, or witnessing. Religions also teach ideals of love, altruism, compassion, forgiveness, hope, dignity, and "goodness."[41] Religions may offer rituals for purification and cleansing, or new beginnings. Religions provide for a compassionate witness in the community, through saints or prophets, fellow congregants, or a divine theistic figure. Religious communities offer social support in times of need. Further, religions foster a positive world view, a sense of control, personal empowerment, shared communal responsibility, and guidance for decision making.[42]

Finally, religions transcend time and place. They serve to bring people into contact with the transcendent, as in Aaqil's search for the heavens. Religions provide answers to "ultimate questions" and systems of meaning and purpose. Elie Wiesel once suggested that the most important question a human being must face is "[w]hy are we here?" When others have died, when one's existence has been threatened, as for refugees, this question looms large. Religions may not offer an answer, but they offer a promise of meaning and pathways for pursuing the question. Finally, for children, especially refugee children, religion may create a powerful bridge across generations. It may link past, present, and future in an otherwise fragmented life history. One's life may shift dramatically, but through the practice of religion one is brought into contact with prayers that have been repeated by millions over generations and across miles.

I would like to share the story of one of my clients. This client is a refugee from a war-torn nation and a devout Muslim. She is the mother of several children. Her eldest child fell in love with a Christian. One day, that child did not return home. For days, the mother searched for this child. She called all known friends and family. She walked the streets and visited hospitals. She went to morgues. There were so many bodies, they could not be kept in the refrigerated rooms. Instead, they lay rotting on the floor. She walked the rows and piles of bodies: men, women, children. These people had been tortured, murdered, decapitated, eviscerated. Limbs had been severed. She walked and walked through the bodies, praying not to find her child, while creating fearful images of how her child might be suffering. Exhausted and bereft, she left the morgue and sat down on a bench. She looked down at her shoes and saw pieces of human flesh stuck to the soles. Horrified and grief-stricken, she lay down on the bench and fell asleep.

As she slept, she dreamt.

In her dream she was awakened from her troubled sleep by two women. These women guided her from the bench and through the city. They led her to a large estate outside of the city, and through a beautiful courtyard. They removed her soiled clothing and bathed her. They washed her hair and cleansed her. Then she was given new white clothing. She was fed and rested. Then she was summoned. She was directed to walk up a very long set of stone stairs, set into the courtyard wall. She climbed the many stairs alone. As she reached the top of the stairs, she was met by Jesus. He greeted her with a smile and took her hand. He led her along the top of the stone wall and past a line of great prophets. She was led to a tent where the prophet Mohammed sat. She stood alone in front of Mohammed who blessed her.

From this dream, my client awoke. She was still grief-stricken, dirty, and frightened. But she no longer felt as alone. She felt stronger. She felt comforted. And she felt somehow "called" or "blessed" in her suffering. In the torturous days and nights that followed, my client survived. She looks back on this experience not as a dream, but as a vision and a calling. From her isolation, she was touched by compassionate love and called to care for others who suffer. Within the local refugee community, this woman is a "mother" to many. She is respected and called upon by others for her wisdom. She generously gives and shares, reaching out to others. She still experiences pain, nightmares, and sorrow. But she remains resilient.

The images of her dream speak to the internalization of the healing elements of religion. She was comforted, fed, and cleansed. She joined the prophets and martyrs. She connected symbols of both her faith and the faith of her child's partner in a benevolent and caring fashion. In treatment, she shared this dream in the same session that I first learned of the details of her child's abduction and murder. In her mind, her suffering and trauma were deeply embedded and contextualized within this dream of care and compassionate love.

Conclusions

Trauma and violence silence. They isolate. Resilience is largely determined by how people come to make sense of horrific, meaningless events, and ultimately come together in community.[43] Traumatic narratives must be spoken, heard, and witnessed. Narratives foster resilience when they become flexible, coherent, culturally contextualized, and allow for connection. Having another bear witness to your suffering restores agency, subjectivity, and relatedness, and promotes reflection. As in the drawings presented in this chapter, traumatic narratives tend to be limited and rigid (the safe house), or chaotic and incoherent (absence of home). But through connecting our story to a larger framework, religion, by experiencing ourselves in relation to others and to something greater than ourselves, we can create more integrated, dynamic, healing narratives and perhaps a more peaceful world. Scholars of truth and reconciliation commissions regarding sociopolitical violence continue to explore whether or not "truth-telling" can prevent future violence.[44] Sharing one's story, however, does seem integral to healing and reparation from past wounds for both individuals and communities.

Religion provides a social and transcendent context in which one can share in, and make meaning of, human suffering. As Rolheiser states, community is a constitutive element of religion and true worship.[45] He describes religion as ultimately communitarian, a shared search, not for self, but for the face of God. He continues, declaring that

> [religious] community is not had by joining others who share our fears and, with them, barricading ourselves against what threatens us. It is had when, on the basis of something more powerful than our fears, we emerge from our locked rooms and begin to take down walls.[46]

Ultimately, religion demands that we are accountable to one another.[47] In praying together, sharing feasts and fears, celebrating daily events and holy rites, mutually managing property and finances, we are knit together in humility and humanity. As part of a community responsible for one another's well-being we are called to create a more peaceful and ethical world. We are called to hear and bear witness to the suffering of those who are oppressed in this world.

> Never be silent whenever and wherever human beings endure suffering and humiliation. We must take sides. Neutrality helps the oppressor, never the victim. Silence encourages the tormentor, never the tormented.[48]

We are called to act on one another's behalf. In the words of Dag Hammarskjold, first secretary general of the United Nations, "the road to holiness necessarily passes through the world of action." We must have the courage to tell stories of atrocity and to hear them, as well. For in this shared subjectivity lie relatedness and love. Like Aaqil, we may keep our eyes on the heavens, recognizing our connection to something greater than ourselves, but we must not fear breaking down the walls.

Notes

1. Daniel Chirot and Martin E. P. Seligman, eds., *Ethnopolitical Warfare: Causes, Consequences, and Possible Solutions* (Washington, D.C.: American Psychological Association, 2001).

2. Compare Roy F. Baumeister, *Evil: Inside Human Violence and Cruelty* (New York: Henry Holt and Company, 1999); and Chirot and Seligman, *Ethnopolitical Warfare*.

3. Peter S. Henne, "The Two Swords: Religion-State Connections and Interstate Disputes," *Journal of Peace Research* 49, no. 6 (November 22, 2012): 753–68.

4. Charles Farhadian and Robert A. Emmons, "The Psychology of Forgiveness in the World Religions," in *Forgiveness and Reconciliation: Psychological Pathways to Conflict Transformation and Peace Building*, ed. Ani Kalayjian and Raymond F. Paloutzian, 55–70 (New York: Springer, 2010); Brandon Hamber, *Transforming Societies after Political Violence: Truth, Reconciliation, and Mental Health* (New York: Springer, 2009).

5. Johan Galtung, "Cultural Violence," *Journal of Peace Research* 27, no. 3 (August 1990): 295.

6. Henry Munson, "Religion and Violence," *Religion* 35, no. 4 (2005): 223–46.

7. Ronald Rolheiser, *The Holy Longing: The Search for a Christian Spirituality* (New York: Image, 1999).

8. Urie Bronfenbrenner, *The Ecology of Human Development: Experiments by Nature and Design* (Cambridge, MA: Harvard University Press, 1979).

9. United Nations High Commissioner for Refugees, *Convention and Protocol Relating to the Status of Refugees* (UNHCR, 1951), http://www.unhcr.org/3b66c2aa10.html.

10. Elaine Scarry, *The Body in Pain: The Making and Unmaking of the World* (New York: Oxford University Press, 1985); Hamber, *Transforming Societies after Political Violence*.

11. Hamber, *Transforming Societies after Political Violence*, 22.

12. Martin Luther King Jr., "Loving Your Enemies" (sermon, Dexter Avenue Baptist Church, Montgomery, AL, November 17, 1957), http://mlkonline.com.

13. Lina S. Millett et al., "Child Maltreatment Victimization and Subsequent Perpetration of Young Adult Intimate Partner Violence: An Exploration of Mediating Factors," *Child Maltreatment* 18, no. 2 (May 2013): 71–84.

14. For example, Matthew K. Nock et al., "Suicide among Soldiers: A Review of Psychosocial Risk and Protective Factors," *Psychiatry: Interpersonal and Biological Processes* 76, no. 2 (June 2013): 97–125; and S. Walker, "Assessing the Mental Health Consequences of Military Combat in Iraq and Afghanistan: A Literature Review," *Journal of Psychiatric and Mental Health Nursing* 17, no. 9 (November 2010): 790–96.

15. Kerrie James, "Domestic Violence Within Refugee Families: Intersecting Patriarchal Culture and the Refugee Experience," *Australian & New Zealand Journal of Family Therapy* 31, no. 3 (September 2010): 275–84.

16. Compare Henri Parens, Harold P. Blum, and Salman Akhtar, *The Unbroken Soul: Tragedy, Trauma, and Resilience* (Lanham, MD: Jason Aronson, 2008); Steven M. Southwick and Dennis S. Charney, *Resilience: The Science of*

Mastering Life's Greatest Challenges (New York: Cambridge University Press, 2013); and Emmy E. Werner and Ruth S. Smith, *Journeys from Childhood to Midlife: Risk, Resilience, and Recovery* (Ithaca, NY: Cornell University Press, 2001).

17. Parens, Blum, and Akhtar, *The Unbroken Soul*, 92–93.
18. Ibid.
19. Boris Cyrulnik and Hon. Causa, "Children in War and Their Resiliencies," in Parens, Blum, and Akhtar, *The Unbroken Soul*, 26.
20. Parens, Blum, and Akhtar, *The Unbroken Soul*.
21. Ibid.
22. Compare Southwick and Charney, *Resilience*; and John Tuskan, "Religion, Spirituality, and Faith in the Care of Torture Survivors" (webinar, National Capacity Building Webinar Series, April 29, 2009), http://vimeo.com/38390246.
23. Compare Thomas G. Plante, "Fruit of Faith, Fruit of the Spirit," in *Religion, Spirituality, and Positive Psychology: Understanding the Psychological Fruits of Faith*, ed. Thomas G. Plante (Santa Barbara, CA: Praeger, 2008), 3–8; and Southwick and Charney, Resilience.
24. Theodore Roethke, "In a Dark Time," in *The Collected Poems of Theodore Roethke* (New York: Anchor Books, 1964), 231.
25. Isaiah D. Wexler, David Branski, and Eitan Kerem, "War and Children," *Journal of the American Medical Association* 296, no. 5 (August 2, 2006): 579–81.
26. Theresa S. Betancourt, "The Social Ecology of Resilience in War-Affected Youth: A Longitudinal Study from Sierra Leone," in *The Social Ecology of Resilience: A Handbook of Theory and Practice*, ed. Michael Ungar (New York: Springer, 2012), 347–56; UN System Task Team on the Post-2015 UN Development Agenda: Peace and Security, http://www.un.org/millenniumgoals/pdf/14_peace_and_security_20July.pdf ; and Rafif Jouejati, "Local Coordination Committees (LCC) in Syria" (2014), http://www.lccsyria.org.
27. Hamber, *Transforming Societies after Political Violence*, 37.
28. United Nations High Commissioner for Refugees, *UNHCR Statistical Yearbook* (UNHCR, 2012), http://www.unhcr.org/52a7213b9.html.
29. Renos K. Papadopoulos, *Therapeutic Care for Refugees: No Place Like Home* (London: Karnac Books, 2002).
30. Laura Simich, Hayley Hamilton, and B. Khamisa Baya, "Mental Distress, Economic Hardship and Expectations of Life in Canada among Sudanese Newcomers," *Transcultural Psychiatry* 43, no. 3 (September 2006): 418–44.
31. All names and details have been changed to protect the privacy of clients. Stories are composites of several cases to reflect general themes and truths.
32. Babette Rothschild, *The Body Remembers: The Psychophysiology of Trauma and Trauma Treatment* (New York: W. W. Norton & Company, 2000).
33. Yael Danieli, "Psychotherapist's Participation in the Conspiracy of Silence about the Holocaust," *Psychoanalytic Psychology* 1, no. 1 (December 1984): 23–42.
34. Jeffrey Kauffman, "On the Primacy of Shame," in *The Shame of Death, Grief, and Trauma*, ed. Jeffrey Kauffman (New York: Routledge, 2010), 3–24.
35. Cyrulnik and Causa, "Children in War and Their Resiliencies," 23.

36. Kelly Oliver, *Witnessing: Beyond Recognition* (Minneapolis: University of Minnesota Press, 2001); D. W. Winnicott, "Mirror-role of Mother and Family in Child Development," in *Playing and Reality* (Abingdon, UK: Tavistock Publications, 1971).

37. Shoshana Felman and Dori Laub, *Testimony: Crises of Witnessing in Literature, Psychoanalysis and History* (New York: Routledge, 1992).

38. Oliver, *Witnessing*, 18.

39. Farhadian and Emmons, "The Psychology of Forgiveness in the World Religions."

40. Ibid.; Plante, *Religion, Spirituality, and Positive Psychology*.

41. King, "Loving Your Enemies"; Plante, *Religion, Spirituality, and Positive Psychology*; and Everett L. Worthington Jr. et al., "Forgiveness," in *Plante, Religion, Spirituality, and Positive Psychology*, 63–78.

42. Plante, Religion, Spirituality, and Positive Psychology.

43. Hamber, *Transforming Societies after Political Violence*; Judith Herman, *Trauma and Recovery: The Aftermath of Violence—from Domestic Abuse to Political Terror* (New York: Basic Books, 1992); Nora Sveaass and Marcia Castillo, "From War Hero to Cripple: An Interview Study on Psychosocial Intervention and Social Reconstruction in Nicaragua," *Peace and Conflict: Journal of Peace Psychology* 6, no. 2 (June 2000): 113–33.

44. Hamber, *Transforming Societies after Political Violence*.

45. Rolheiser, *The Holy Longing*.

46. Ibid., 116.

47. Ibid.

48. Elie Wiesel, "Acceptance Speech" (speech, Nobel Peace Prize, Oslo, Norway, December 10, 1986), http://www.nobelprize.org/nobel_prizes/peace/laureates/1986/wiesel-acceptance_en.html.

BIBLIOGRAPHY

Abdul Rauf, Feisal. *Moving the Mountain: A New Vision of Islam in America*. New York: Free Press, 2012.

Abu-Nimer, Mohammed. *Dialogue, Conflict Resolution, and Change: Arab-Jewish Encounters in Israel*. Albany: State University of New York Press, 1999.

Abu-Nimer, Mohammed, Emily Welty, and Amal I. Khoury. *Unity in Diversity: Interfaith Dialogue in the Middle East*. Washington, D.C.: United States Institute of Peace, 2007.

Accattoli, Luigi. *Quand le pape demande pardon*. Paris: Albin Michel, 1997.

Ahlstrom, Sydney E. *A Religious History of the American People*. New Haven, CT: Yale University Press, 1972.

Allan, Pierre, and Alexis Keller, eds. *What Is a Just Peace?* Oxford: Oxford University Press, 2006.

Anderson, Timothy, Kirk M. Lunnen, and Benjamin M. Ogles. "Putting Models and Techniques in Context." In *The Heart and Soul of Change: Delivering What Works in Therapy*, edited by Barry L. Duncan et al. 2d ed. Washington, D.C.: American Psychological Association, 2010.

Angelou, Maya. *On the Pulse of Morning*. New York: Random House, 1993.

Appleby, Scott. "Pope John Paul II." *Foreign Policy* 119 (summer 2000): 12–25.

Armstrong, Karen. *Fields of Blood: Religion and the History of Violence*. New York: Anchor Books, 2015.

Auerbach, Yehudith. "National Narratives in a Conflict of Identity." *In Barriers to Peace in the Israeli-Palestinian Conflict*, edited by Yaacov Bar-Sima-Tov, 99–134. Jerusalem: Jerusalem Institute for Israel Studies, 2010.

Avruch, Kevin, and Beatriz Vejarano. "Truth and Reconciliation Commissions: A Review Essay and Annotated Bibliography." *The Online Journal of Peace and Conflict Resolution* 4, no. 2 (spring 2002): 37–76.

Aziz, Parwen. "Damn Tree: A Reflection about Colombian Oil Palm Trees." ECAP Colombia (March 21, 2014). http://www.ecapcolombia.org/en/2014/03/damn-tree-a-reflection-about-colombian-oil-palm-trees/.

Baird, Robert. *Religion in America*. New York: Harper & Brothers, 1844.

Barrera, Jorge, and Kenneth Jackson. "Chiefs Take Fight to House of Commons' Doorstep." *APTN National News* (December 4, 2012). http://aptn.ca/news/2012/12/04/chiefs-take-fight-to-house-of-commons-doorstep/.

Baumeister, Roy F. *Evil: Inside Human Violence and Cruelty*. New York: Henry Holt and Company, 1999.

Bellah, Robert N. "Civil Religion in America." In *Beyond Belief: Essays on Religion in a Post-Traditionalist World*, 168–89. Berkeley: University of California Press, 1991.

———. "Civil Religion in America." *Daedalus: Journal of the American Academy of Arts and Sciences*, 96, no. 1 (winter 1967): 1–21.

Bellah, Robert N., et al. *Habits of the Heart: Individualism and Commitment in American Life*. New York: Perennial, 1985.

Bellinger, Charles K. "Religion and Violence: A Bibliography." *Hedgehog Review* 6, no. 1 (spring 2004): 111–19.

Bercovitch, Sacvan. *The American Jeremiad*. Madison: University of Wisconsin Press, 1978.

Berlinerblau, Jacques. *Thumpin' It: The Use and Abuse of the Bible in Today's Presidential Politics*. Louisville, KY: Westminster John Knox Press, 2008.

Bermanzohn, Sally A. *Through Survivors' Eyes: From the Sixties to the Greensboro Massacre*. Nashville: Vanderbilt University Press, 2003.

Betancourt, Theresa S. "The Social Ecology of Resilience in War-Affected Youth: A Longitudinal Study from Sierra Leone." *In The Social Ecology of Resilience: A Handbook of Theory and Practice*, edited by Michael Ungar, 347–56. New York: Springer, 2012.

Breggin, Peter R., and David Cohen. *Your Drug May Be Your Problem: How and Why to Stop Taking Psychiatric Medications*. New York: Da Capo Press, 2000.

Bronfenbrenner, Urie. *The Ecology of Human Development: Experiments by Nature and Design*. Cambridge, MA: Harvard University Press, 1979.

Brown, Emma. "Texas Officials: Schools Should Teach that Slavery Was 'Side Issue' to Civil War." *Washington Post* (July 5, 2015).

Butler, Jon. *Awash in a Sea of Faith: Christianizing the American People*. Cambridge, MA: Harvard University Press, 1990.

Carlson, John D. "A Just or Holy War of Independence? The Revolution's Legacy for Religion, Violence, and American Exceptionalism." In Carlson and Ebel, *From Jeremiad to Jihad*, 197–219.

———. "Religion and Violence: Coming to Terms with Terms." *In The Blackwell Companion to Religion and Violence*, edited by Andrew R. Murphy, 7–22. Oxford: Wiley-Blackwell, 2011.

Carlson, John D., and Jonathan H. Ebel, eds. *From Jeremiad to Jihad: Religion, Violence, and America*. Berkeley: University of California Press, 2012.

Cavanaugh, William T. "Does Religion Cause Violence?" *Harvard Divinity Bulletin* 35, nos. 2–3 (spring/summer 2007).

———. *The Myth of Religious Violence: Secular Ideology and the Roots of Modern Conflict*. Oxford: Oxford University Press, 2009.

Chafe, William H. *Civilities and Civil Rights: Greensboro, North Carolina, and the Black Struggle for Freedom*. New York: Oxford University Press, 1981.

Chenoweth, Erica, and Maria J. Stephan. *Why Civil Resistance Works: The Strategic Logic of Nonviolent Conflict*. New York: Columbia University Press, 2011.

"Chief Theresa Spence to End Hunger Strike Today." *CBC News* (last updated January 24, 2013). http://www.cbc.ca/1.1341571.

Chirot, Daniel, and Martin E. P. Seligman, eds. *Ethnopolitical Warfare: Causes, Consequences, and Possible Solutions.* Washington, D.C.: American Psychological Association, 2001.

Chodron, Pema. *Practicing Peace in Times of War.* Boston: Shambhala, 2003.

Christiansen, Drew. "John Paul II Peacemaker: A Nonviolent Pope in a Time of Terror." Unpublished paper, 2005.

Clinebell, Howard. *Ecotherapy: Healing Ourselves, Healing the Earth.* New York: Haworth Press, 1996.

"COLOMBIA: The Body Shop Terminates Trading Relationship with Daabon—a Great Step Forward for the People of Las Pavas." *Christian Peacemaker Teams* (October 4, 2010). http://www.cpt.org/cptnet/2010/10/04/colombia-body-shop-terminates-trading-relationship-daabon%E2%80%94-great-step-forward-peop.

"COLOMBIA: Rural Families Celebrate Ruling on Las Pavas." *Christian Peacemaker Teams* (November 26, 2012). http://www.cpt.org/cptnet/2012/11/26/colombia-rural-families-celebrate-ruling-las-pavas.

Corrigan, John. "New Israel, New Amalek: Biblical Exhortations to Religious Violence." In Carlson and Ebel, *From Jeremiad to Jihad*, 111–27.

Cose, Ellis. *Bone to Pick: Of Forgiveness, Reconciliation, Reparation, and Revenge.* New York: Simon and Schuster, 2004.

Coward, Harold, and Gordon Smith, eds. *Religion and Peacebuilding.* Albany: State University of New York Press, 2004.

"CPT INTERNATIONAL: Mission, Vision and Values." *Christian Peacemaker Teams* (June 21, 2012). http://www.cpt.org/cptnet/2012/06/21/cpt-international-mission-vision-and-values.

"Damn Tree: A Reflection about Colombian Oil Palm Trees." *ECAP Columbia* (March 20, 2014). http://www.cpt.org/cptnet/2014/03/20/iraqi-kurdistan-reflection-damn-tree.

Danieli, Yael. "Psychotherapist's Participation in the Conspiracy of Silence about the Holocaust." *Psychoanalytic Psychology* 1, no. 1 (December 1984): 23–42.

Daye, Russell. *Political Forgiveness: Lessons from South Africa.* Maryknoll, NY: Orbis Books, 2004.

De Lubac, Henri. *At the Service of the Church: Henri De Lubac Reflects on the Circumstances That Occasioned His Writings.* San Francisco, CA: Ignatius Press, 1993.

Derezotes, David. "Ideology Identification as Psychosocial-Spiritual Disorder: A Framework for Assessment and Intervention." *Journal of Religion & Spirituality in Social Work* 32, no. 2 (April/June 2014): 145–59.

———. *Transforming Historical Trauma through Dialogue.* Thousand Oaks, CA: Sage Publications, 2013.

Derezotes, David, et al. "Spiritual Maturity: An Exploratory Study and Model for Social Work Practice." *Currents: New Scholarship in the Human Services* 7, no. 1 (2008): 1–18.

Ebel, Jonathan H. "From Covenant to Crusade and Back: American Christianity and the Late Great War." In Carlson and Ebel, *From Jeremiad to Jihad*, 62–77.

Elshtain, Jean Bethke. "International Justice as Equal Regard and the Use of Force." In *Ethics & International Affairs* 17, no. 2 (September 2003): 63–75.

Enns, Elaine, and Ched Myers. *Ambassadors of Reconciliation: Diverse Christian Practices of Restorative Justice and Peacemaking.* Vol. 2. Maryknoll, NY: Orbis Books, 2009.

Fahey, Joseph J. "On Peace and War." *America* 193, no. 11 (October 17, 2005).

Farhadian, Charles, and Robert A. Emmons. "The Psychology of Forgiveness in the World Religions." In *Forgiveness and Reconciliation: Psychological Pathways to Conflict Transformation and Peace Building,* edited by Ani Kalayjian and Raymond F. Paloutzian, 55–70. New York: Springer, 2010.

"Featured Religions and Beliefs." Religions. *BBC* (2013). http://www.bbc.co.uk/ religion/religions/.

Felman, Shoshana, and Dori Laub. *Testimony: Crises of Witnessing in Literature, Psychoanalysis, and History.* New York: Routledge, 1992.

Fisher, Simon, et al. *Working with Conflict: Skills and Strategies for Action.* New York: Zed Books, 2000.

Flannery, Austin, ed. *Vatican Council II: Constitutions, Decrees, Declarations.* Northport, NY: Costello Publishing, 1996.

Frederickson, Jon. *Psychodynamic Psychotherapy: Learning to Listen from Multiple Perspectives.* Hove, UK: Psychology Press, 1999.

Friedman, Maurice S. *The Confirmation of Otherness, in Family, Community, and Society.* New York: Pilgrim Press, 1983.

Galtung, Johan. "Cultural Violence." *Journal of Peace Research* 27, no. 3 (August 1990): 291–305.

Goodstein, Laurie. "Falwell: blame abortionists, feminists and gays." *The Guardian* (September 19, 2001), http://gu.com/p/xv7c9/stw.

Gopin, Marc. "Religion, Violence, and Conflict Resolution." *Peace & Change* 22, no. 1 (January 1997): 1–31.

"Grabación especial en CD y/o DVD (Poll Closed)." Shock, http://www.shock.co/ grabacion-especial-en-cd-yo-dvd. Accessed May 7, 2014.

Grandin, Greg, and Thomas Miller Klubock. *Truth Commissions: State Terror, History, and Memory.* Durham, NC: Duke University Press, 2007.

Hamber, Brandon. *Transforming Societies after Political Violence: Truth, Reconciliation, and Mental Health.* New York: Springer, 2009.

Hanson, Rick. *Hardwiring Happiness: The New Brain Science of Contentment, Calm, and Confidence.* New York: Harmony, 2013.

Harada, Masazumi, et al. "Mercury Poisoning in First Nations Groups in Ontario, Canada: 35 Years of Minamata Disease in Canada." Translated from Japanese. *Journal of Minamata Studies* 3 (2011): 3–30.

Harding, Vincent. *Hope and History: Why We Must Share the Story of the Movement.* Maryknoll, NY: Orbis Books, 1990.

———. *Martin Luther King: The Inconvenient Hero.* 2d ed. Maryknoll, NY: Orbis Books, 2008.

Harris, Sam. *The End of Faith: Religion, Terror, and the Future of Reason.* New York: W.W. Norton and Company, 2005.

Hart, Lawrence. Story recounted at the Fresno Pacific University Center for Peacemaking and Conflict Studies' Seventh Annual Restorative Justice Conference, Fresno Pacific University, February 25–26, 2000.

Hatch, Thom. *Black Kettle: The Cheyenne Chief Who Sought Peace but Found War.* Hoboken, NJ: John Wiley & Sons, 2004.

Hatton, Christopher. "LONDON: UK CPT Trainees Call on The Body Shop to Put People Before Palm Oil." *Christian Peacemaker Teams* (November 17, 2009). http://www.cpt.org/cptnet/2009/11/17/london-uk-cpt-trainees-call-body-shop-put-people-palm-oil.

Hauerwas, Stanley. "Why War Is a Moral Necessity: Realism, Sacrifice, and the Civil War." In Carlson and Ebel, *From Jeremiad to Jihad*, 83–85.

Heft, James L. "John Paul II and the 'Just War' Doctrine: 'Make Peace through Justice and Forgiveness, Not War.'" In *Religion, Identity, and Global Governance: Ideas, Evidence, and Practice*, edited by Patrick James, 203–19. Toronto, Canada: University of Toronto Press, 2011.

Hehir, J. Bryan. "Reordering the World: John Paul II's *Centesimus annus.*" *Commonweal* 118 (June 14, 1991): 393–94.

Henne, Peter S. "The Two Swords: Religion-State Connections and Interstate Disputes." *Journal of Peace Research* 49, no. 6 (November 22, 2012): 753–68.

Herberg, Will. *Protestant-Catholic-Jew: An Essay in Religious Sociology.* Garden City, NJ: Doubleday, 1955.

Herman, Judith. *Trauma and Recovery: The Aftermath of Violence—From Domestic Abuse to Political Terror.* New York: Basic Books, 1992.

Hinz-Penner, Raylene. *Searching for Sacred Ground: The Journey of Chief Lawrence Hart, Mennonite.* Telford, PA: Cascadia Publishing House, 2007.

Hitchens, Christopher. God Is Not Great: How Religion Poisons Everything. New York: Twelve Books, 2007.

Hogan, Wesley C. *Many Minds, One Heart: SNCC's Dream for a New America.* Chapel Hill: University of North Carolina Press, 2007.

Hogue, Andrew. *Stumping God: Reagan, Carter, and the Invention of a Political Faith.* Waco, TX: Baylor University Press, 2012.

Hoig, Stan. *Peace Chiefs of the Cheyennes.* Norman: University of Oklahoma Press, 1980.

Honey, Michael Keith. *Black Workers Remember: An Oral History of Segregation, Unionism, and the Freedom Struggle.* Berkeley: University of California Press, 1999.

Hubbard, Amy S. "Understanding Majority and Minority Participation in Interracial and Interethnic Dialogue." In *Reconciliation, Justice, and Coexistence: Theory and Practice*, edited by Mohammed Abu-Nimer. Lanham, MD: Lexington Books, 2001.

Hughes, Richard T. *Myths America Lives By.* Urbana: University of Illinois Press, 2003.

"IRAQI KURDISTAN: CPT Releases Video about Exxon Mobil's Confiscation of Kurdish Villagers' Land." *Christian Peacemaker Teams* (November 25, 2013). http://www.cpt.org/cptnet/2013/11/25/iraqi-kurdistan-cpt-releases-video-about-exxon-mobil%E2%80%99s-confiscation-kurdish-villag.

Jafari, Sheherazade, and Abdul Aziz Said. "Islam and Peacemaking." In *Peacemaking: From Practice to Theory*, edited by Susan Allen Nan, Zachariah Cherian Mampilly, and Andrea Bartoli, 228–43. Santa Barbara, CA: Praeger, 2012.

Jakobsen, Janet R. "Is Secularism Less Violent than Religion?" *In Interventions: Activists and Academics Respond to Violence*, edited by Elizabeth A. Castelli and Janet R. Jackobsen, 53–69. New York: Palgrave Macmillan, 2004.

James, Kerrie. "Domestic Violence within Refugee Families: Intersecting Patriarchal Culture and the Refugee Experience." *Australian & New Zealand Journal of Family Therapy* 31, no. 3 (September 2010): 275–84.

Jewett, Robert, and John Shelton Lawrence. *Captain America and the Crusade against Evil: The Dilemma of Zealous Nationalism*. Grand Rapids, MI: Wm. B. Eerdmans Publishing, 2003.

John Paul II. *Centesimus annus*. Boston: St. Paul Books and Media, 1991.

———. *Evangelium vitae*. Boston: St. Paul Books and Media, 1995.

———. "If You Want Peace, Reach Out to the Poor." Message given at the XXVI Annual World Day of Prayer for Peace, January 1, 1993.

———. *Laborem exercens*. Boston: St. Paul Books and Media, 1981.

Jouejati, Rafif. "Local Coordination Committees (LCC) in Syria." 2014. http://www.lccsyria.org.

Juergensmeyer, Mark. *Terror in the Mind of God: The Global Rise of Religious Violence*. Berkeley: University of California Press, 2003.

Kauffman, Jeffrey. "On the Primacy of Shame." In *The Shame of Death, Grief, and Trauma*, edited by Jeffrey Kauffman, 3–24. New York: Routledge, 2010.

Kelly, J. N. D. *The Oxford Dictionary of the Popes*. New York: Oxford University Press, 1986.

Kern, Kathleen. "Corporate Complicity in Congo's War." *Tikkun* 21, no. 2 (March/April 2006): 38–44.

———. *In Harm's Way: A History of Christian Peacemaker Teams*. Eugene, OR: Cascade Books, 2009.

———. "The Human Cost of Cheap Cellphones." In *A Game As Old As Empire: The Secret World of Economic Hit Men and the Web of Global Corruption*, edited by Steven Hiatt, 93–112. San Francisco, CA: Berrett-Koehler Publishers, 2007.

———. "Victims as Pariahs." *The Christian Century* 123, no. 2 (January 24, 2006).

Kerstetter, Todd M. "State Violence and the Un-American West: Mormons, American Indians, and Cults." In Carlson and Ebel, *From Jeremiad to Jihad*, 143–58.

Khan, Irene. *The Unheard Truth: Poverty and Human Rights*. New York: W. W. Norton & Company, 2009.

Kimball, Charles. *When Religion Becomes Evil*. New York: HarperCollins, 2008.

King, Martin Luther, Jr. "Loving Your Enemies." Sermon delivered at Dexter Avenue Baptist Church, Montgomery, AL, November 17, 1957. http://mlkonline.com/.

Krishnamurti, J. *The First & Last Freedom*. New York: Harper & Row, 1975.

Las Casas, Bartolomé de. *Brevísima Relación de la Destrucción de las Indias*. 1542. http://www.rae.es/sites/default/files/HOJEAR_Brevisima_relacion_de_la_destruicion_de_las_Indias.pdf. Accessed April 13, 2017.

"Las Pavas Writes to President Santos Regarding Continued Attacks on Their Community." *Christian Peacemaker Teams* (March 20, 2014). http://www.cpt.org/cptnet/2014/03/20/las-pavas-writes-president-santos-regarding-continued-attacks-their-community.

Lederach, John Paul. *Reconcile: Conflict Transformation for Ordinary Christians.* Harrisonburg, VA: Herald Press, 1999. 61–68.

Lieberman, Matthew D. *Social: Why Our Brains Are Wired to Connect.* New York: Crown, 2013.

Lincoln, Bruce. *Holy Terrors: Thinking about Religion after September 11.* 2d ed. Chicago: University of Chicago Press, 2006.

Little, David, ed. *Peacemakers in Action: Profiles of Religion in Conflict Resolution.* Cambridge: Cambridge University Press, 2007.

Llewellyn, Karl N., and E. Adamson Hoebel. *The Cheyenne Way: Conflict and Case Law in Primitive Jurisprudence.* 1941; reissue, Buffalo, NY: William S. Hein & Co., 2002.

Long, Michael G., and Tracy Wenger Sadd, eds. *God and Country?: Diverse Perspectives on Christianity and Patriotism.* New York: Palgrave Macmillan, 2007.

Lowen, Alexander. *The Voice of the Body.* Alachua, FL: Bioenergetics Press, 2005.

Mahoney, Liam, and Luis Enrique Eguren. *Unarmed Bodyguards: International Accompaniment for the Protection of Human Rights.* West Hartford, CT: Kumarian Press, 1997.

Mallat, Chibli. "Nonviolence from Damascus and Manama to Moscow and Beijing: Why the Middle East Revolution Makes Dictatorships Tremble." Lecture presented at Initiatives for China's Seventh Annual Interethnic/Interfaith Leadership Conference, Los Angeles, CA, April 21, 2012. http://www.righttononviolence.org/mallat-addresses-7th-annual-initiatives-for-china-leadership-conference/.

———. "Obstacles to Democratization in Iraq: A Reading of Post-Revolutionary Iraqi History through the Gulf War." In *Rules and Rights in the Middle East: Democracy, Law and Society*, edited by Ellis Goldberg, Resat Kasaba, and Joel Migdal, 224–47. Seattle: University of Washington Press, 1993.

———. *Philosophy of Nonviolence: Revolution, Constitutionalism, and Justice beyond the Middle East.* New York: Oxford University Press, 2015.

———. "Voices of Opposition: The International Committee for a Free Iraq." In *Rules and Rights in the Middle East: Democracy, Law and Society*, edited by Ellis Goldberg, Resat Kasaba, and Joel Migdal, 174–87. Seattle: University of Washington Press, 1993.

Mallat, Chibli, and Edward Mortimer. "The Background to Civil Resistance in the Middle East." In *Civil Resistance in the Arab Spring: Triumphs and Disasters*, edited by Adam Roberts et al. Oxford: Oxford University Press, 2016, 1–29.

Mallat, Chibli, and Jason Gelbort. "Constitutional Options for Bahrain." *Virginia Journal of International Law* 2 (April 12, 2011): 1–16.

Mallat, Chibli, et al. "The Efficacy of Lustration Laws within the Pyramid of Accountability: Libya Compared." *Yale Journal of International Law* (Online) 39 (Spring 2014): 112–33.

Marsh, Charles. *The Beloved Community: How Faith Shapes Social Justice from the Civil Rights Movement to Today.* New York: Basic Books, 2005.

Martin, Michael T., and Marilyn Yaquinto, eds. *Redress for Historical Injustices in the United States: On Reparations for Slavery, Jim Crow, and Their Legacies.* Durham, NC: Duke University Press, 2007.

Marty, Martin E. "Insights of a Family Friend." *America* 192, no. 13 (April 18, 2005).

———. *Pilgrims in Their Own Land: 500 Years of Religion in America*. New York: Little, Brown and Company, 1984.

Maslow, Abraham H. *The Farther Reaches of Human Nature*. New York: Viking Press, 1971.

McCarthy, Cormac. *Blood Meridian; or, The Evening Redness in the West*. New York: Vintage Books, 1985.

McCormick, Richard A. "Deeds Not Words." In *John Paul II: Reflections from The Tablet*, edited by Catherine Pepinster, 105–10. London: Burns & Oates, 2005.

McCutcheon, Russell T. "A Direct Question Deserves a Direct Answer: A Response to Atalia Omer's 'Can a Critic Be a Caretaker Too?'" *Journal of the American Academy of Religion* 80, no. 4 (December 2012): 1077–82.

Mennonite Central Committee. "The Long Journey Home." 1997. Slightly edited transcript of video with footage from segments of Jane Brayden, Fox 5 News Tonight.

Metzger, Yona. "Yesterday, Today and Tomorrow." *America* 193, no. 12 (October 24, 2005).

Miles, Jack. "The Iraqi Dead: Respect Must Be Paid." *Commonweal* 130, no. 13 (July 18, 2003).

Millett, Lina S., et al. "Child Maltreatment Victimization and Subsequent Perpetration of Young Adult Intimate Partner Violence: An Exploration of Mediating Factors." *Child Maltreatment* 18, no. 2 (May 2013): 71–84.

Moore, Christopher W. *The Mediation Process: Practical Strategies for Resolving Conflict*. San Francisco, CA: Jossey-Bass, 2003.

Moran, Daniel J. "The Three Waves of Behavior Therapy: Course Corrections or Navigation Errors?" *The Behavioral Therapist*, Special Issue (Winter 2008): 147–57.

Morrison, Sylvia. "Could This Be Our Finest (H)Our?" *Christian Peacemaker Teams* (March 1, 2009). http://www.cpt.org/content/undoing-racism.

Munson, Henry. "Religion and Violence." *Religion* 35, no. 4 (2005): 223–46.

Murphy, Andrew R., and Elizabeth Hanson. "From King Phillip's War to September 11: Religion, Violence, and the American Way." In Carlson and Ebel, *From Jeremiad to Jihad*, 29–47.

Myers, Ched. *Who Will Roll Away the Stone?: Discipleship Queries for First World Christians*. Maryknoll, NY: Orbis Books, 1994.

———. "Word and World: A People's School." *The Clergy Journal* 78, no. 9 (September 2002): 9–10.

Myers, Ched, and Elaine Enns. "'Ambassadors of Reconciliation': Witnessing to the Restorative Justice of God." In Enns and Myers, *Ambassadors of Reconciliation*, 1–17.

Neufeldt, Reina C. "Interfaith Dialogue: Assessing Theories of Change." *Peace & Change* 36, no. 3 (July 2011): 344–72.

Nock, Matthew K., et al. "Suicide among Soldiers: A Review of Psychosocial Risk and Protective Factors." *Psychiatry: Interpersonal and Biological Processes* 76, no. 2 (June 2013): 97–125.

Norwood, George. "Emotions." *Deepermind*. http://www.deepermind.com/o2clarty.htm.

Obama, Barack. Nobel Peace Prize address given at Oslo City Hall, Oslo, Norway, December 10, 2009. http://www.nobelprize.org/nobel_prizes/peace/laureates/2009/obama-lecture_en.html.

O'Gorman, Ned. "From Jeremiad to Manifesto: The Rhetorical Evolution of John Foster Dulles's 'Massive Retaliation.'" In Carlson and Ebel, *From Jeremiad to Jihad*, 78–90.

Oliver, Kelly. *Witnessing: Beyond Recognition*. Minneapolis: University of Minnesota Press, 2001.

Omer, Atalia. "Can a Critic Be a Caretaker Too? Religion, Conflict, and Conflict Transformation." *Journal of the American Academy of Religion* 79, no. 2 (June 2011): 459–96.

Page, Richard C., James F. Weiss, and Germain Lietaer. "Humanistic Group Psychotherapy." In *Humanistic Psychotherapies: Handbook of Research and Practice*, edited by David J. Cain and Julius Seeman, 339–68. Washington, D.C.: American Psychological Association, 2002.

Pahl, Jon. *Empire of Sacrifice: The Religious Origins of American Violence*. New York: New York University Press, 2010.

Papadopoulos, Renos K., ed. *Therapeutic Care for Refugees: No Place Like Home*. London: Karnac Books, 2002.

Parens, Henri, Harold P. Blum, and Salman Akhtar, eds. *The Unbroken Soul: Tragedy, Trauma, and Human Resilience*. Lanham, MD: Jason Aronson, 2008.

Philpott, Daniel, and Gerard Powers, eds. *Strategies of Peace: Transforming Conflict in a Violent World*. Oxford: Oxford University Press, 2010.

Plante, Thomas G., ed. Religion, *Spirituality, and Positive Psychology: Understanding the Psychological Fruits of Faith*. Santa Barbara, CA: Praeger, 2012.

"Pope John Paul II." *Time* 165, no. 15 (April 3, 2005).

Portier, William L. "Are We Really Serious When We Ask God to Deliver Us from War? The Catechism and the Challenge of Pope John Paul II." *Communio* 23, no. 1 (spring 1996): 47–63.

Powers, Gerard. "Religion and Peacebuilding," in Philpott and Powers, *Strategies of Peace*, 317–52.

Rauf, Feisal Abdul. *Moving the Mountain: A New Vision of Islam in America*. New York: Free Press, 2012.

Renard, John, ed. *Fighting Words: Religion, Violence, and the Interpretation of Sacred Texts*. Berkeley: University of California Press, 2012.

Rincón, Sandra Milena. "The Challenge Continues." Translated by Carol Rose. Address given at the Mennonite World Conference, Asunción, Paraguay, July 2009. http://www.cpt.org/resources/writings/rincon-challenge-continues.

Robert, Mackey. "Updates on Day 18 of Egypt Protests." *The Lede, New York Times* (February 11, 2011). http://nyti.ms/1XwkX5K.

Robson, Susan. *Living with Conflict: A Challenge to a Peace Church*. Plymouth, UK: Scarecrow Press, 2013.

Roethke, Theodore. "In a Dark Time." In *The Collected Poems of Theodore Roethke*, 231. New York: Anchor Books, 1964.

Rolheiser, Ronald. *The Holy Longing: The Search for a Christian Spirituality*. New York: Image, 1999.

Rose, Wendy. "For Some, It's a Time of Mourning." In *Without Discovery: A Native Response to Columbus*, edited by Ray Gonzalez, 3–7. Seattle: Broken Moon Press, 1992.

Ross, Brian, and Rehab El-Buri. "Obama's Pastor: God Damn America, U.S. to Blame for 9/11." *ABC News*, March 13, 2008.

Rothschild, Babette. *The Body Remembers: Continuing Education Test: The Psychophysiology of Trauma and Trauma Treatment*. New York: W. W. Norton & Company, 2000.

Scarry, Elaine. *The Body in Pain: The Making and Unmaking of the World*. New York: Oxford University Press, 1985.

Sider, Ronald J. "God's People Reconciling." Speech presented at the Mennonite World Conference, Strasbourg, France, Summer 1984.

———. *Nonviolence: The Invincible Weapon?* Dallas, TX: W Publishing Group, 1989.

Simich, Laura, Hayley Hamilton, and B. Khamisa Baya. "Mental Distress, Economic Hardship and Expectations of Life in Canada among Sudanese Newcomers." *Transcultural Psychiatry* 43, no. 3 (September 2006): 418–44.

Smith, Gordon S., and Harold Coward, eds. *Religion and Peacebuilding*. Albany: State University of New York Press, 2004.

Smith, Henry Nash. *Virgin Land: The American West as Symbol and Myth*. Cambridge, MA: Harvard University Press, 1950, 1970.

Smock, David R. *Interfaith Dialogue and Peacebuilding*. Washington, D.C.: United States Institute of Peace, 2002.

———. *Religion in World Affairs: Its Role in Conflict and Peace*. Washington, D.C.: United States Institute of Peace, 2008.

Sniegocki, John. "Catholic Teaching on War, Peace, and Nonviolence since Vatican II." In *Vatican II: Forty Years Later*, edited by William Madges, 224–44. Maryknoll, NY: Orbis Books, 2006.

Southwick, Steven M., and Dennis S. Charney. *Resilience: The Science of Mastering Life's Greatest Challenges*. New York: Cambridge University Press, 2013.

Stout, Harry S. *Upon the Altar of the Nation: A Moral History of the Civil War*. New York: Viking, 2006.

Summerfield, Derek. "Childhood, War, Refugeedom and 'Trauma': Three Core Questions for Mental Health Professionals." *Transcultural Psychiatry* 37, no. 3 (September 2000): 417–33.

Sveaass, Nora, and Marcia Castillo. "From War Hero to Cripple: An Interview Study on Psychosocial Intervention and Social Reconstruction in Nicaragua." *Peace and Conflict: Journal of Peace Psychology* 6, no. 2 (June 2002): 113–33.

Thich Nhat Hanh. *The Art of Communicating*. New York: HarperCollins, 2013.

Thiessen, Kathy Moorhead. "Aboriginal Justice: Welcome to Idle No More." *Christian Peacemaker Teams* (March 31, 2013). http://www.cpt.org/news/sott/articles/2013/aboriginal-justice-welcome-idle-no-more.

Tuskan, John. "Religion, Spirituality, and Faith in the Care of Torture Survivors." Webinar organized as a part of the National Capacity Building Webinar Series, April 29, 2009. http://vimeo.com/38390246.

Tutu, Desmond. *No Future without Forgiveness*. New York: Doubleday, 1999.

Tyson, Timothy B. *Blood Done Sign My Name: A True Story*. New York: Three Rivers Press, 2004.

United Nations High Commissioner for Refugees. *Convention and Protocol Relating to the Status of Refugees*. UNHCR, 1951. http://www.unhcr.org/3b66c2aa10.html.

———. *UNHCR Statistical Yearbook*. UNHCR, 2012. http://www.unhcr.org/52a7213b9.html.

Van Voorst, Robert E. *RELG: World*. New York: Cengage Learning, 2013.

Volkan, Vamık D. "Transgenerational Transmissions and Chosen Trauma." Opening Address, XIII International Congress, International Association of Group Psychotherapy, London, August 1998.

Vriesinga, Stewart. "COLOMBIA ANALYSIS: Las Pavas—The Criminalization of Victims." *Christian Peacemaker Teams* (February 14, 2012). http://www.cpt.org/cptnet/2009/11/17/london-uk-cpt-trainees-call-body-shop-put-people-palm-oil.

Walker, S. "Assessing the Mental Health Consequences of Military Combat in Iraq and Afghanistan: A Literature Review." *Journal of Psychiatric and Mental Health Nursing* 17, no. 9 (November 2010): 790–96.

Waller, Signe. *Love and Revolution, A Political Memoir: People's History of the Greensboro Massacre, Its Setting and Aftermath*. Lanham, MD: Rowman & Littlefield, 2002.

Webb, Stephen H. "American Providence, American Violence." In Carlson and Ebel, *From Jeremiad to Jihad*, 91–108.

Werner, Emmy E., and Ruth S. Smith. *Journeys from Childhood to Midlife: Risk, Resilience, and Recovery*. Ithaca, NY: Cornell University Press, 2001.

Wexler, Isaiah D., David Branski, and Eitan Kerem. "War and Children." *Journal of the American Medical Association* 296, no. 5 (August 2, 2006): 579–81.

Wiesel, Elie. "Acceptance Speech." Speech on the occasion of the award of the Nobel Peace Prize, Oslo, Norway, December 10, 1986. http://www.nobelprize.org/nobel_prizes/peace/laureates/1986/wiesel-acceptance_en.html.

Wilber, Ken. *The Spectrum of Consciousness*. Wheaton, IL: Theosophical Publishing House, 1977.

Winnicott, D. W. "Mirror-role of Mother and Family in Child Development." In *Playing and Reality*, 149–59. Abingdon, UK: Tavistock Publications, 1971.

Wood, Graeme. "What ISIS Really Wants." *The Atlantic* (March 2015).

Woolford, Andrew. *The Politics of Restorative Justice: A Critical Introduction*. Halifax, Nova Scotia, Canada: Fernwood Publishing, 2009.

Worthington, Everett L., Jr., et al. "Forgiveness." In *Plante, Religion, Spirituality, and Positive Psychology*, 63–78.

Wright, Jeremiah. "Confusing God and Government." Sermon given at Trinity United Church of Christ, April 13, 2003. Transcription online at http://www.sluggy.net/forum/viewtopic.php?p=315691&sid=4b3e97ace4ee8ceeo2bd6850e52f50b7.

Yellow Horse Brave Heart, Maria, and Lemyra M. DeBruyn. "The American Indian Holocaust: Healing Historical Unresolved Grief." *American Indian and Alaska Native Mental Health Research* 8, no. 2 (1998): 60–82.

CONTRIBUTORS

Mohammed Abu-Nimer
Mohammed Abu-Nimer, of the International Peace and Conflict Resolution program, serves as director of the Peacebuilding and Development Institute at the American University in Washington, D.C. He has conducted interreligious conflict resolution training and interfaith dialogue workshops in conflict areas around the world, including Palestine, Israel, Egypt, Northern Ireland, the Philippines (Mindanao), and Sri Lanka. In addition to his articles and publications, Dr. Abu-Nimer is the cofounder and coeditor of the *Journal of Peacebuilding and Development*. Professor Abu-Nimer also serves as senior advisor to the KAICIID International Dialogue Center in Vienna, Austria.

Abbas Aroua
Medical and health physicist Abbas Aroua is adjunct professor at the Lausanne Faculty of Medicine. He is the founder (in 2002) and director of the Cordoba Foundation of Geneva (CFG), dedicated to violence prevention, conflict transformation, and peace promotion. CFG's current activities cover North Africa, West Asia, and the Sahel. Building on local capacities and resources, the CFG empowers people, promotes dialogue, and creates safe mediation spaces. Abbas Aroua has authored *The Work of Goodness: A Comprehensive Approach to Human Security* (in Arabic, CFG, Geneva 2010) and *The Quest for Peace in the Islamic Tradition* (Kolofon Press, Oslo 2013).

Laura M. Bennett-Murphy
Dr. Laura Bennett Murphy is an associate clinical professor at the University of Utah School of Medicine. She received her PhD in clinical

psychology from Duke University and completed a pediatric psychology fellowship at Nationwide Children's Hospital and The Ohio State University. Dr. Murphy specializes in the psychological and health needs of medically ill children, refugees, and those who have experienced trauma.

John Carlson

John D. Carlson is associate professor of Religious Studies at Arizona State University, where he also serves as associate director of the Center for the Study of Religion and Conflict. He is coeditor of three books, including *From Jeremiad to Jihad: Religion, Violence, and America*, and has authored over twenty-five academic articles and book chapters as well as dozens of shorter essays and reviews. He is currently codirecting a multiyear project on "Religion and Global Citizenship," funded by the Henry R. Luce Foundation.

David Derezotes

David Derezotes is a professor at the University of Utah, where he is director of Peace and Conflict Studies in the College of Humanities, director of the Bridge Training Clinic and of the Mental Health program at the College of Social Work, and a program director at the Center for Teaching and Learning Excellence (CTLE). He is currently involved in many training and dialogue projects, including the Transforming Classrooms into Inclusive Communities CTLE project, which he directs on campus. He can be found wandering in the deserts of southern Utah on warm days.

Elaine Enns

Elaine Enns has been working in the field of restorative justice and conflict transformation since 1989 as victim-offender dialogue facilitator, consultant, educator, and trainer. She recently completed her Doctor of Ministry degree and holds an M.A. in Theology and Peacemaking from the Mennonite Brethren Biblical Seminary in Fresno as well. She provides mediation and consultation services for individuals, churches, schools, community organizations, and businesses, travels throughout North America teaching and training, and serves as the program director for Restorative Justice Services with Bartimaeus Cooperative Ministries. Her most recent publication is *Ambassadors of Reconciliation: A New Testament Theology and Diverse Christian Practices of Restorative Justice and Peacemaking* (with Ched Myers, Orbis Books, 2009).

James L. Heft

James L. Heft, S.M. (Marianist), is the Alton Brooks Professor of Religion and president of the Institute for Advanced Catholic Studies at the University of Southern California. He has published over two hundred articles and is the author and editor of twelve books, including his most recent, *In the Logos of Love: Promise and Predicament in Catholic Intellectual Life* (Oxford, 2016). He is currently organizing an interdisciplinary study on the "spiritual but not religious movement" and working on a book on Catholic higher education.

Kathleen Kern

Kathleen Kern has worked with *Christian Peacemaker Teams* since 1993, serving on assignments in Haiti, Palestine, Washington, D.C., Colombia, and Indigenous communities in North America. She has authored two histories of CPT: *In Harm's Way: a History of Christian Peacemaker Teams* and *As Resident Aliens: Christian Peacemaker Teams in the West Bank, 1995–2005*.

John Paul Lederach

John Paul Lederach is professor of International Peacebuilding at the University of Notre Dame. Widely known for his pioneering work in conflict transformation, Lederach is involved in conciliation work in Colombia, the Philippines, and Nepal, plus countries in East and West Africa. In August 2013, Lederach was appointed director of the Peace Accords Matrix at the Kroc Institute. Lederach is the author of twenty-two books, including *When Blood and Bones Cry Out: Journeys Through the Soundscape of Healing and Reconciliation* (University of Queensland Press, 2010), *The Moral Imagination: The Art and Soul of Building Peace* (Oxford University Press, 2005), and *Building Peace: Sustainable Reconciliation in Divided Societies* (USIP, 1997).

Chibli Mallat

Chibli Mallat is Presidential Professor of Middle Eastern Law and Politics at the University of Utah, and EU Jean Monnet Professor of European Law at Saint Joseph's University, Lebanon. He has been active in the Arab Spring with Right to Nonviolence, an international NGO based in Beirut, and is the author of *Philosophy of Nonviolence: Revolution, Constitutionalism, and Justice Beyond the Middle East* (Oxford University Press 2015).

Ched Myers

Ched Myers is an activist theologian who has worked in social change movements for forty years. With a degree in New Testament Studies from the Graduate Theological Union, he is a popular educator who animates scripture and issues of faith-based peace and justice. He has authored over one hundred articles and more than a half-dozen books, including *Binding the Strong Man: A Political Reading of Mark's Story of Jesus* (Orbis, 1988/2008), *The Biblical Vision of Sabbath Economics* (Tell the Word, 2001), *Ambassadors of Reconciliation: A N.T. Theology and Diverse Christian Practices of Restorative Justice and Peacemaking* (with Elaine Enns, Orbis, 2009), and *Our God Is Undocumented: Biblical Faith and Immigrant Justice* (with Matthew Colwell, Orbis, 2012). Most recently he curated, edited, and contributed to an anthology entitled *Watershed Discipleship: Reinhabiting Bioregional Faith and Practice* (Cascade Press, 2016). Ched is adjunct faculty at St. Andrew's College in Saskatoon, Saskatchewan, and has taught at many seminaries around the United States, Canada, and Australia.

Tim Nafziger

Tim Nafziger is a Mennonite writer and organizer for social change who thrives on cross-pollination. Since 2003, he has been a reservist with *Christian Peacemaker Teams* and served as part of CPT's administrative team from 2008 to 2014. He lives with his wife, Charletta, in Oak View, California, on the traditional lands of the Chumash. He is involved locally as a leader in the Ventura County chapter of Showing Up for Racial Justice.

Muriel Schmid

Muriel Schmid holds a PhD in Protestant Theology from the University of Neuchâtel in Switzerland and is an ordained minister in the Swiss Reformed Church. She taught for ten years at the University of Utah where she founded and directed the Religious Studies program. She left her position at the University of Utah in 2014. Since then, she has been directing programs for faith-based nonprofit organizations. She holds a postgraduate certificate in Peace and Conflict Studies from the European Peace University and a graduate certificate in Conflict Resolution from the University of Utah. She has traveled to Palestine, Iraqi Kurdistan, Colombia, and Costa Rica, where she was involved in various grassroot peace initiatives. Her publications range from the history of Christian thought to the history of the prison system, religion and peacemaking, and Christian nonviolence.

INDEX